An Innocent Eye

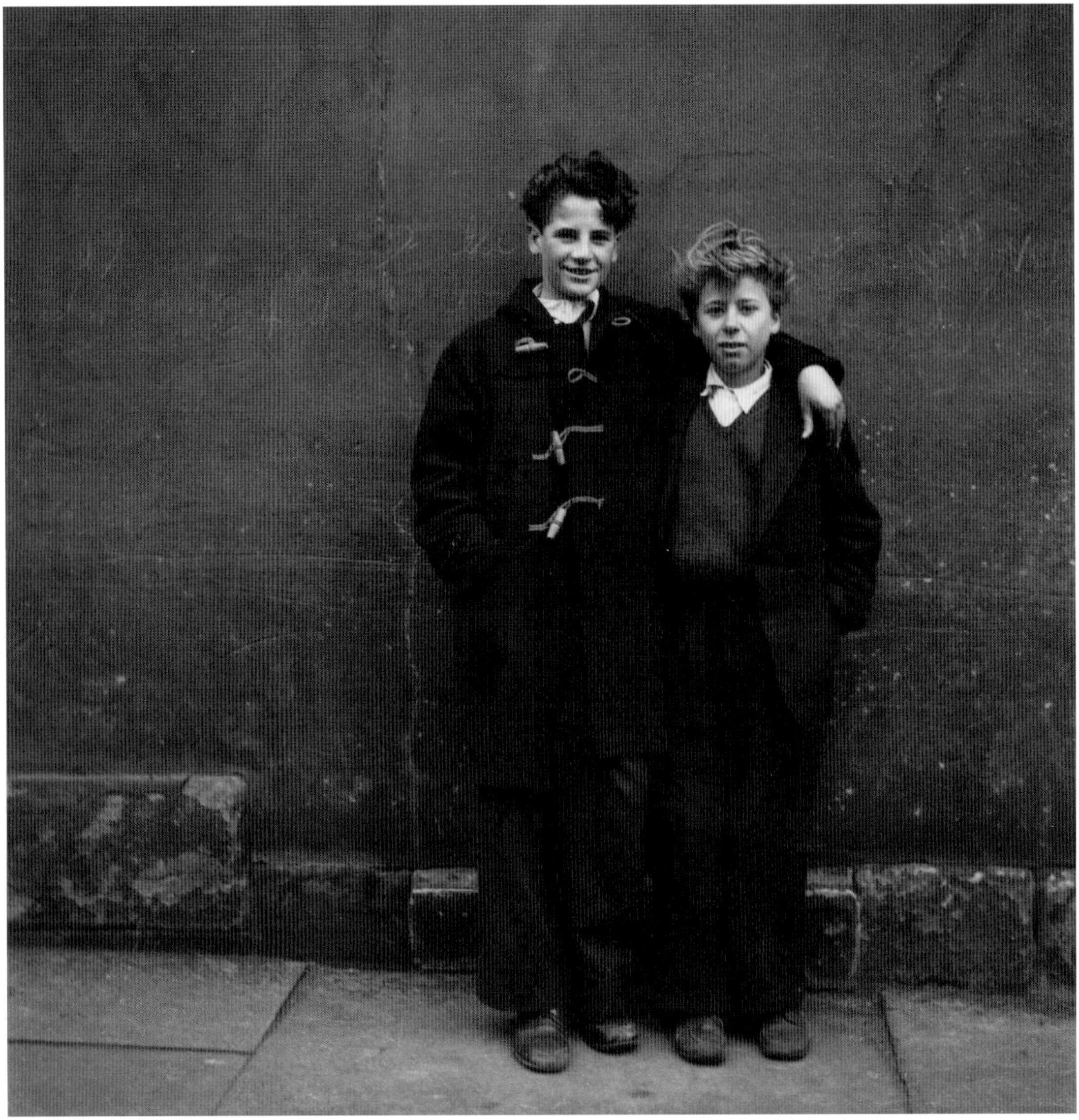

Snuggy Sample and Derek Wall, 1957.

An Innocent Eye

Jimmy Forsyth

Tyneside Photographer

Anthony Flowers

Tyne Bridge Publishing

in association with
Amber Film & Photography Collective and Tyne & Wear Archives & Museums

Acknowledgements

Tyne Bridge Publishing, and the author, warmly thank the following for their generous help: Liz Rees, Tyne & Wear Archives & Museums; Graeme Rigby and Peter Scott, Side Gallery (Amber Film & Photography Collective); Michael Chaplin for permission to quote from Sid Chaplin's *The Watchers and the Watched*; Keith Pattison; Derek Smith.

Cover photograph of Jimmy Forsyth in his flat at The Cedars, Newcastle upon Tyne, July 1990, by Keith Pattison.

Published by:
City of Newcastle upon Tyne
Newcastle Libraries & Information Service
Tyne Bridge Publishing, 2013

www.tynebridgepublishing.co.uk
www.newcastle.gov.uk/libraries

ISBN: 978-1-85795-214-8

Printed by Elanders UK Ltd, North Tyneside

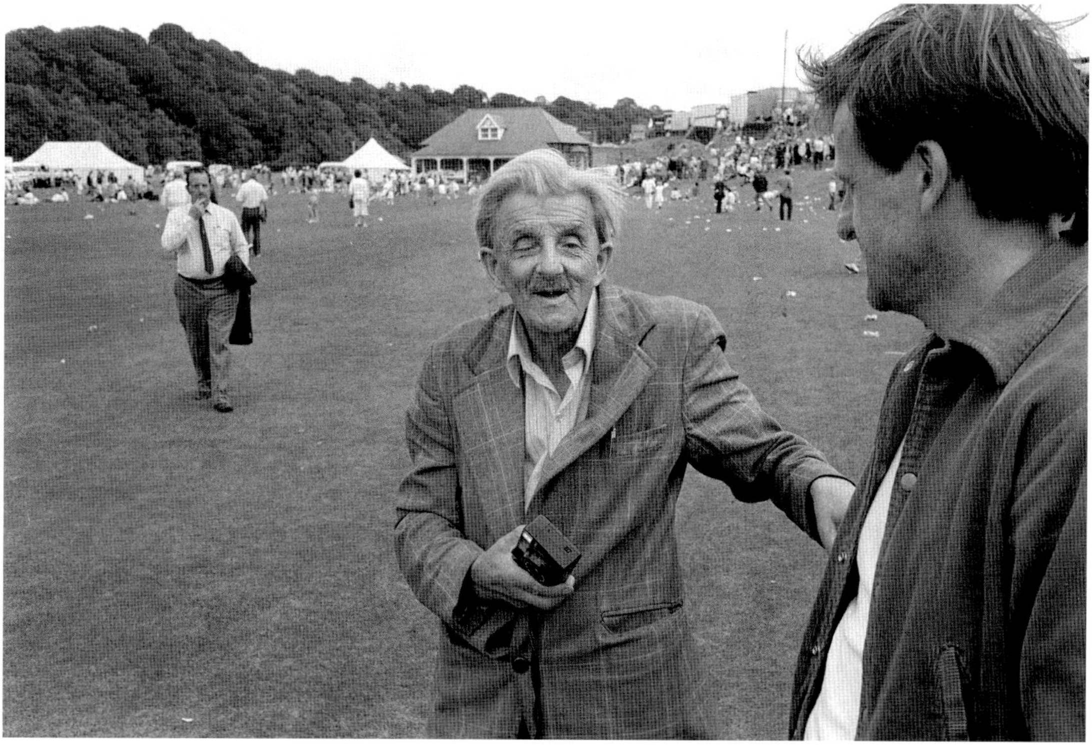

Keith Pattison

Jimmy Forsyth, photographed by Keith Pattison at Durham Miners' Gala, 1987, with Ian Tinwell of the Side Gallery.

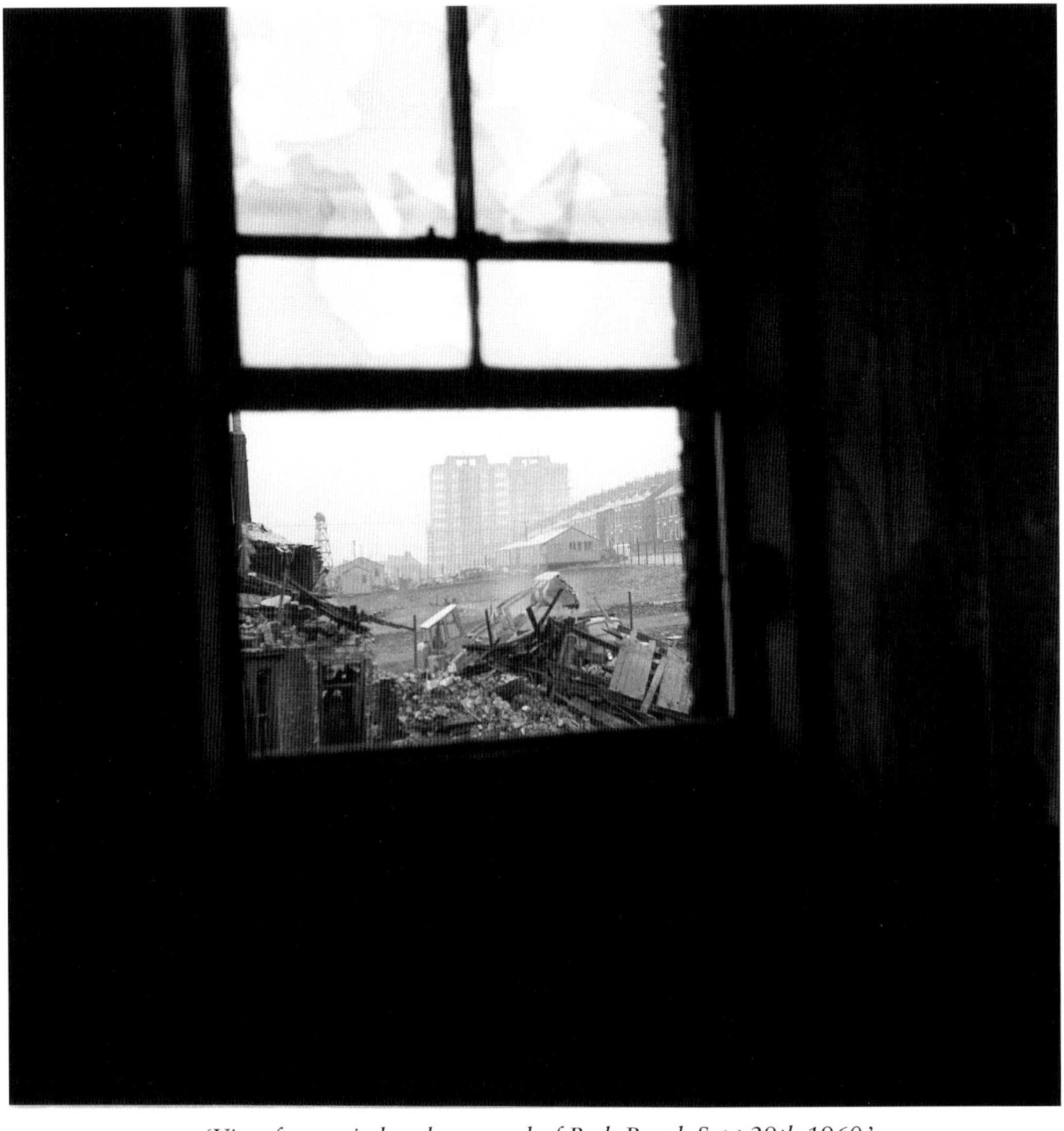

'View from window lower end of Park Road. Sept 29th 1960.'

Nobody was forced to stay in the rotting houses of lower Blucher and a dozen like it along the Road. It needed little effort to move. But now the city was in their bones, they feared the wilderness of flats and isolated houses without a centre, they instinctively rejected amenities without that highway of shops and pubs which constitutes the ganglion of a living place. The Road was their life, and they clung to it. As long as they could, as long as they were allowed, they would stay. And yet their days were numbered. The Road was being demolished and the people were shifting. Some went, then returned from the desert, paying double the old rent rather than be dead, content to keep one wall between themselves and the demolition gang. Some stayed and were lost.

Sid Chaplin,
'The Watchers and the Watched' Eyre and Spottiswood, 1962

An Innocent Eye

JIMMY FORSYTH will always be associated with Scotswood Road in the west end of Newcastle upon Tyne. It provided the title for his first exhibition, *Scotswood Road with a Box Camera*, in 1979, and for the long awaited book of his photographs *Scotswood Road*, published by Bloodaxe Books in 1986, which established his reputation. Jimmy lived on or near Scotswood Road for almost all of his adult life. It was on Scotswood Road that he found his subjects among his friends and neighbours. Scotswood Road stretches for around three miles west through Elswick from Newcastle's long demolished Marlborough Crescent Bus Station to the site of the old Scotswood or Chain Bridge.

In the 1940s and 1950s Elswick was still a densely populated part of the city, reflected in the fifty or so pubs that were to be found along the length of Scotswood Road. It was a microcosm of working-class Tyneside life. Jimmy's remarkable photographs of this now vanished Tyneside were mostly taken between 1954 and 1967 and they represent what has been recognised as one of the most important records of twentieth-century working-class society that anyone has produced. Considering the circumstances under which they were taken, it is amazing that they have survived at all.

James 'Jimmy' Forsyth was born to John and Bertha Forsyth, on 15 August 1913, at 24 Trinity Street in Barry, an industrial town built on the rich coalfields of Glamorganshire in South Wales. It had been the major exporter of coal until the Great Western Railway extended its reach to Cardiff. For Jimmy, Barry was a fascinating fusion of the rural, marine and industrial. It was, in fact, not unlike his eventual adoptive Tyneside.

The Forsyths came from Garmouth, not far from the mouth of the Spey in Elgin, north-east Scotland. Jimmy's grandfather, James, was a stonemason. Like his grandson would in the 1950s, James walked to find work, making his way to Liverpool and then to Bangor in North Wales, where Jimmy's father, John, was born in 1881. Eventually James was to find work in the docks of Barry and Cardiff.

When Jimmy was born he was not expected to live, and remained a slight child with a pronounced cast to his left eye. He went to High Street School, Barry, and left at 14, without formal qualifications. On leaving school, he became an apprentice fitter in a cement works repair shop. Jimmy successfully completed his apprenticeship in 1934 but he found it hard to get regular work. At his father's suggestion he then joined the Merchant Navy, going to Newport to sign on as an assistant engineer. He eventually rose to the rank of fourth engineer, and worked on board several ships throughout 1936 and 1937.

His career as a merchant seaman seems to have come to an abrupt end on 26 August 1937 when he signed off from the SS *St Helena* at Sunderland and returned to Wales. In 1938 he went to work, for the Ministry of Supply, on the construction of a small arms factory owned by ICI at Hirwaun near Merthyr Tydfil. He then learned that fitters were required in Mossend, Glasgow, so he volunteered along with three workmates, but by 1940, with the Second World War underway, he had returned to Merthyr.

Jimmy Forsyth arrived in Newcastle from South Wales, aged thirty, in 1943. He had come to work as a fitter at ICI in Prudhoe, a short train journey west along the Tyne. He found a room in Grove Street, just off the north side of Elswick Road. As a volunteer in Merthyr he had agreed to come north for a period of three months to help with the frantic effort to maintain munitions for the war. Tragically, he was at ICI for just four days before an accident, while he was working on a boiler, left him blind in his right eye – a metal splinter from a broken chisel tore into the pupil. After a period of convalescence in a hospital at Wylam, in the Tyne Valley, he returned to Elswick to find that his room had been re-let. A workmate's family at Crawcrook, a few miles from Gateshead, offered him lodgings. Despite his accident he returned to work. In 1945 he moved to Prudhoe, on the south bank of the Tyne, while continuing at ICI, but the eventual return of former employees from the demobilising forces created tensions, and issues came to a head late in 1946 when a dispute with a foreman led to his dismissal. He was still keen to stay on Tyneside and decided to remain temporarily in Prudhoe, though his disability had significantly reduced his chances of employment.

In 1946, with rationing still on and little prospect of work, Jimmy needed to find cheaper lodgings. He landed up in what he described as a 'half-brothel' in Suffolk Street, Elswick. He survived there, in somewhat unusual circumstances, until 1951, but by 1952 he had found a Tyneside flat at 353 Scotswood Road.

Most of Jimmy's time was taken up with the search for a job and with no money for bus or train fares, daylight hours were spent walking from place to place in the hope of employment. The dole was usually £2 but 'if you said that you lived in digs you got more'. The search for work took him to London, Reading, Manchester and Nottingham, then to Canterbury and London again before he returned to Tyneside, only to be told by the Labour Exchange at Manors in Newcastle that he was no longer eligible for the dole. These were difficult times.

Jimmy eventually found temporary work as a cleaner in the kitchens of the Station Hotel. Later, a handyman's job at an ironworks across the river near Blaydon ended in near disaster when a crane jib struck him, fracturing his skull. Jimmy's independent spirit and forthright nature did not make him an easy employee so he tried self-employment in 1955, when he took on a general dealer's shop in Pine Street, Elswick, financed, it is said, by compensation for the accident. However, this was no more successful because he gave too much credit to his customers.

It is uncertain in which year Jimmy first acquired a camera. Some photographs that appear in his 'tartan albums' (photograph albums with a distinctive tartan cover that Jimmy used to contain his earliest work) seem to predate the demolition of Newcastle's old Infirmary in 1954, which provided Jimmy with the impetus to begin recording places that were disappearing. In 1986 he explained why he started to take his photographs: 'When they knocked down the Infirmary in 1954, a curious crowd gathered to watch. It was then that I realised someone should make a record of what was left of the community. I had nothing to do, [so] why not make a record of Scottie Road to pass the time? It would show future generations what we looked like and how we lived.'

These early photographs were mostly taken with a Coronet 020 Box camera made in Birmingham, bought in a junk shop: 'I've never had any fancy gear – I've never had any money to buy fancy gear – I've only had old box cameras'. The Coronet, which was one of the cheapest cameras on the market, had a lens that produced an image that inadequately covered the film, leading to vignetting at the edges of the 6 x 9cm negative. Jimmy was to tell Jools Holland in 1987 that he had used a Kodak Brownie to take the pictures for *Scotswood Road*: 'I used this Kodak Brownie – a good many years like, and then later I bought a cheap Agfa – a second-hand Agfa Camera like'. Jools, commenting on the sharpness of the photographs in the book, produced the following response from Jimmy: 'That's because Kodaks makes good cameras see ... You have to have a decent camera – like these modern ones like – these disc cameras – the negatives are too small really – a lot of people are finding that out now.'

It is important not to underestimate what an undertaking this was to become for an unemployed man with few resources, though he said that by selling prints to his neighbours 'for pennies' he was able to manage to buy more film. This was a constant worry for Jimmy, that he might miss something worth photographing through lack of film.

A natural curiosity about the history of the city also led to him making exposures of interesting buildings he saw as he walked about. The tartan albums began to contain, alongside pictures of friends and their children, views of places he had visited, parts of the surviving Town Walls, supposed Roman remains; almost anything that looked historic seemed to require a photograph and appropriate caption: 'View look[ing] west up Neville Street – note; island absent from up road centre as it has not been laid', or in a more historical vein 'Southern Postern gateway – note; believed to be [the] only completely preserved Norman postern in England.'

On the night of December 23-24 1955 the Tyne Tees Coaster, *Cyprian Coast* sank in the Tyne between the Newcastle and Gateshead quaysides. It had previously been in collision with a Swedish ship *Arabert* and sank within five minutes, the ten-man crew having had a remarkable escape. Jimmy, obviously attracted by this dramatic maritime subject, returned many times to record the salvage operation during the months of January and February 1956.

A more sustained period of employment, of over a year, saw Jimmy working as part of a Trinidad Lake asphalting team. Even when supposed to be labouring he took a sequence of photographs of his workmates as they replaced roads south of the river in County Durham.

He was taking pictures of local children when a neighbour told him that Scotswood Road and the surrounding area was to be demolished, and suggested he make a record of where he lived: 'A wife said to me you should take some pictures of Scotswood Road because they are going to knock it down, and I said to me-self ain't she stupid because they never do them sort of things, but luckily I took the pictures just the same because then they started knocking them down around the back where I was living like and that was the start of it!'

It was the perfect subject – combining history and the gritty reality of what had become an extremely rundown working-class area. An indication of how systematic he was to become in his recording of Scotswood Road is evident in a sequence of photographs taken in 1956 along the road from Churchill Street to Park Road, Park Road to Rendell Street, and Rendell Street to School Street. He went on to photograph the remainder of the area over the next three years. In fact, such is the entirety of his record that when Newcastle Libraries came to make a book on the forty or so Scotswood Road pubs, many of which had disappeared by 1988, they were able to source the illustrations largely from Jimmy's photographs.

The next five years were to be a time of almost feverish activity for Jimmy. During these years he produced the majority of his most memorable and remarkable images.

In the mid 1950s Jimmy came to know a local photographer, Steve Wood. Steve was manager of Turner's Photographic Dealers shop at 62 Clayton Street. Steve thought that Jimmy had been attracted by photographs of old Newcastle which he had taken, and displayed in the shop window. In any case they had much in common, a passion for local history and Jimmy's growing interest in photography. Jimmy was often in the shop telling Steve of the impending demolition of local landmarks: 'He used to tell me all about the pubs and buildings of note that were being pulled down … I would make a note of these so that I could include them on my Sunday morning forays'. Jimmy showed him prints that he had taken, and Steve would give him film, 'then I would tell him to bring the film in when he had finished it. If there was anything I wanted, I would keep the print,' from which Steve would make a transparency for use in slideshows he put on in the area. The relationship developed, though Steve could find Jimmy's presence in the shop distracting, and encouraged him to choose slack periods for his visits. 'Jimmy was not in the market for buying things, and I think I kept him in films at first. Then I had a sale in the shop, where I offered five shillings for any old camera, regardless of state, in part-exchange. It does not seem much, does it? But this was the

1950s. I just put them all in a bin, and let Jimmy when he came in, pick out anything he was interested in. The rest were packed in a box for the bin men.'

It was Steve who offered Jimmy a twenty-year-old Rolleiflex camera for £15, which was a huge sum of money for a man on the dole. He was allowed to pay off the purchase price in instalments.

Although Jimmy has always denied anything but a rudimentary acquaintance with photographic technique, it is difficult not to conclude that Steve Wood gave Jimmy much practical advice with regards to exposure and instruction in the use of flash for interiors. When Jimmy's father died in 1960 Steve Wood gave him one of his old suits and a shirt to wear for the funeral (he was told by Steve's wife to polish the shoes he was wearing). His train fare to Barry was covered by a discretionary grant from National Assistance.

'Jimmy knew Scotswood like a book, and was a treasure of information' and, as Steve Wood was to discover, he also had considerable knowledge of Newcastle's history: 'Well, whilst I was in his house, he took a key and opened a bedroom door. Here on shelves there were racks of tomes, by all the best-known [local] historians, Bourne, McKenzie, Welford, Charleton and many others. He had a fortune tied up there … I asked where he got them. Oh, he said, he saved up and used to go to Stedemans [Robert D. Steedman, a well known antiquarian book dealer] at the bottom of Grey Street and buy them, or put them aside, till he could. As he would only be on Assistance allowance, he must have starved himself to buy them.'

Jimmy recorded the contents of his personal library, which at that time was approaching three hundred volumes covering a variety of subjects, in a blue Monarch exercise book. There were autobiographies and biographies; the study of language and dictionaries; an extensive section devoted to works about Scotland (Jimmy had always been immensely proud of his Scottish roots); atlases and a number of periodicals, many of which were of antiquarian interest and of considerable value. It has not been possible to establish what happened to them.

Living in Elswick brought Jimmy into contact with some of the notorious families that lived there in the late 1950s and 1960s. Steve Wood described how Jimmy 'knew all the villains':

> At least twice, things happened with my shop, and when things sorted themselves out I was sure Jimmy helped in his way. For instance, one customer of mine had an electric[al] store in Newgate Street facing the Empire and on the corner of Nuns Lane. He was talking to me one day in the front shop, and said he had been broken into the previous evening, and the thieves had got away with a lot of gear. I have forgotten his name, but think he traded under 'Newgate Electrics'. He lived at Tweedmouth and had a hotel near the corner of the main road leading over the old Tweed Bridge. On occasions he used to pop in for a bit chat, and at times left a parcel on the counter. Always a nice slice of salmon. Now about a week or two after he had been broken into. I suffered a smash and grab. My shop had no back, so is [was] difficult to get into. But cameras, [were] on display in my four windows in the arcade. Always smash and grab. Even though over the years I had had gates, wire netted frames, and metal tape alarms fitted [which were] no deterrent. Smash the gate and wrench the wire grid off [!] They just waited till the police car had done its round, and when out of hearing, a brick through the glass and grab what they could, or wanted. [This had happened] eleven times in my tenancy. Well this time this time they had got numerous cameras and accessories.

Within a week a 'large brown envelope' arrived which contained a message that said that if police were to call at a certain address 'they would find something of interest'. When the police carried out a raid at the address they found an 'Aladdin's Cave of stolen property'. Steve Wood was in no doubt as to who had provided the information, which led to a successful prosecution. Jimmy, himself, was a victim of crime on more than one occasion. When his flat on Scotswood Road was broken into he hurried home to find that only an electric kettle was missing. As he commented 'most of the nickable wealth in my house and neighbour's houses was in the gas meter'.

Jimmy's flat, too, was swept away by the developers. As the condemned houses were demolished and the land was cleared for the new flats to house displaced families, the developers had to keep one step ahead. Jimmy followed the progress with his camera, driven by a compulsion to get things down simply and quickly without too much concern for his own personal safety: 'You don't think that things are going to change that quick, you believe some things will be there for ever'. This urgency is captured in Jimmy's description of one such photographic assignment: 'Mary Rutherford had a second-hand shop along here, I looked down into the Rolleiflex as the digger started like, and when I looked up there was nothing to be seen, down it fell, it had gone in a cloud of dust.'

Eventually those left behind wanted to move as the dust, disruption, the vermin and the opportunist thieves made life impossible. Jimmy moved to Woodland Crescent on a 1930s estate off Delaval Road. With this move he was now in the heart of an area that was to become notorious in the 1960s for the Mary Bell murders.

In 1964 Jimmy began documenting the demolition of another important landmark which was nearer to where he was now living, the old Scotswood Chain Bridge (Scotswood Suspension Bridge). This was to be a lengthy project, as it was not until 1967, after the opening of the replacement bridge, that it was finally removed. At night he worked as a watchman on a sheltered housing development near Benwell, and by day he watched and recorded the progress of the contractors. In 1971 he moved again, to a house in Forest Road, which he shared with friends from his early years on the Scotswood Road.

Throughout the late 1960s and well into the 1970s Jimmy seems to have used several cameras; the Rolleiflex having been dropped and beyond repair, while on a trip to Jesmond Dene. Most notably there is the gradual introduction of colour into his photography. He had taken some colour pictures in the 1950s but these were for special occasions – parties or weddings. The high cost of colour film was obviously an important consideration, which prevented him from exploiting its special qualities more frequently. The colour work from the 1970s has not worn well, the photographic paper used in processing has proved unstable and many prints, contained in albums in Tyne & Wear Archives are in poor condition. Jimmy's often rather erratic and haphazard methods of storage during this period have not helped. The same subjects are in evidence but it has to be said that few from this period have the compelling visual interest of his earlier work. He nevertheless continued to record all the major construction projects that took place during those years, including the construction of the Western Bypass and the development of Eldon Square into a modern shopping centre.

In the Jimmy Forsyth collection at Tyne and Wear Archives, there is an interesting two-page document [written on paper torn from a Nielsen Shopping Survey Pad] in Jimmy's handwriting, recording the demolition of the Redheugh Bridge, which was to be replaced by a modern concrete road bridge. This detailed narrative record, seems to suggest that Jimmy was beginning to consider writing as an additional way of fixing his observations. It makes for a compelling read: 'A lot of the expansion joints are now lying on the north approach road. Two large mechanical picks are now pounding away at the roadway on the bridge & the rollers can be seen on which the spans moved when expanded by heat…' certainly, I have not read anything quite like this, apart from in some of Jimmy's detailed captions to his early photographs. It seems a form of writing without precedent.

For a long time Jimmy's photographs remained largely hidden from public view and few people had any idea of his ongoing project. In 1956 Desmond Walton, a librarian based in the west of the city, met Jimmy in Elswick. 'I didn't realise at the time that he was taking photographs. The only clue I had was that I saw Jimmy standing on Park Road with a camera in his hand talking to some people.' Eventually, however, in 1974, 'Jimmy came in out of the blue with his albums, all the tiny contact prints of work going back to 1954 right up to the present day. I was absolutely staggered to see what he had done – it was a systematic approach with a proper index. Finally, he asked if he could leave the negative albums with me at the library because he was afraid that if anything happened to him they might be thrown out and destroyed. No one would understand their value.'

Recognising the significance of what Jimmy had shown him, Des arranged for prints to be made from the negatives and mounted a number of exhibitions in local libraries. The first of these exhibitions, in January 1979 at Denton Park Library, entitled *Scotswood Road with a Box Camera* was well received by local people many of whom had been relocated there from the Elswick area, prompting an outpouring of memories. Des began to interview and collect their stories in an attempt to gain an understanding of the area, and of the people who lived there. This material is now housed in West End Library at West Newcastle Picture History Collection and has grown to become a substantial archive of memories and documentary material.

In March and April 1981, Newcastle's innovative Side Gallery brought Jimmy's work to a wider public. Derek Smith (himself a fine photographer, film maker and researcher) spent many hours uncovering Jimmy's story, arranging for exhibition prints to be made from the negatives by Isabella Jedrzejczyk, and patiently transcribing Jimmy's (often extensive) captions. Jimmy was pleased with the result as it was the first time that he had seen his negatives professionally printed. This exhibition created enormous interest, and demand for publication in book form grew.

In 1983 Jimmy moved from Forest Road to a high-rise block, The Cedars, off Park Road. It was almost full circle to this part of Scotswood Road, where he had arrived forty years before. The move brought very mixed feelings, as he remained sceptical about the motives of the planners with their preference for this form of housing. As he caustically remarked: 'Planners unfortunately never live in their constructions or they would be more careful. High-rise flats for instance are only makeshift establishments, cannot and never will compare to a house of one's own and communities cannot naturally exist in such conditions. Living here I know about only eight or nine of the ninety or so people who live here. All on my floor are new, as you go out you meet in the lift, not as in a street where you pass people on doorsteps. Nobody stands at the flat door and you are too quickly away to see anyone. IF I HAD MY WAY I WOULD BLOW THEM ALL UP.'

After a number of years, concerns about his declining mobility led to him being relocated to a flat nearer ground level, sadly without the views that he cherished.

The Tyne Tees Television documentary *Jimmy Forsyth: No Fancy Shades*, which was transmitted on 9 October 1986, after a press preview the previous day, was to prove to be a turning point in interest in Jimmy and in his photographs. *No Fancy Shades*, is a remarkable film, the title taken from an interview with Jimmy that formed part of the soundtrack of the film: 'People say to me today, how did you get all those fancy shades? But I wasn't looking for fancy shades. I was just taking what was there, the things I was interested in and the things I liked, and tried to make them look real.'

Jimmy, who, at 72 (most of the footage was shot in 1985) looks surprisingly well, if a little frail, is shown photographing a demolition site and climbing the stairs at the Cedars to his flat (the lifts were often 'out of order'). 'And this is where I have ended up – The Cedars – a posh name for a block of council flats'. The film interweaves footage of Jimmy with archive film to tell his story. It also brings him together with Chris Killip, a founder member of the Side Gallery in 1976, who was, and remains, a great supporter of Jimmy and his work.

A particularly poignant encounter with Sid Chaplin, recorded two weeks before he died, is touching for Sid's obvious empathy with Jimmy and his photographs. Sid particularly liked the portraits of 'The men with caps' (he had contributed a piece to the *Guardian,* 8 September 1960, on the decline of the cloth clap in Newcastle; and he talks at length about the ways in which the older working men chose to place them very straight on the head, with the peaks facing forward shielding their eyes). In a voice over he reads a passage from what is perhaps his best book, *The Watchers and the Watched,* a novel set against the changing landscape along the Scotswood Road. Jimmy is also seen in an affectionate meeting with local politician T. Dan Smith, who defends his reasons for supporting the re-development of Elswick, as they walk together in a bleak landscape of empty streets. What comes through in the film is Jimmy's loneliness, the long hours spent reading with the aid of a large magnifying glass, and the hours tramping the streets. 'If I stopped in the house all day I had an awful job getting to sleep at night – you have to work yourself tired'. The film also shows how Jimmy used photography as a form of engagement with the characters he met on his travels around the west end of the city.

Scotswood Road grew out of *No Fancy Shades*, and was published in the same year by Bloodaxe Books, in association with Tyne Tees Television. The book also coincided with an expanded exhibition of Jimmy's photographs at the Side Gallery. An initial print run of six thousand copies quickly sold out forcing a reprint two years later. Interest in his work brought about greater self-awareness: 'I'm pleased when people pull me up in the street and say "Are you the man who took all those photographs?" It gives you a bit of pride in yourself.' In 1987 Jimmy received the Halina Award for Photography, travelling to London to collect his award and acquiring a particularly striking if ill fitting suit for the presentation. Recognition brought its rewards. Jimmy's work has found its way into mixed exhibitions across the country, and many articles about him have appeared in local and national newspapers and magazines. The media attention and his constant presence on the city streets during the 1980s helped Jimmy acquire something of a folk status on Tyneside. The film director Mike Figgis cast him as a newspaper seller in his 1988 feature film *Stormy Monday*. More bizarrely, in January 1987 Jimmy was invited, with his cameras and albums of photographs, to the studios of Tyne Tees Television, to be interviewed live by Jools Holland on the rock and pop programme *The Tube*. In what must be one of the strangest encounters ever to be broadcast, lasting barely two minutes, Jimmy talked about cameras and why he took his pictures, and why in his view, re-development was de-humanising. The interview with Jimmy was followed by a montage of his photographs taken from *Scotswood Road*, set to a backing track.

Although Jimmy's celebrity status gradually meant that the business of making street portraits and recording a changing Newcastle became easier (he was to receive royalties for the *Scotswood Road* book, which was a local best seller), the remarkable achievements of the 1950s and 60s were never to be matched.

By the early 1990s, Jimmy, now in his late seventies, was increasingly vulnerable. In 1992 he returned to Barry. The award of a Northern Arts travel bursary allowed him to make the trip with local journalist Veronica Johnson who first met Jimmy in the early 1980s. She had become a close friend and was preparing to write his biography, but tragically this was to remain unrealised as Veronica died suddenly in 1999. Jimmy hoped that this trip to his birthplace would give him an opportunity to take photographs that could be used in the proposed biography. In Barry, Jimmy was drawn to the docks and railway sidings where his father had worked. In the evening Veronica and Jimmy were entertained 'by members of the railway club'. Veronica contacted High Street School and they made Jimmy guest of honour for the day. Delighted by the response of the pupils and teachers, he left copies of his book *Scotswood Road* in the school library. The next day *The Barry and District News* ran a feature on the return journey and Jimmy's work as a documentary photographer. Sadly, he was unable to trace any surviving relatives. His mother had died in 1958, his father in 1960 and afterwards he had lost contact with his half-brother John; it seems that he had died just before the trip. As part of the journey had been to search for lost relatives, Jimmy was visibly moved on his return to Tyneside having found no one from his generation still in Barry.

Declining health from 2000 onwards meant that Jimmy was largely confined to his flat at The Cedars. The days of his wandering were finally over, though he did manage to get to the opening of the Gateshead Millennium Bridge. However, his appetite for taking photographs remained undiminished as he fired off shots of visitors with his Olympus Trip camera. There is also a series of photographs of images taken from his wide screen television.

The days now were spent reading, despite his failing eyesight. Appropriately, he particularly enjoyed travel writing 'older ones preferably'. He was fascinated by accounts of the sinking of the *Titanic*. Unable to get to libraries he made full use of the contacts he had made over the years, with requests for increasingly obscure books.

In June 2001 Jimmy, was visited in his flat by the writer Gordon Burn who was researching a piece on him. The resulting article was published in the *Guardian Weekend* magazine on 30th June, under the heading 'Little Brother is Watching You'. Burn, who was no stranger to writing about controversial subjects, having already tackled Fred and Rosemary West and the 'Yorkshire Ripper' Peter Sutcliffe, did not spare Jimmy. The opening sentence 'Jimmy Forsyth looks like a tramp and lives like a tramp, and in the course of a day many people no doubt take him for a tramp, rather than what he is: Newcastle's holy innocent, the city's tireless recording angel' sets the tone of the article. Jimmy hated this strident account of him and his life's work. It was not the first time someone had commented in print on his dishevelled appearance, but it seemed particularly unfair as by that time he was almost blind and unable to walk far. He was struggling to survive on his own in very difficult circumstances and waiting to be re-housed by the council. As he was to tell Derek Smith: 'The quality of my life is much better compared to twenty years ago when you had to struggle for everything. We're a lot higher above the poverty line than we were but not as high as Mr Blair thinks we are! I'm unsteady on my feet now but I don't have to wait for buses, I can take a taxi. I have a home help too. And I'm talking to the doctor about me cataract. It's only lately I've been put off reading, and I used to read a lot. It's helped me cope with loneliness.'

Burn's article nevertheless reawakened interest in Jimmy and his photographs. By late July Jimmy had completed the arrangements to hand over all his negatives to Tyne and Wear Archives. The *Evening Chronicle* for 31 July reported that 'Jimmy 87, said: "I'm glad the negatives will be well looked after I'm proud of the pictures and hope future generations will be able to look at them and see how much the city has changed"'.

In May 2002 Jimmy was awarded an honorary degree of Master of the University by the Open University. On being told that he could now put M Univ. after his name, he commented with his characteristic humour that he was now a 'Master of the Universe'. BBC *Close up North* made a film about him entitled *Lives through a Lens*. They succeeded in tracking down a number of the children, who had posed for him nearly fifty years before. The publication of *Out of One Eye: The Photography of Jimmy Forsyth* later that year brought together a wider selection of his photographs with invaluable oral testimony of a selection of his subjects from the 1950s and 1960s.

Although he never married (rumours of romantic attachments persist) he always had several dedicated friends who helped him to maintain his independence. After a series of falls it became clear that he could no longer look after himself, and he was moved to a care home. Initially he was taken on trips to the Grainger Market, the Quayside and the Baltic Centre for Contemporary Art (where he expressed his opinions on the exhibitions forcibly) and further afield to Gibside, Alnwick Fair, Belsay and Bamburgh. Eventually it became clear that he found these outings an ordeal and his deteriorating health confined him within his room. Jimmy died at Elswick Hall Care Home at 2.20am on Saturday 11 July 2009; he had been ill for most of the preceding week. His funeral at West Road Crematorium, the following Thursday, was well attended by friends and some of his subjects from the Scotswood Road. The service was conducted by the vicar of St Stephen's, Low Elswick, Reverend G.R. Curry, who had known Jimmy for nearly thirty years. It was very warm in the chapel, humid and airless, a foretaste of the heavy storm that broke later in the afternoon.

Jimmy Forsyth left a remarkable legacy. He is now seen as one of the region's finest chroniclers, someone to be mentioned in the same breath as the Tyneside novelists Jack Common and Sid Chaplin. His portraits of children are breathtaking for their innocence and reflect the empathy he had with his subjects. In 2002 while researching for *Out of One Eye*, Derek Smith interviewed some of the children, now adults, who had appeared in Jimmy's photographs. They provided some remarkable memories of life along the Scotswood Road. It is rare for the subject of a photograph to get a right of reply, to describe the circumstances under which it was taken and why. Pat Logan proudly held up an original print (extremely creased and with areas of the print surface missing) of the photograph Jimmy had taken of her and her friend Pat Norman in 1957. 'We'd been to a shop in Suffolk Street for chews and just come round the corner into Sycamore Street. We came across Jimmy and he said, "Just stand there and I'll take your photos."' She has kept this battered print of herself as a child in every handbag she has ever owned.

Placing Jimmy's photographs in a gallery context changes them; we see them differently. Mick Bidewell, responding to an article about Jimmy in *Amateur Photographer*, wrote: '... thanks to Jimmy's decision to record what was around him while it was still there, I can revisit the very location where – aged five – I crashed my pedal car, resulting in a bump on the head on which my mum resorted to the rather dubious cure of rubbing it with a knob of butter.'

This association of the personal with the inconsequential, the easily overlooked with the dispassionate record of appearance, gives the photographs a life way beyond the circumstances of their taking. Nothing seems to have escaped his eye. He notices the stirrings of adolescence, the beginnings of self-consciousness in the teenage girls, the lads striking a pose for the camera, the resignation of many of the adults. The young 'Ted' sitting on the roadside kerb clutching a pigeon nervously, is as fine a portrait of 1950s northern youth as we are likely to get.

We can come back to the topographic views and attempt to reconstruct the position of a building or the course of a road but we cannot place individuals in the same way, they have moved on with their lives. At such a distance in time it is also impossible to place Jimmy within his photographs; occasionally his shadow intrudes, but he is mostly missing. There are a few photographs where he appears part of the scene, usually in the background, an elusive presence that states that he was there, a witness concerned with photographing history.

In Tyne & Wear Archives there is a substantial collection of albums, negative files, cardboard boxes brimming with seemingly endless folders of processed films, documents of his life, letters and royalty statements for the *Scotswood Road* book. Most of this material was rescued from Jimmy's flat during his last years, it is still being catalogued and conserved:

a daunting task, as much that has survived is understandably in poor condition. Jimmy seems never to have decided what to keep and what to discard, preferring to leave those decisions to posterity. Obviously, things have been lost during the many moves, and doubtless negatives and photographs will have been borrowed and never returned.

From the early tartan albums with their corresponding negative files, Jimmy meticulously recorded the locations of his pictures, including in one instance on the reverse a detailed sketch-map. As an activity it was the patient recording of an unfolding personal history, initially for his eyes only; though he came later to realise the significance of his work as a record of Tyneside as it was then. In the 1980s as his photographs became more widely appreciated this careful organisation was disrupted when his negatives were professionally printed and exhibited and the demand for prints increased. It proved difficult to keep things as he had intended. Eventually Jimmy temporarily placed his negatives in the care of West Newcastle Local Studies. He remarked philosophically, 'It's no good burying the pictures. They should be given out to more people, and they should be free, after all they belong to their subjects, to the people themselves'.

Jimmy's generosity of spirit is admirable, and his photographs have been extensively reproduced over the years. A 1960 photograph of the hole in the bedroom wall of a house in Pine Street, after a runaway beer wagon from the Hope and Anchor brewery had run backwards into it, taken up by the *Evening Chronicle* ('though I didn't get much for it, 7s 6d'), provides an early example of his work reaching a wider audience.

In the 1980s Jimmy made separate agreements with Bloodaxe Books and the West Newcastle Local Studies Group regarding the reproduction, exhibition and copying of his original negatives. This led inevitably to complications, coming to a head in February 1988 when he signed an agreement with West Newcastle Local Studies that appeared to conflict with an agreement that he had signed with Bloodaxe in 1986. On 19 February this was cancelled – Jimmy writing across the document 'signed under harras[s]ment before being understood properly by signee'. The matter was eventually resolved satisfactorily, with Jimmy receiving two thirds of any proceeds from the sale of his work; the remaining third was payable to West Newcastle Local Studies. After the publication of *Scotswood Road* Jimmy seems not to have appreciated that his photographs were now perceived and valued as outstanding examples of documentary photography. This aspect of the wider photographic world did not interest him. He continued to give away prints as he had done in the 1950s and 1960s, accepting small amounts in return for the cost of films and processing. Jimmy was never to make much from his photographs, though his local fame in the 1980s led some to think that he was suddenly well off. Twenty years earlier Jimmy had been known in Elswick as 'the Duke', a nickname that perhaps grew out of a similar misunderstanding of his actual situation. This perception had also occurred to an *Evening Chronicle* reporter, Jack Saltman, in October 1961, when he went along the Scotswood Road talking to residents who were about to be displaced: 'Perhaps my biggest surprise came with my visit to the home of Mr. James Forsyth. In his small front room at No. 353, I found a library that would have done credit to many a stately home. Around his walls were volumes ranging from books on old Newcastle to works by classical authors.'

There is an amusing story told by Jimmy of a visit from Lady Ridley who came to collect a piece of Sunderland Ware that he had offered to her. The arrival of her chauffeur driven car 'led to lots of heads sticking out of windows down the street to see who it was'. Jimmy's unfailing generosity led, on more than one occasion, to his being taken advantage of, though he seems to have accepted this as a reflection of human nature and was not unduly concerned. As he was to say in *No Fancy Shades,* he was 'an honest citizen who helps everybody when he could'.

Jimmy had an innocent eye; his photographs show without affectation, what he saw around him. There is something intensely engaging in the way in which he had an instant rapport with his subjects; they seem completely at ease, comfortable in his presence. The intimacy of these photographs is a rare and wonderful achievement, because they represent a vanished community seen and photographed from within.

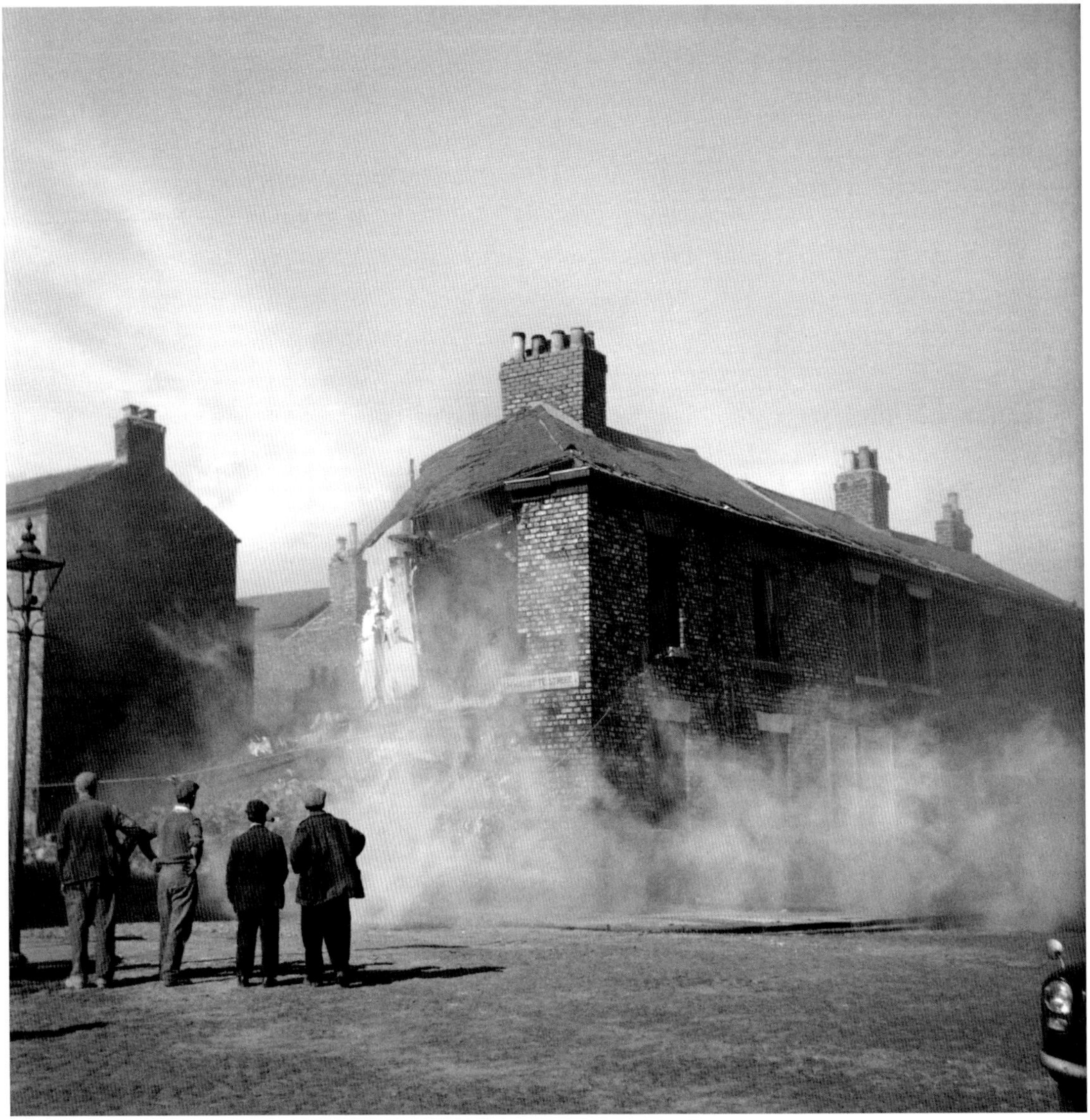

Demolition of Charlotte Street, 1959.

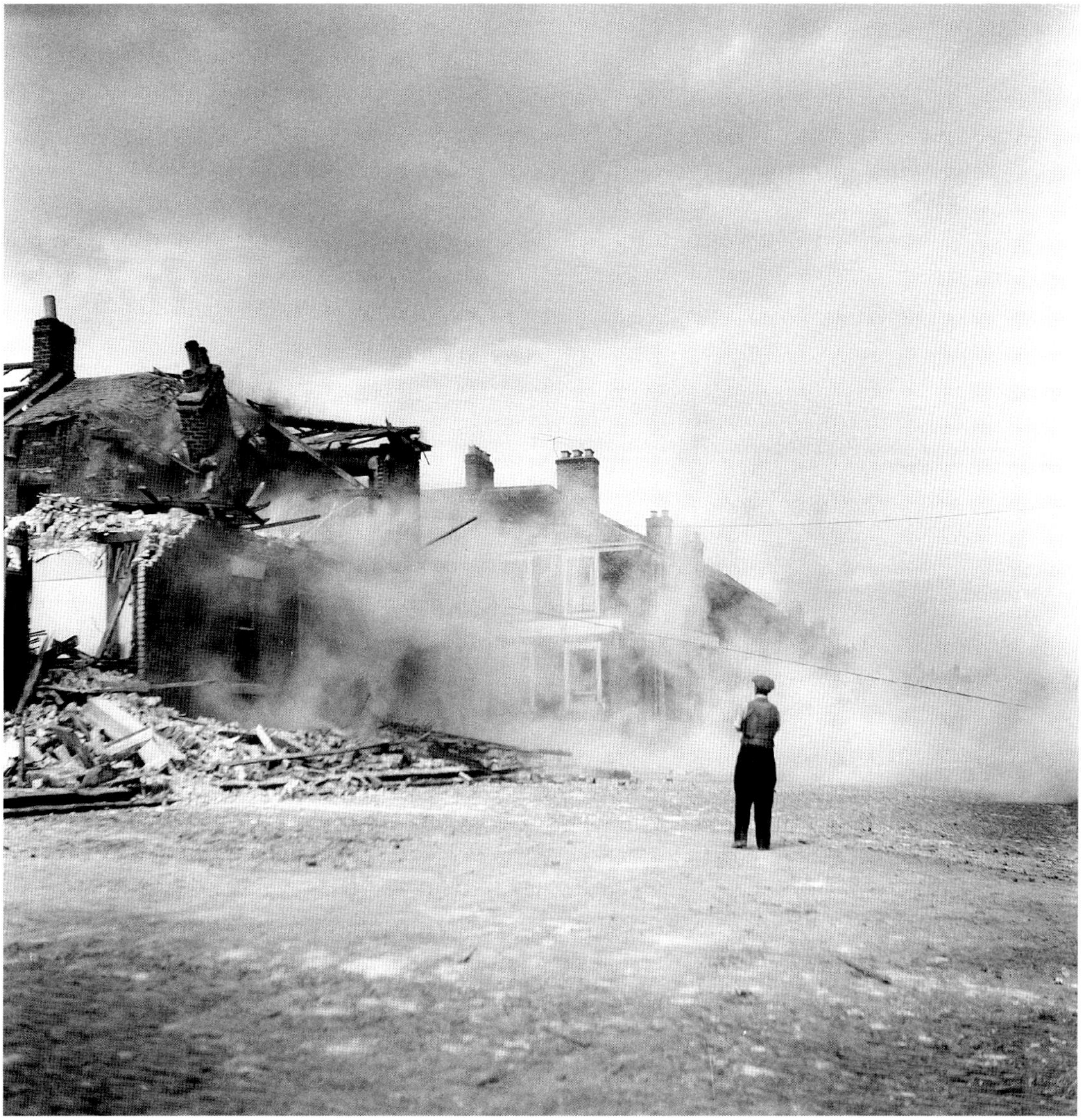

Pushing down a chimney in Sycamore Street, August 1960.

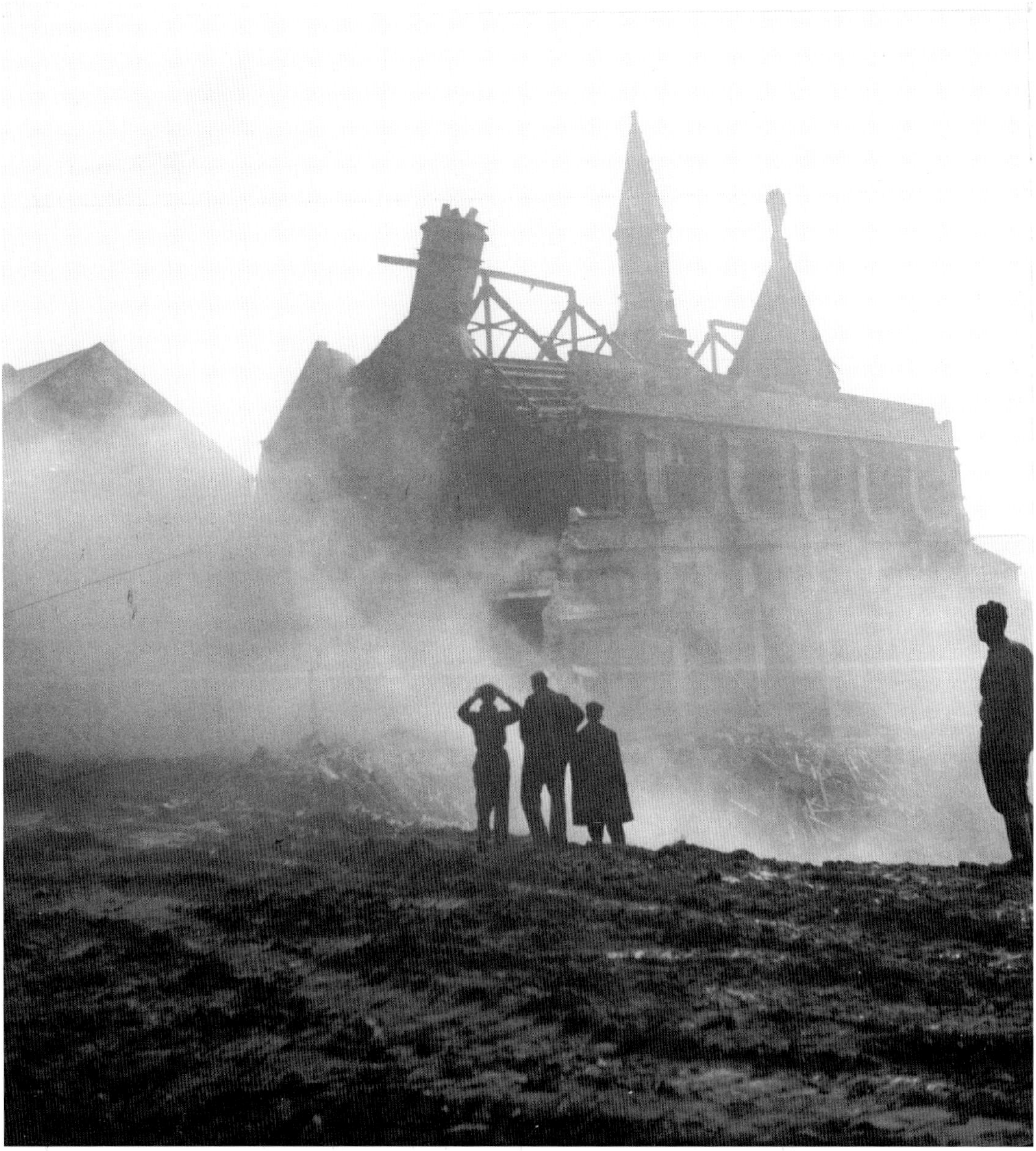

Demolition of St Stephen's Parish Hall, October 1960.

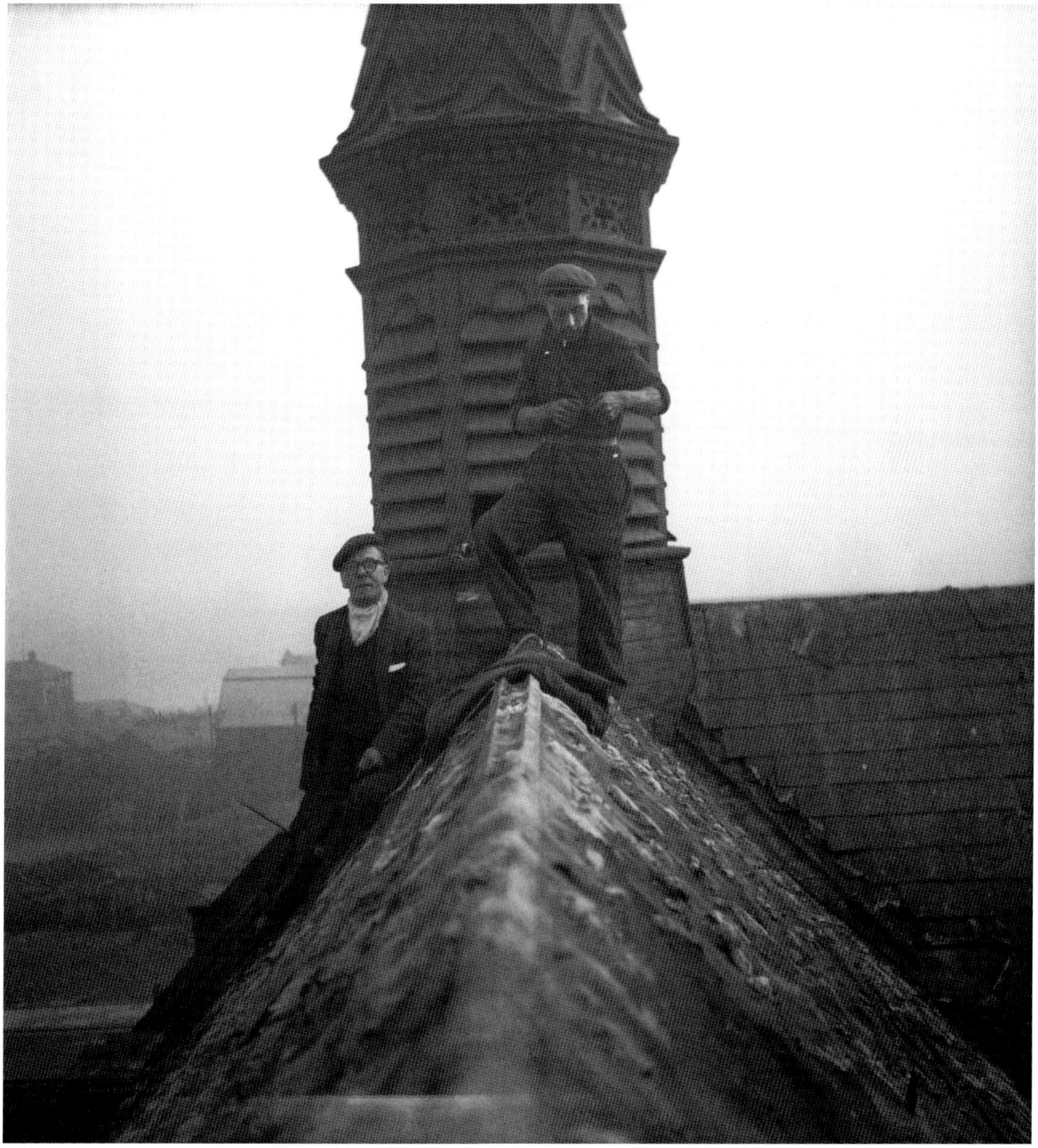

Roof of St Stephen's Parish hall in Tulloch Street.
Vic Summers and Edward Turnbull, 6 October 1960.

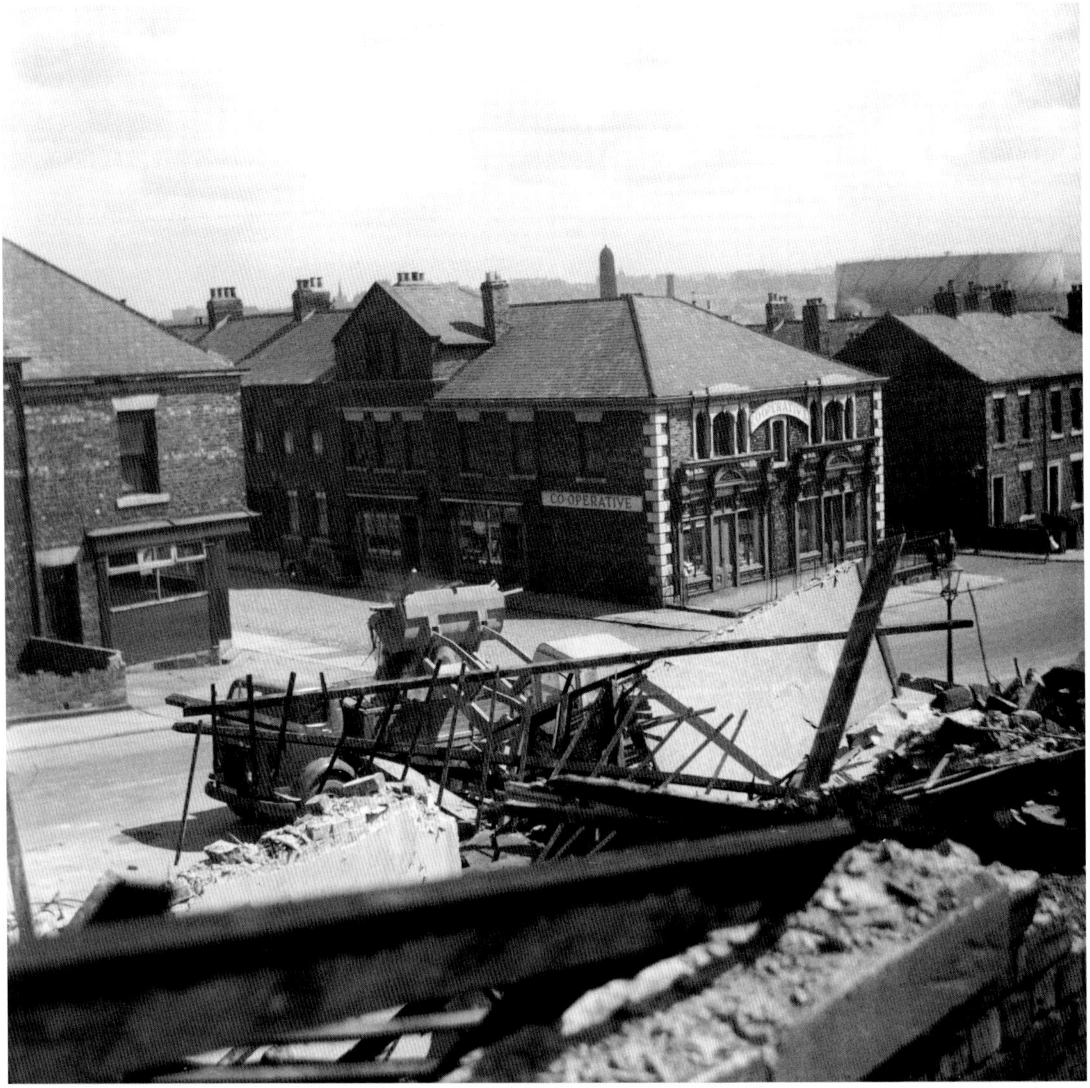

View from the rear steps of Gloucester Street.

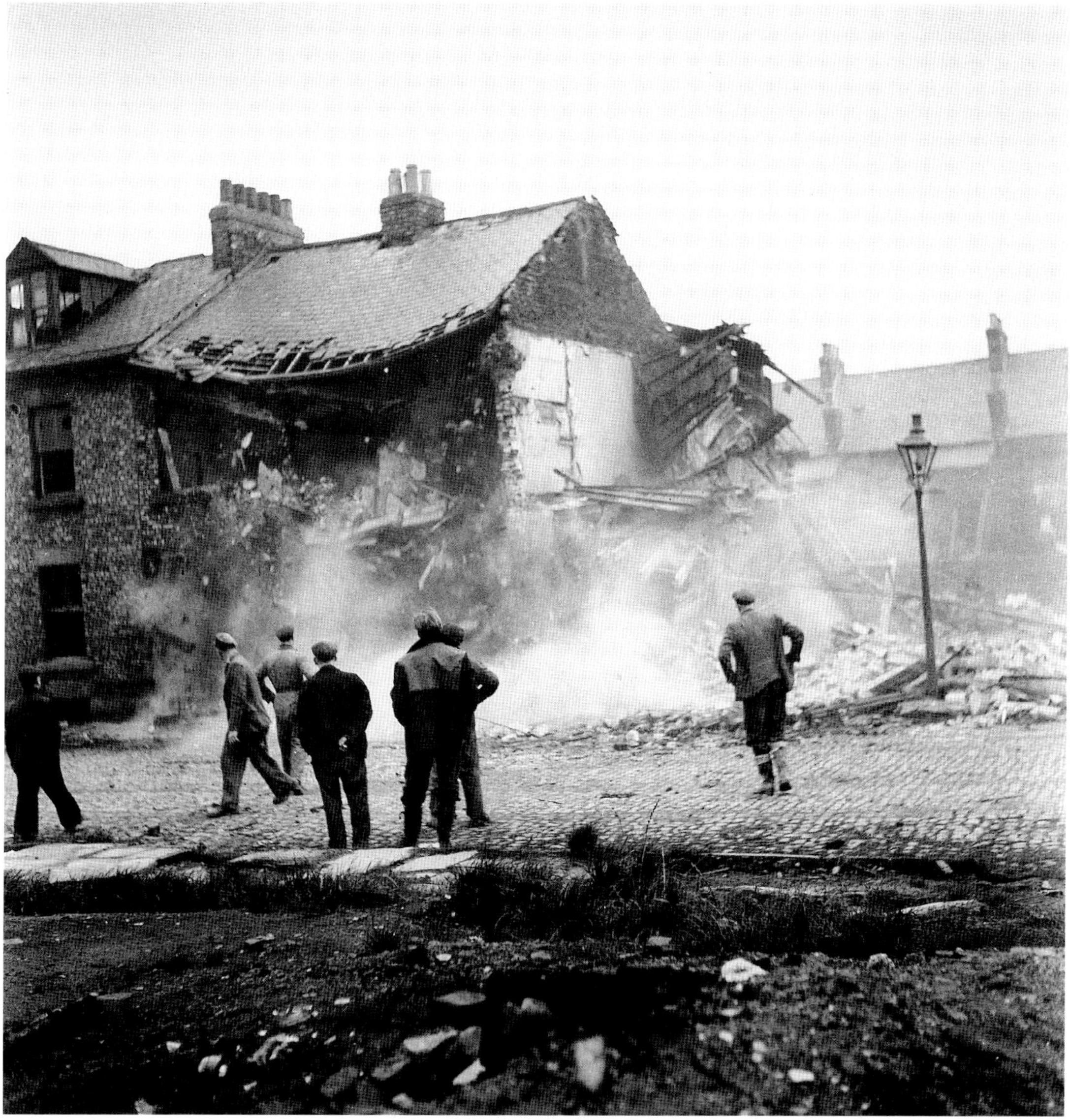

Sycamore and Suffolk Street demolition, 1961.

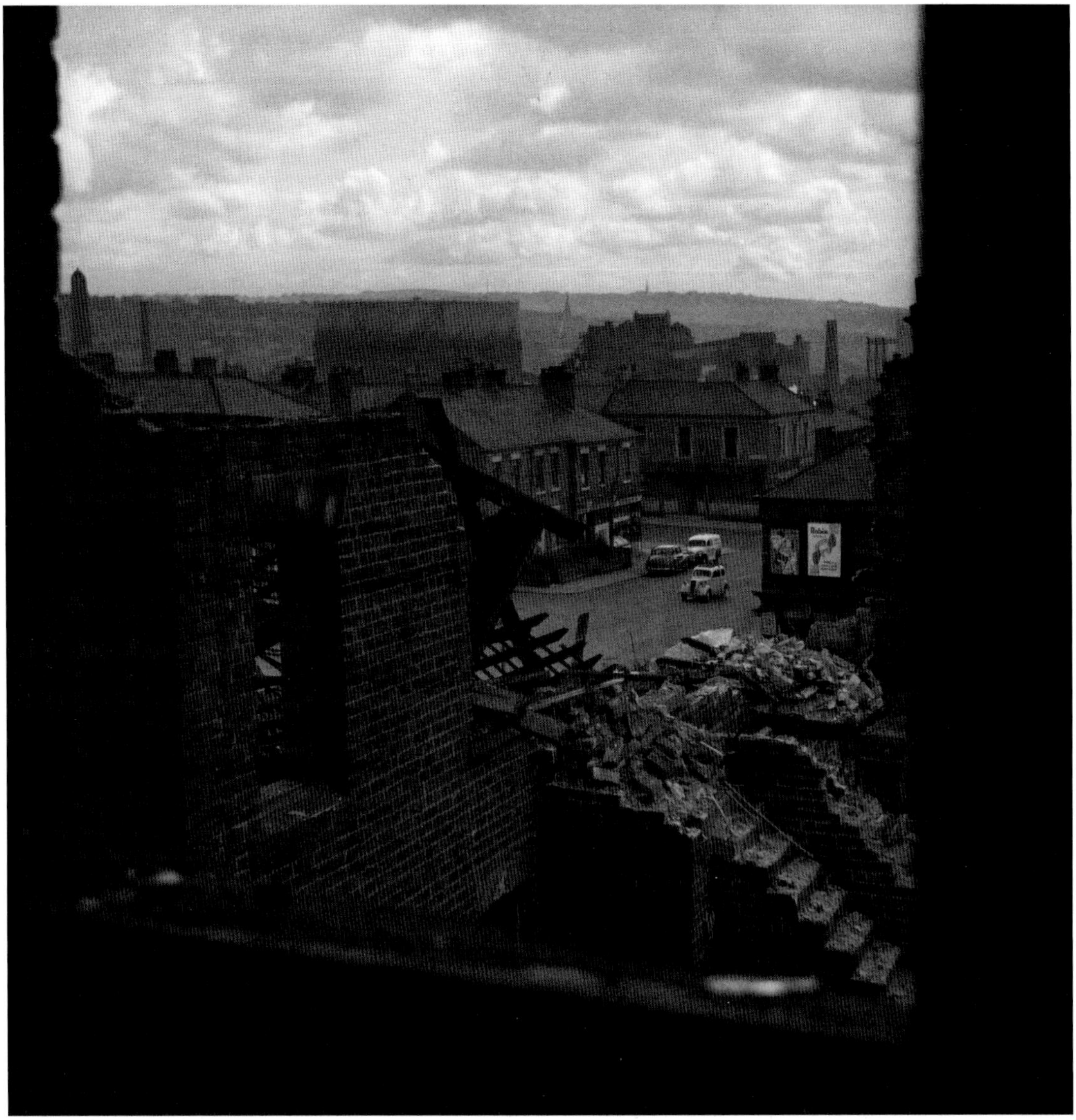

View from the rear window of 107 Pine Street, August 1960.

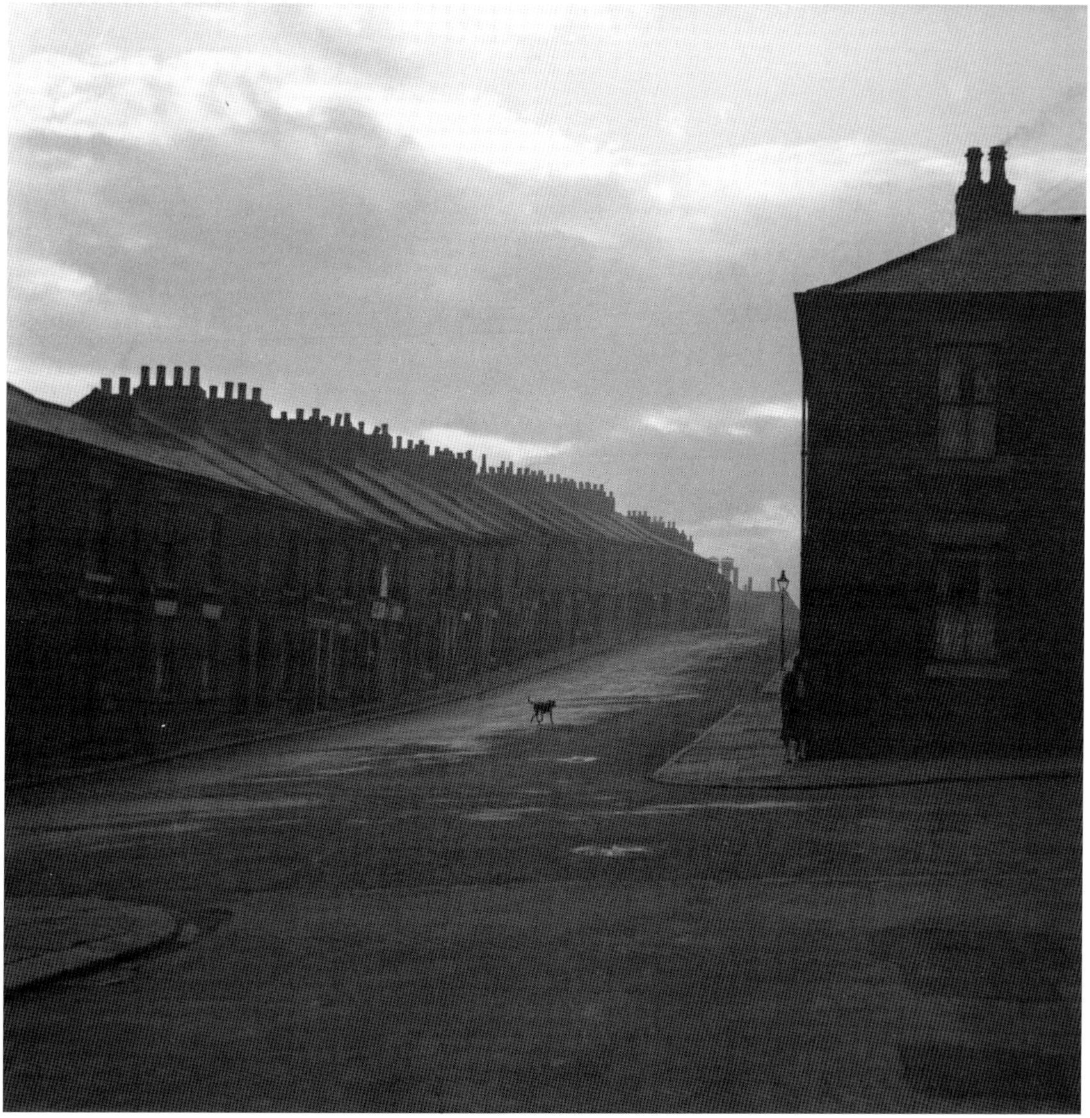

Looking up Penn Street, c1957.

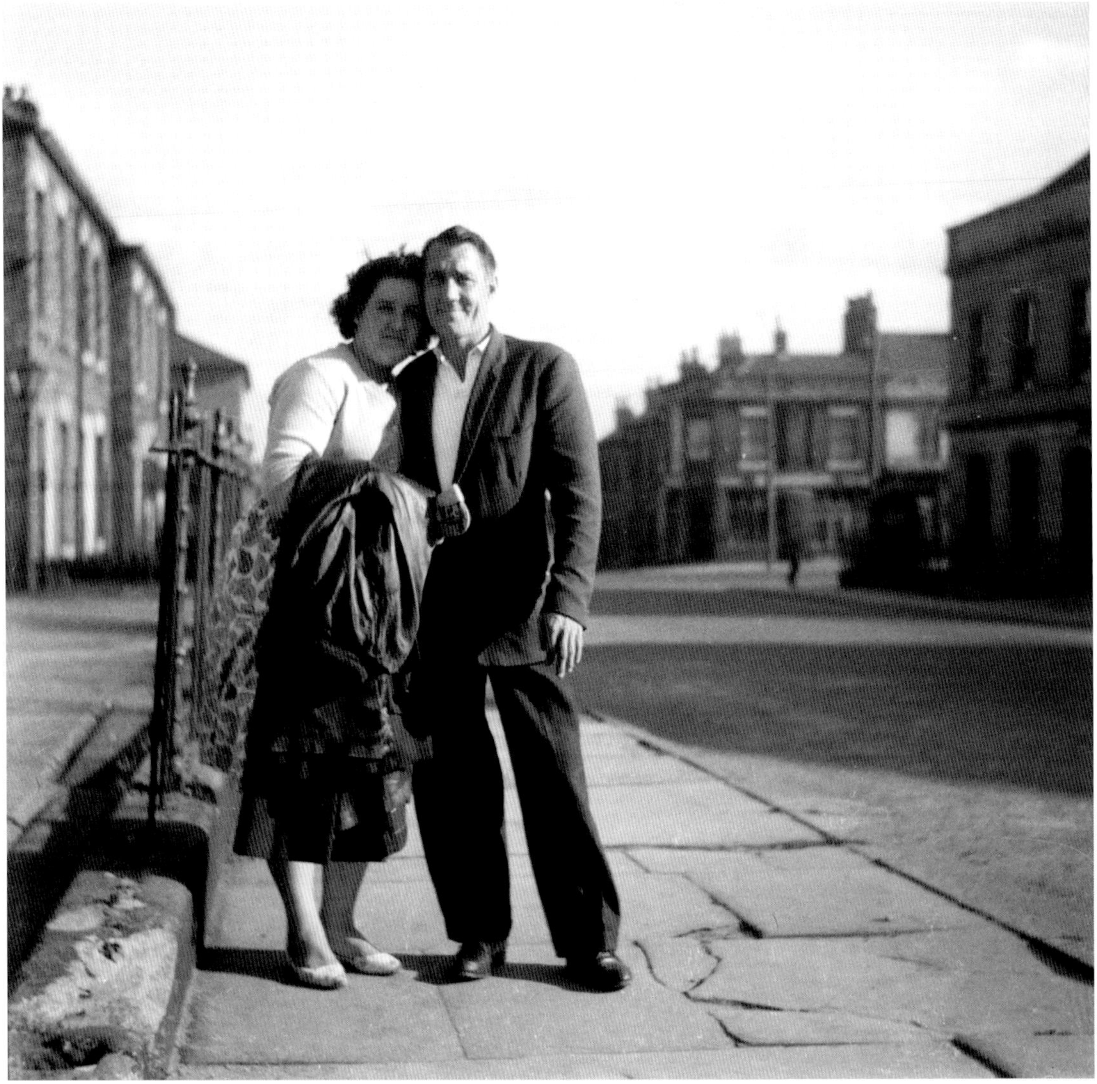

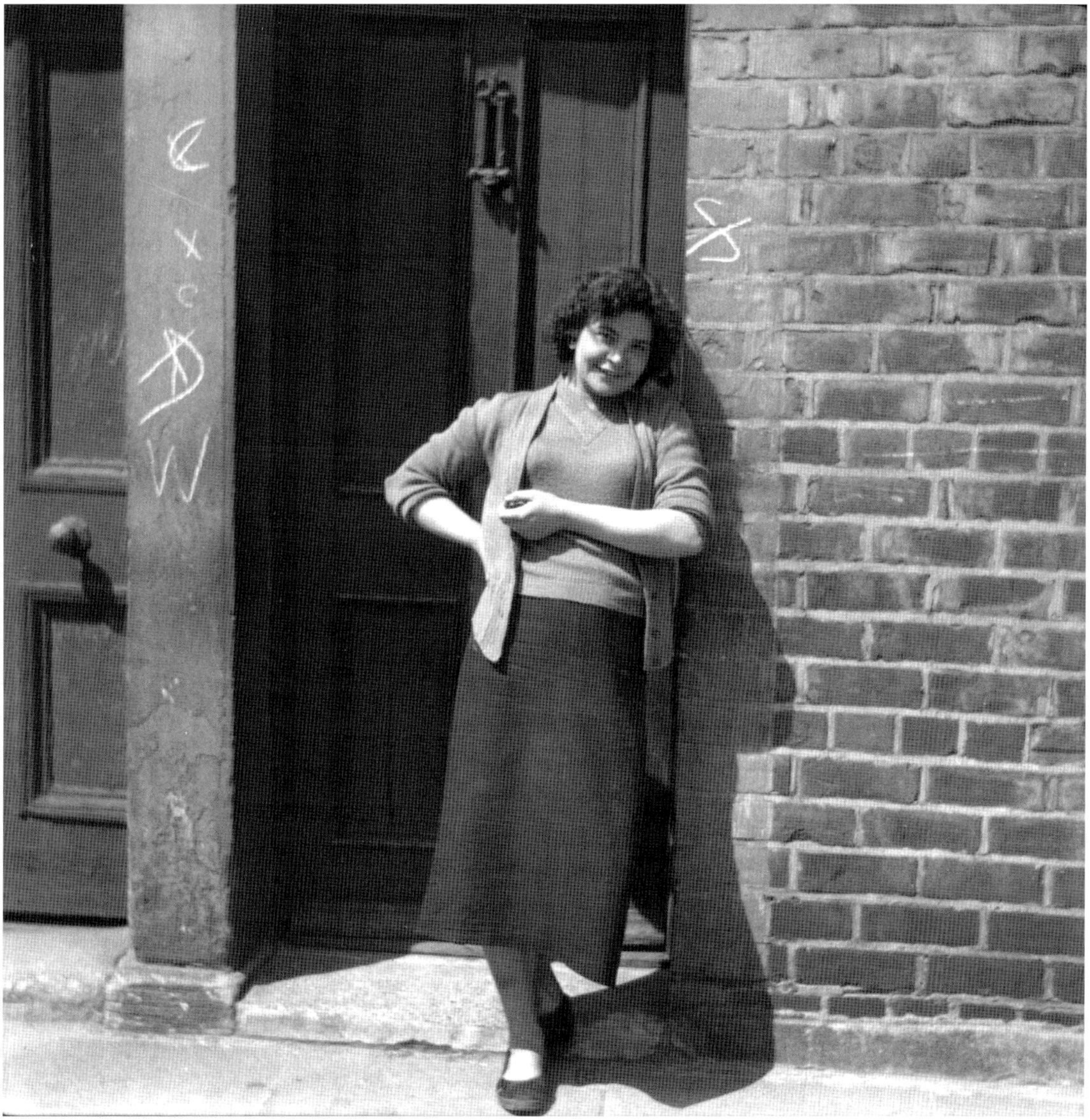

Betty Young on her doorstep, Scotswood Road, 1958.

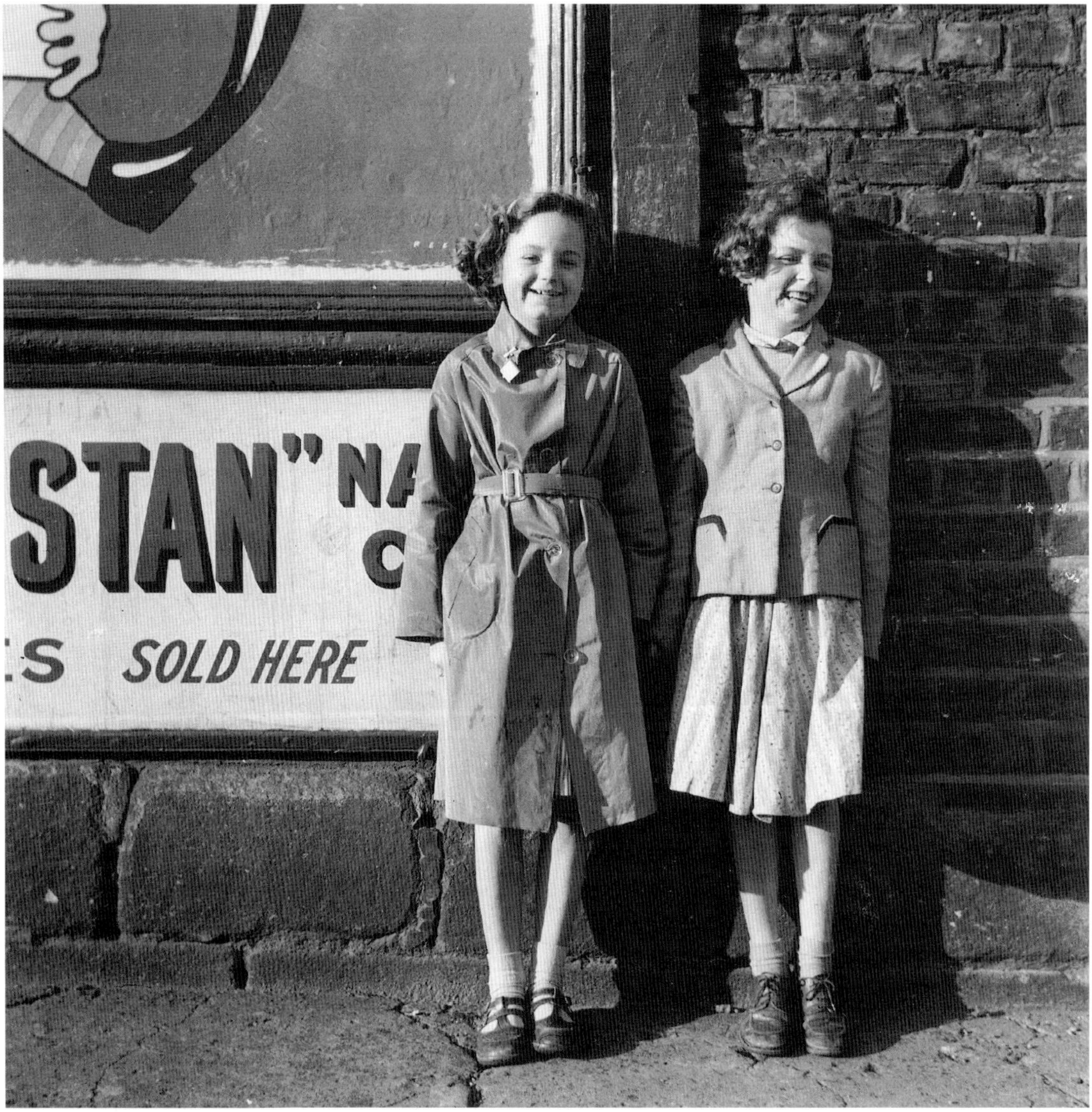

Pat Logan and Pat Curry, Sycamore Street, 1957.

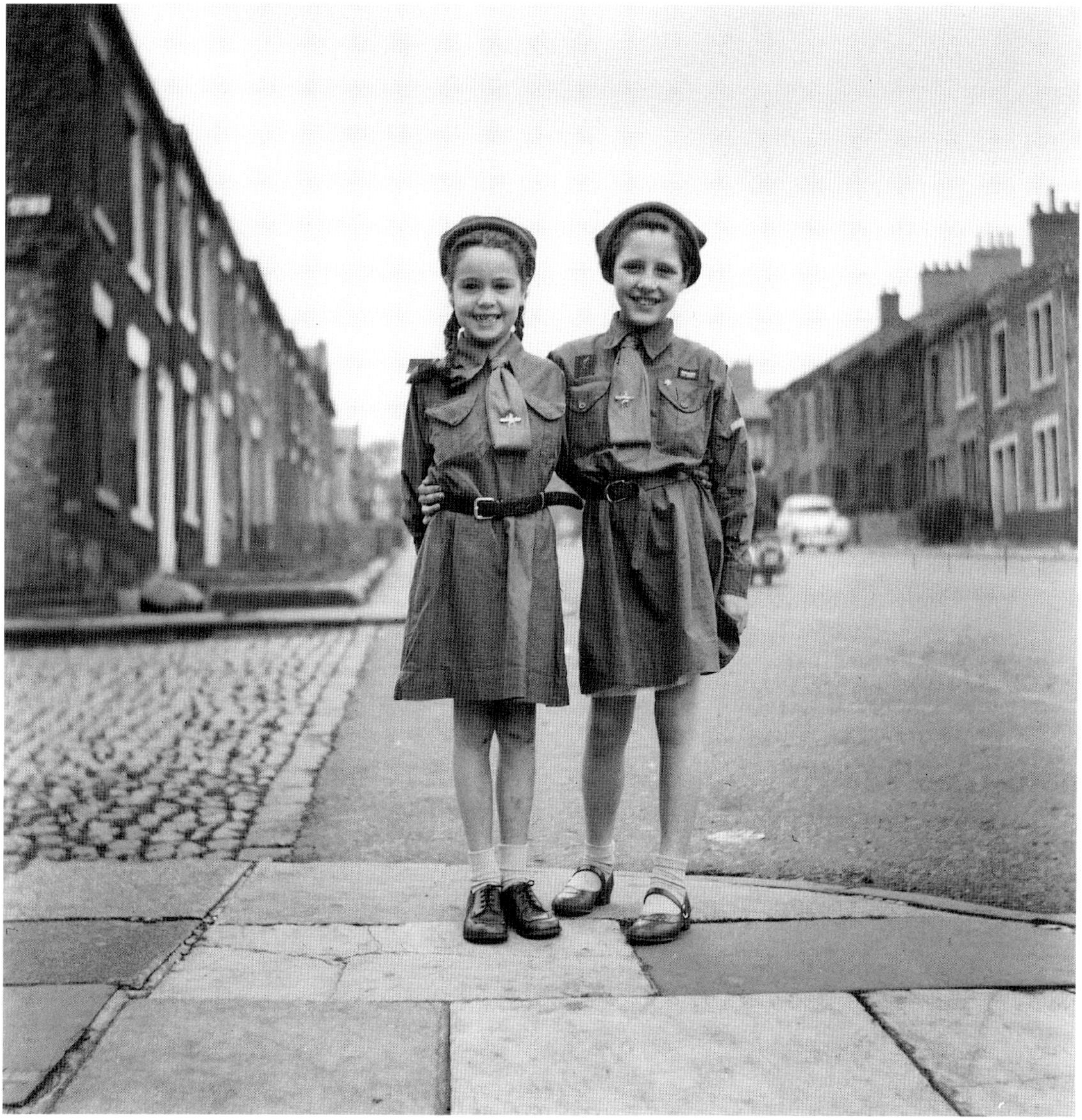

Brownies, 26 July 1958. Maureen Beveridge and Carol.

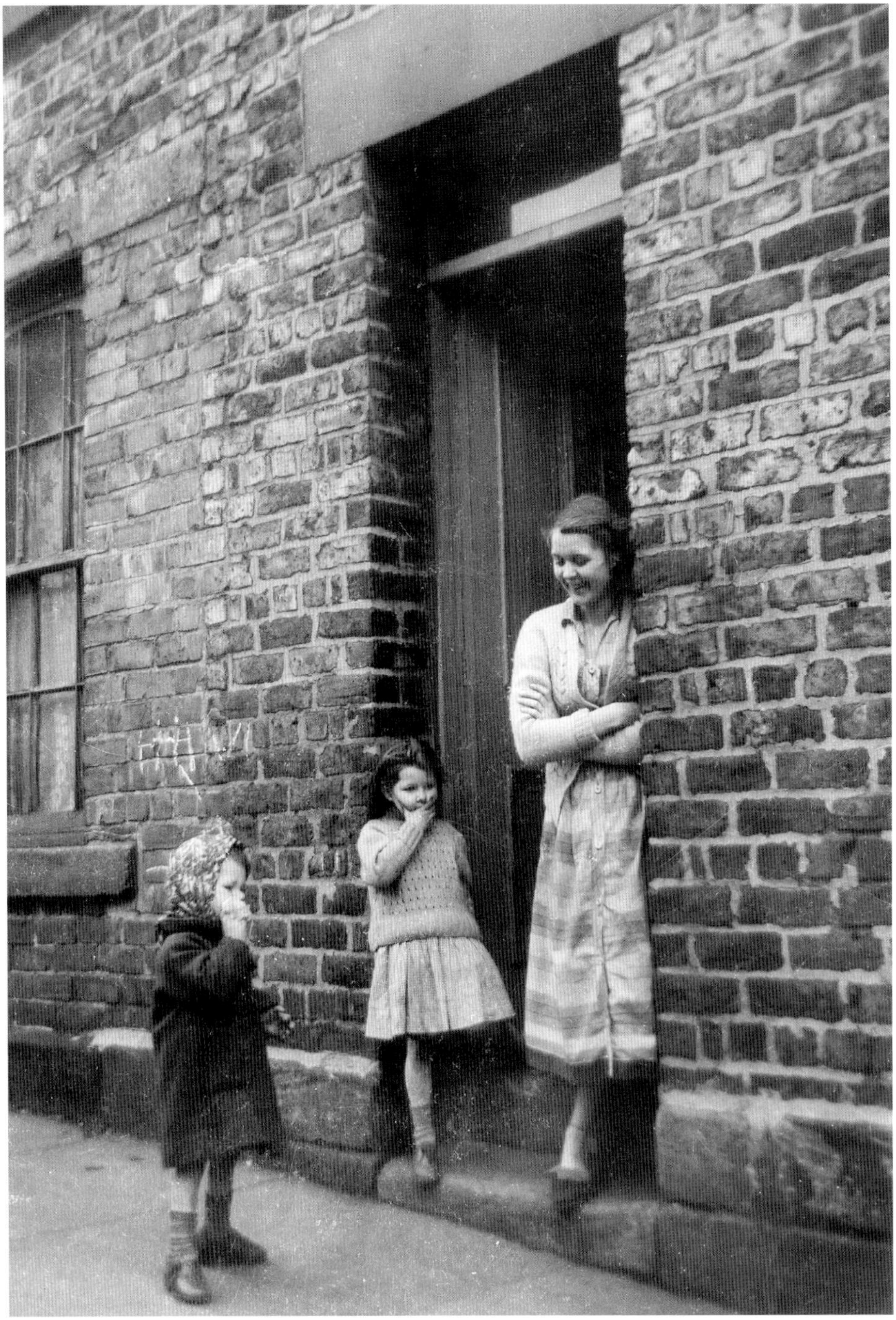

Nancy Bates with Ralph and Shirley Ann, Laurel Street.

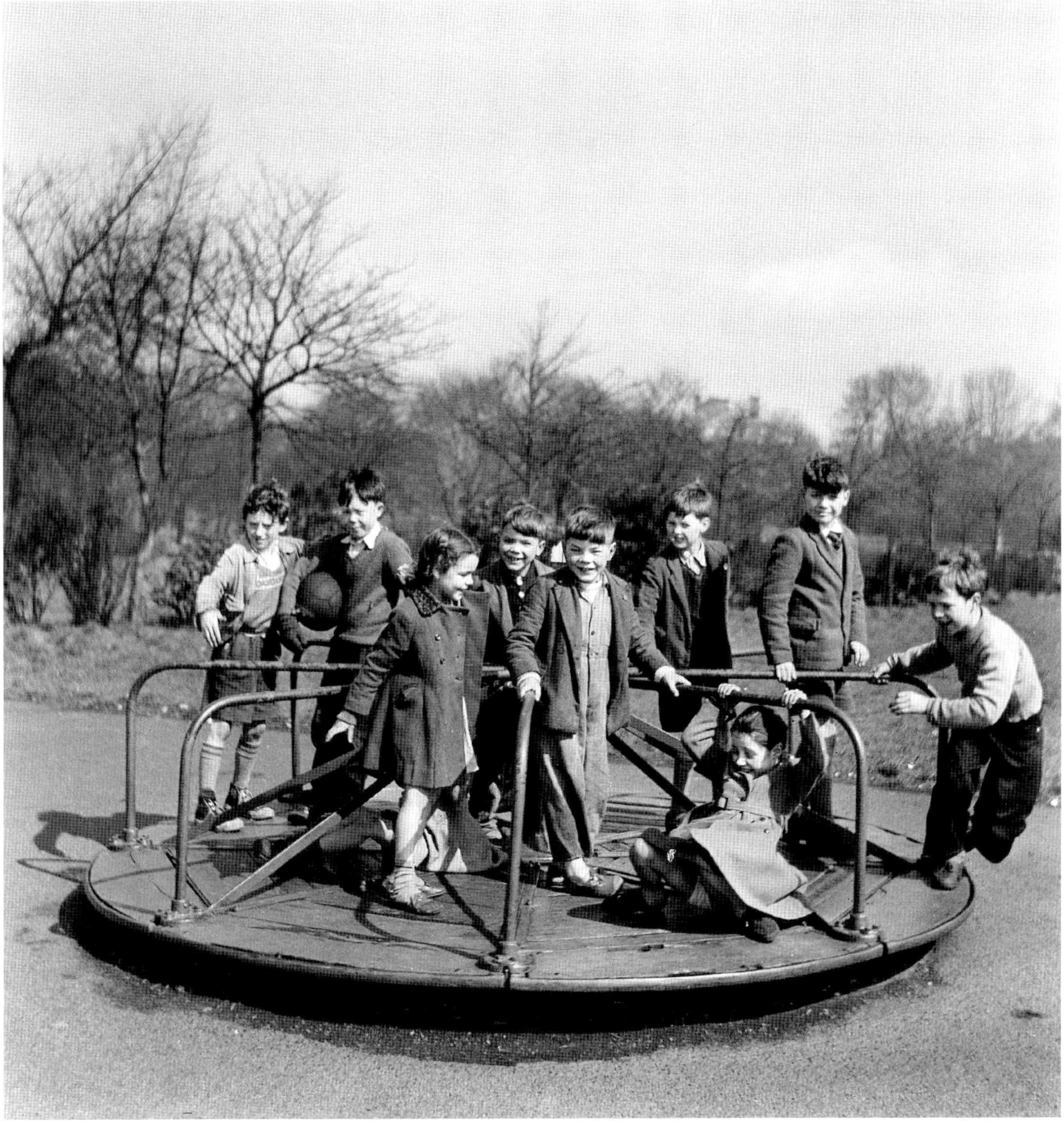

Children in Leazes Park, April 1957.

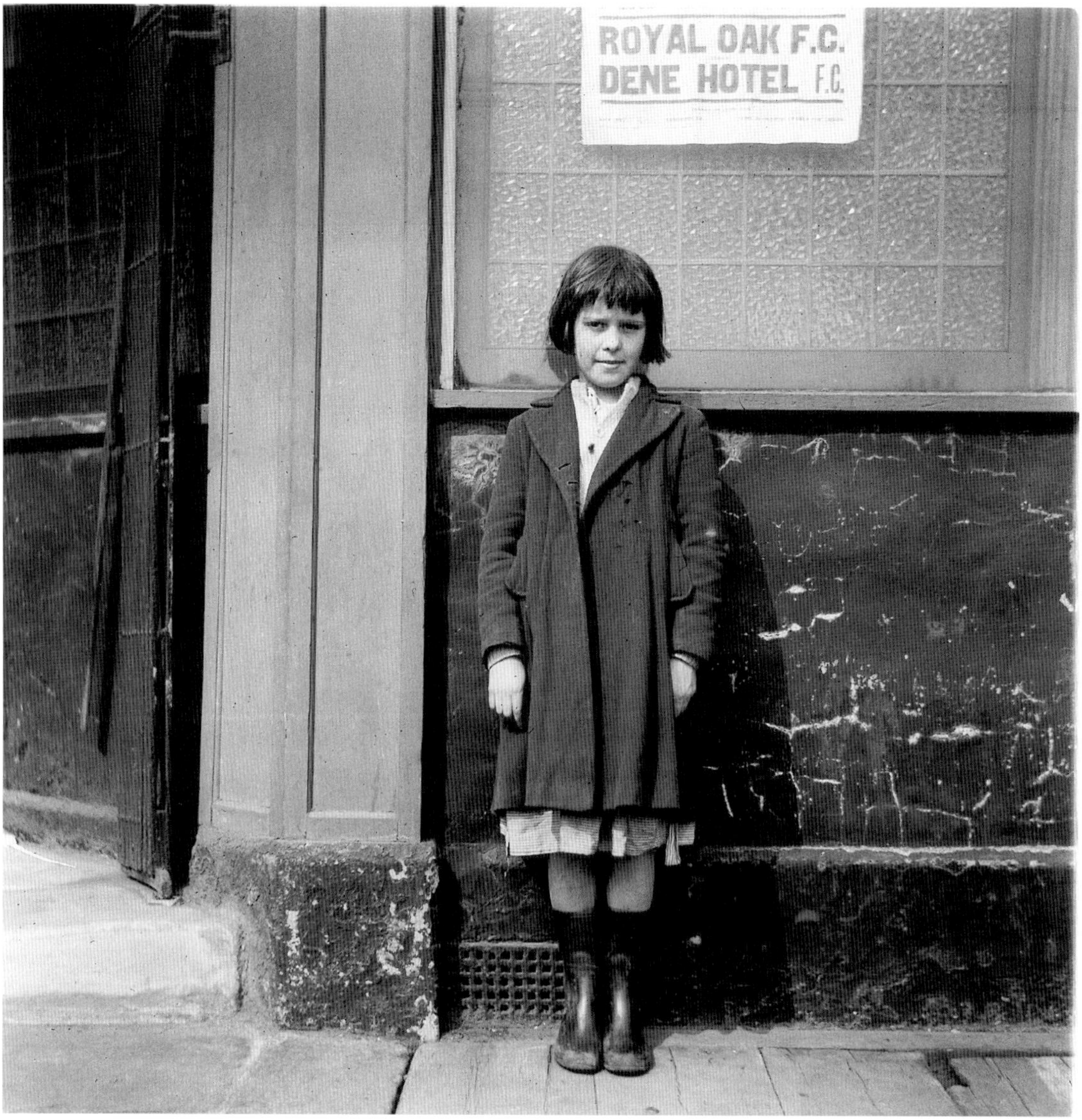

The Royal Oak, Scotswood Road, 1956.

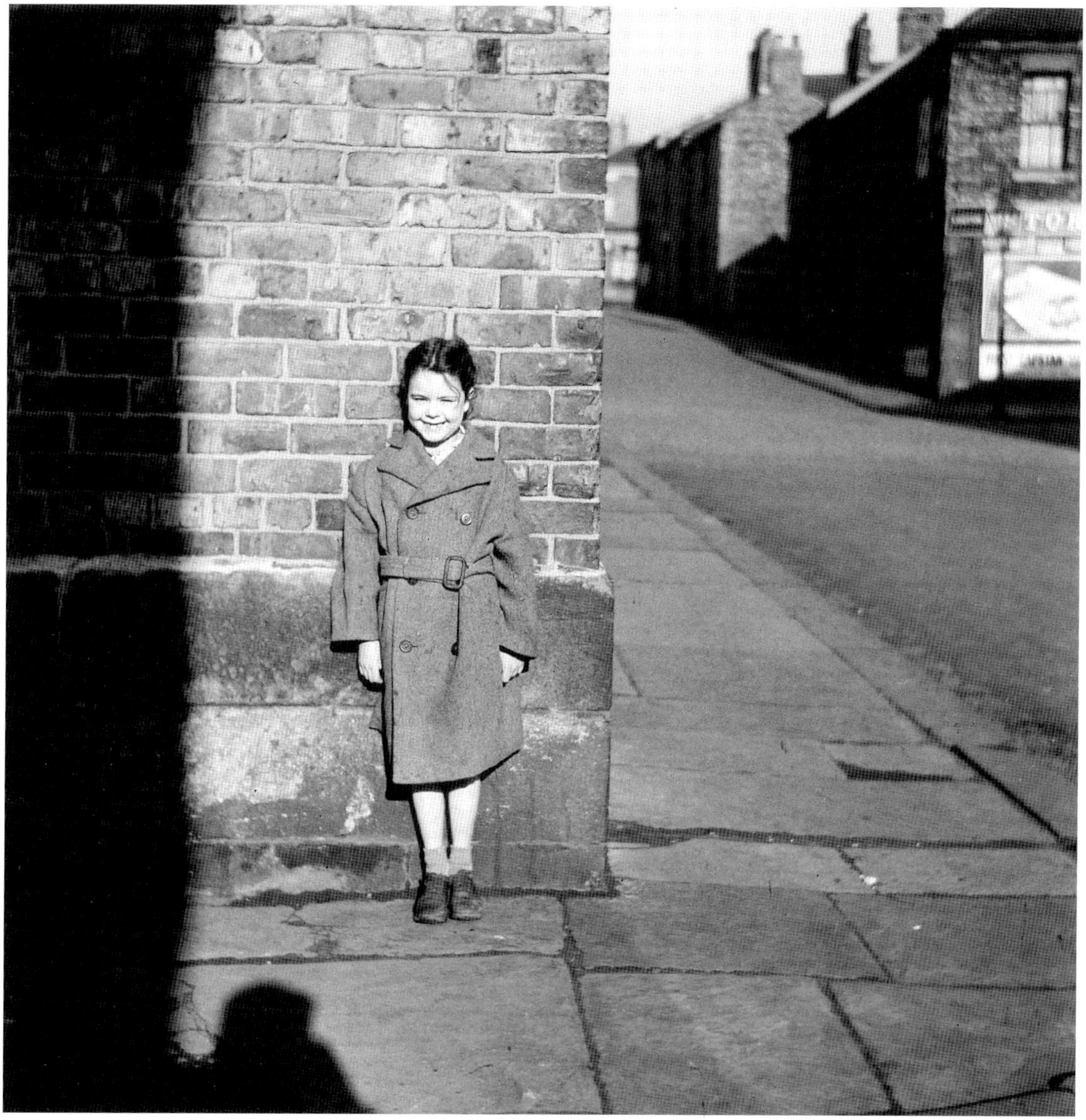

Maureen Beveridge, Sycamore Street, July 1958. North side of Scotswood Road.
'The New Coat'.

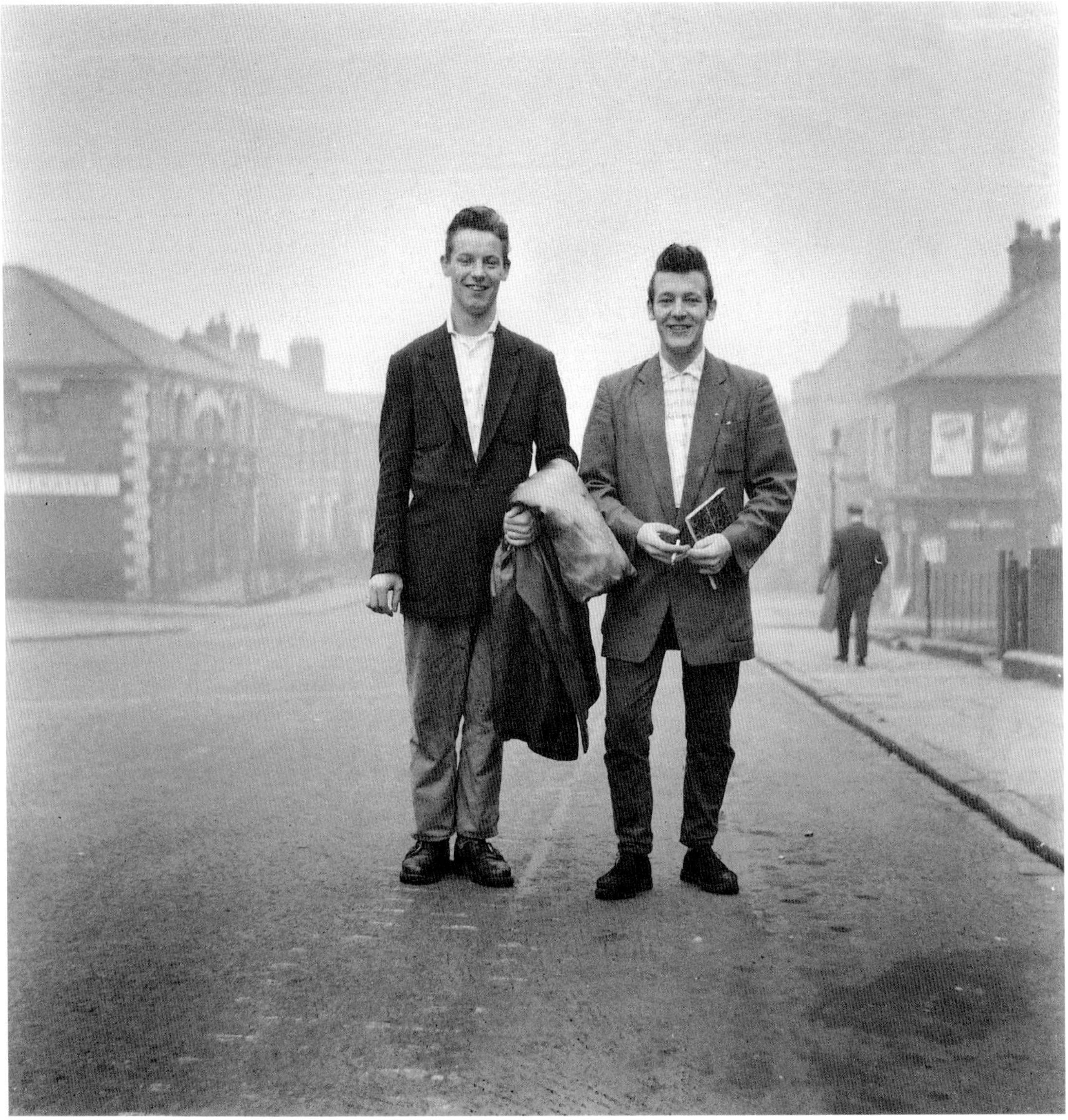

'Tallymen collecting in the Gloucester Street area for the ticket shops.'

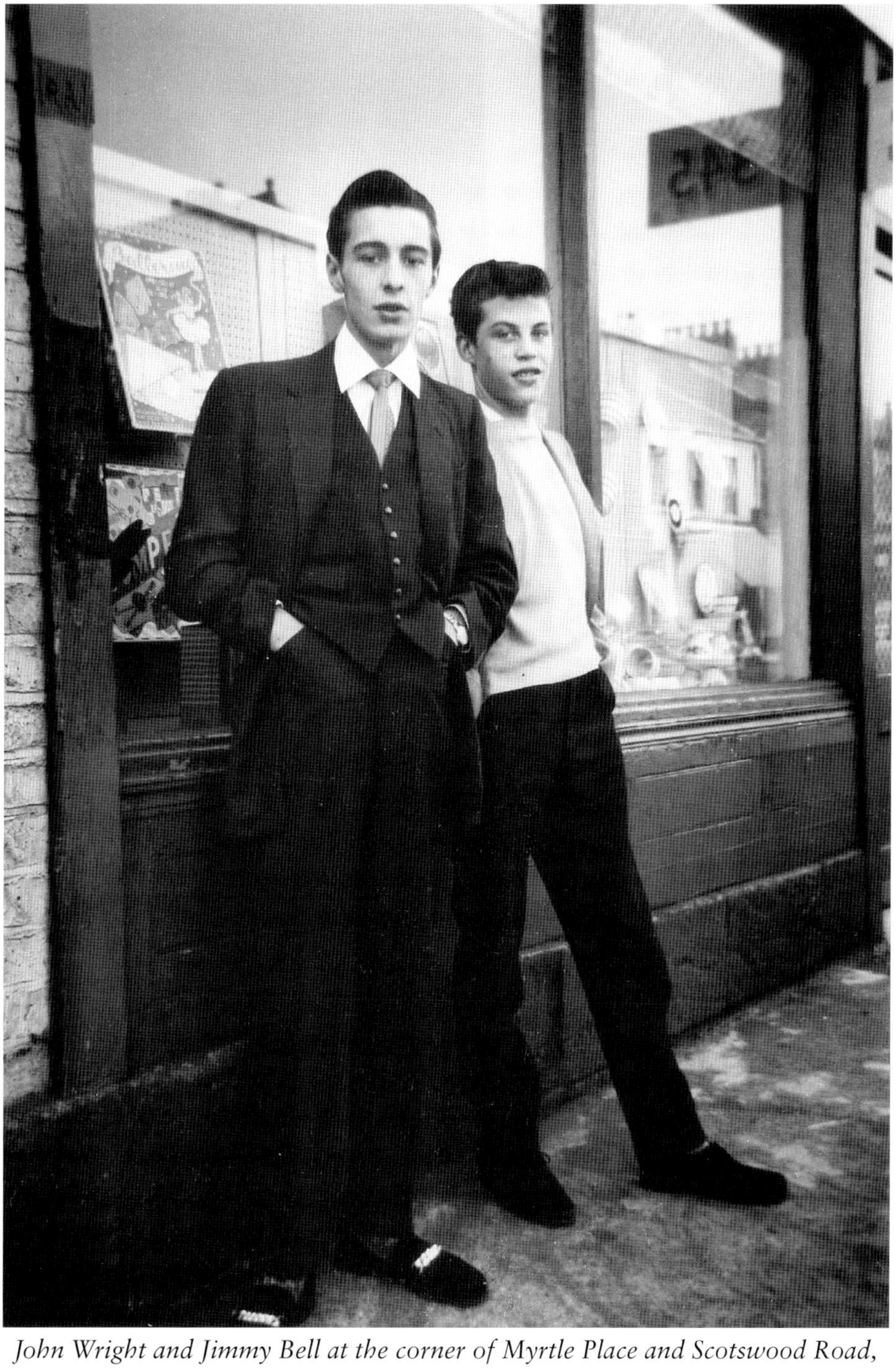

John Wright and Jimmy Bell at the corner of Myrtle Place and Scotswood Road, 1958.

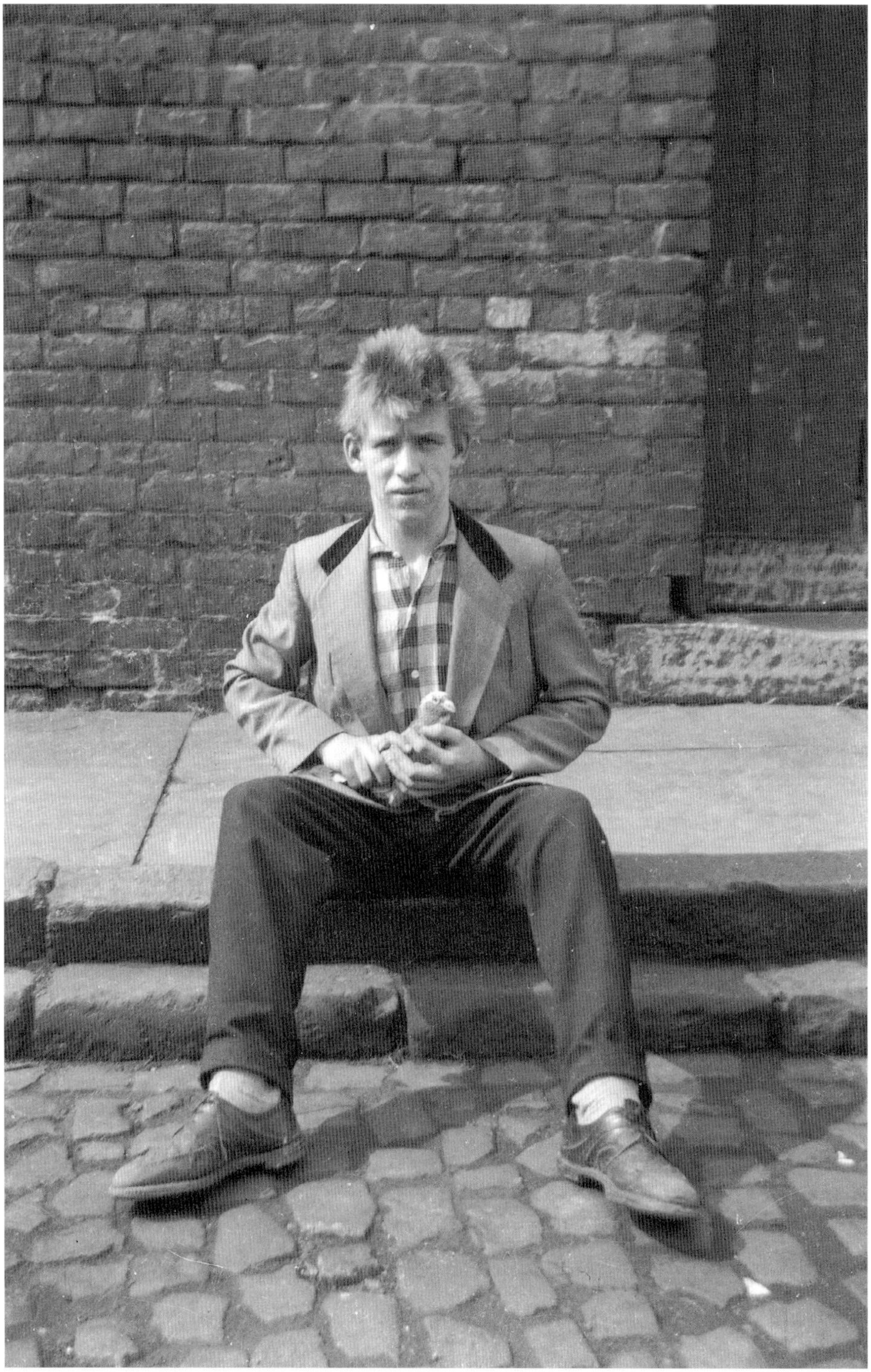

Jackie Prendergast, 1956.

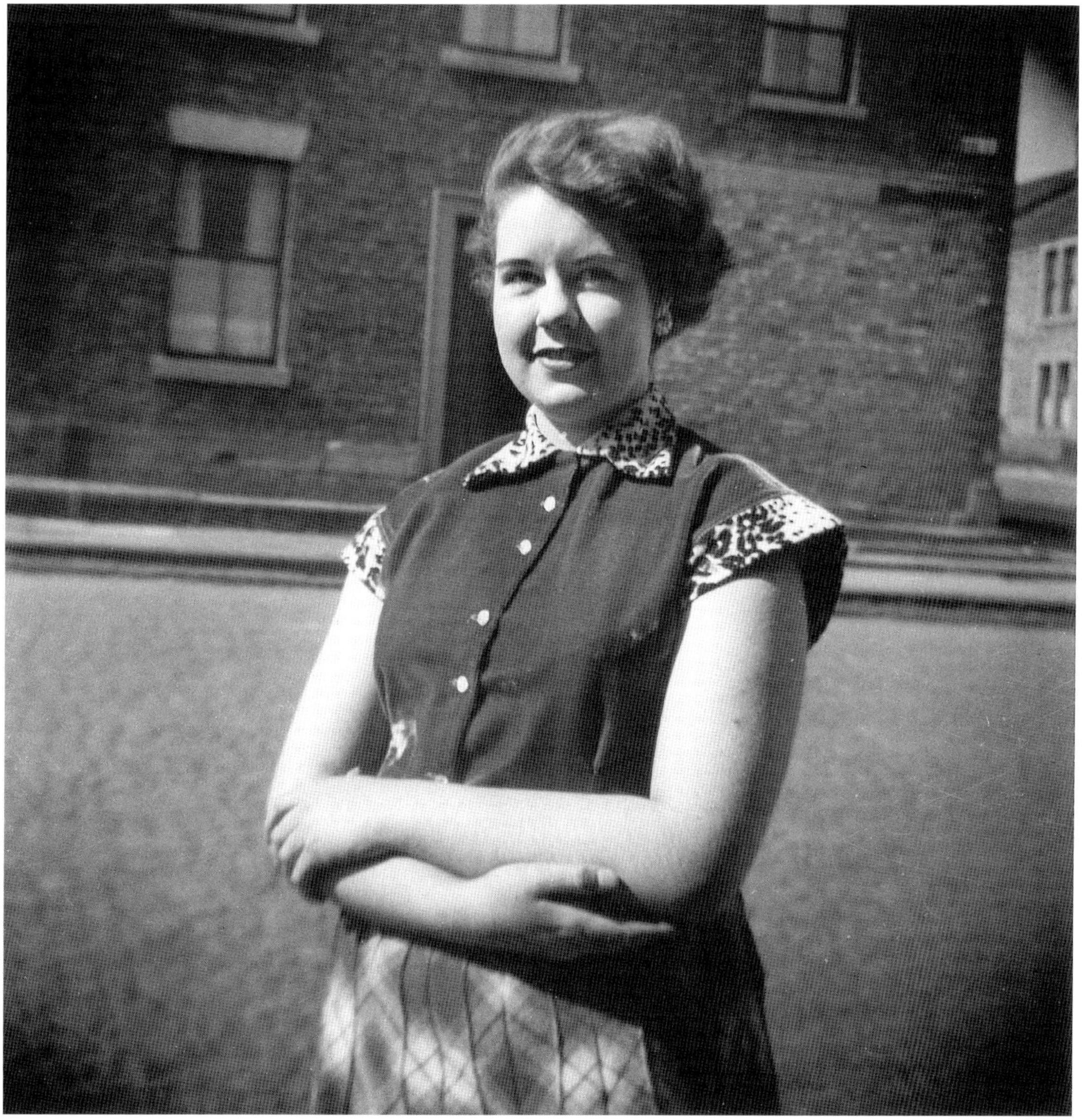

Eric Charlton's girlfriend, Gloucester Street 1954.

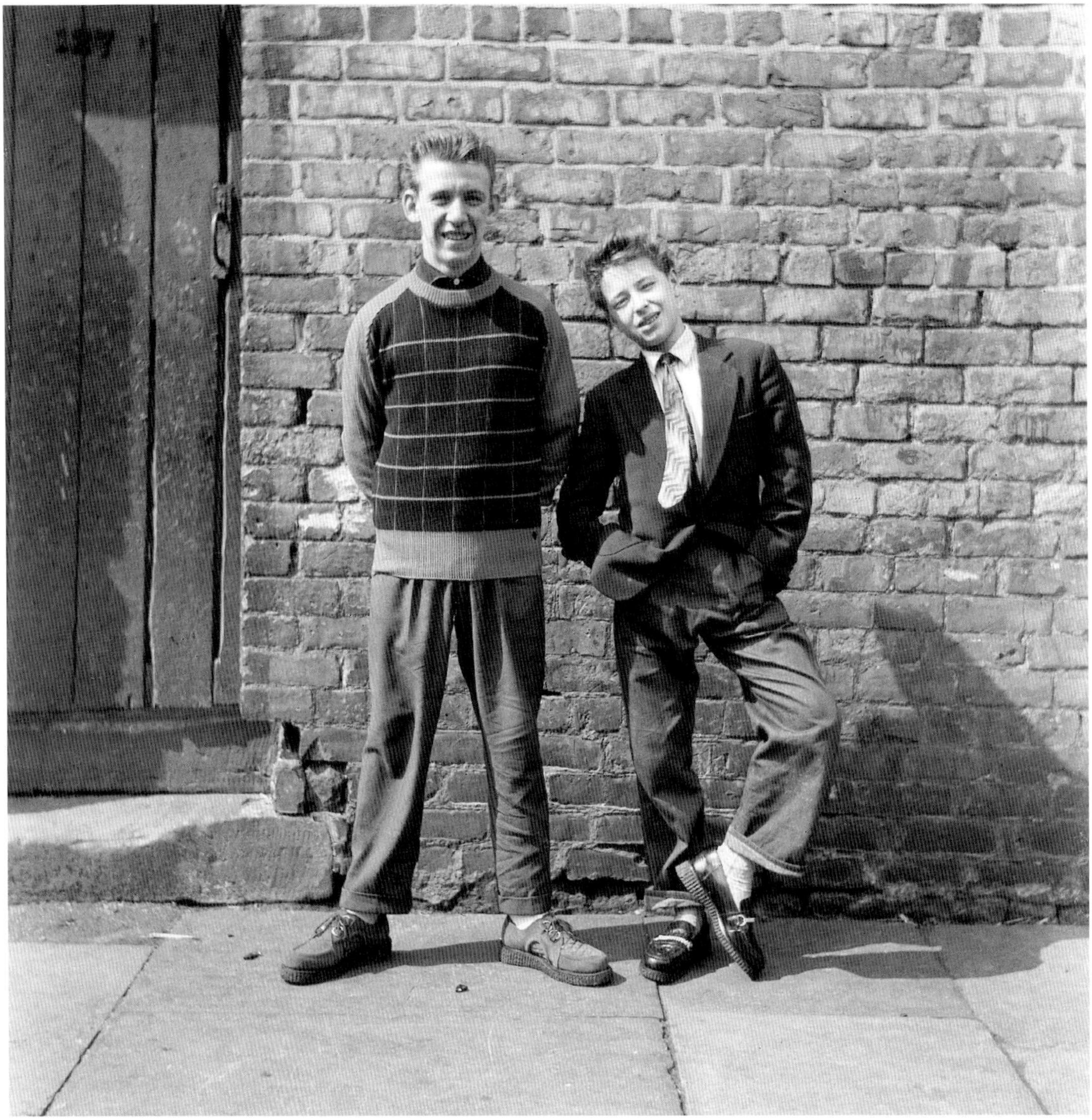

Jackie Prendergast and friend. May 1957.

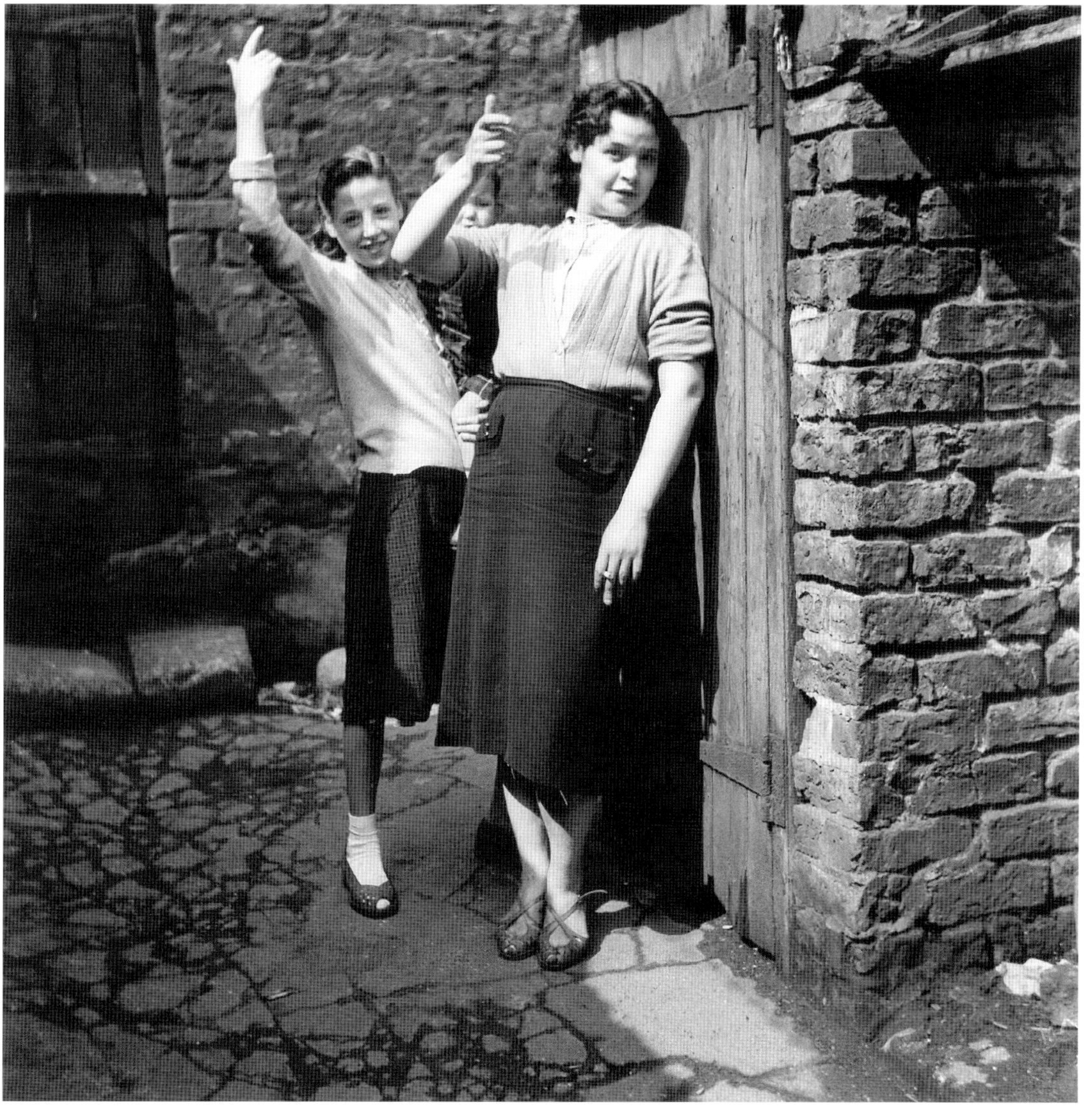

Betty Young and relatives. 1957.

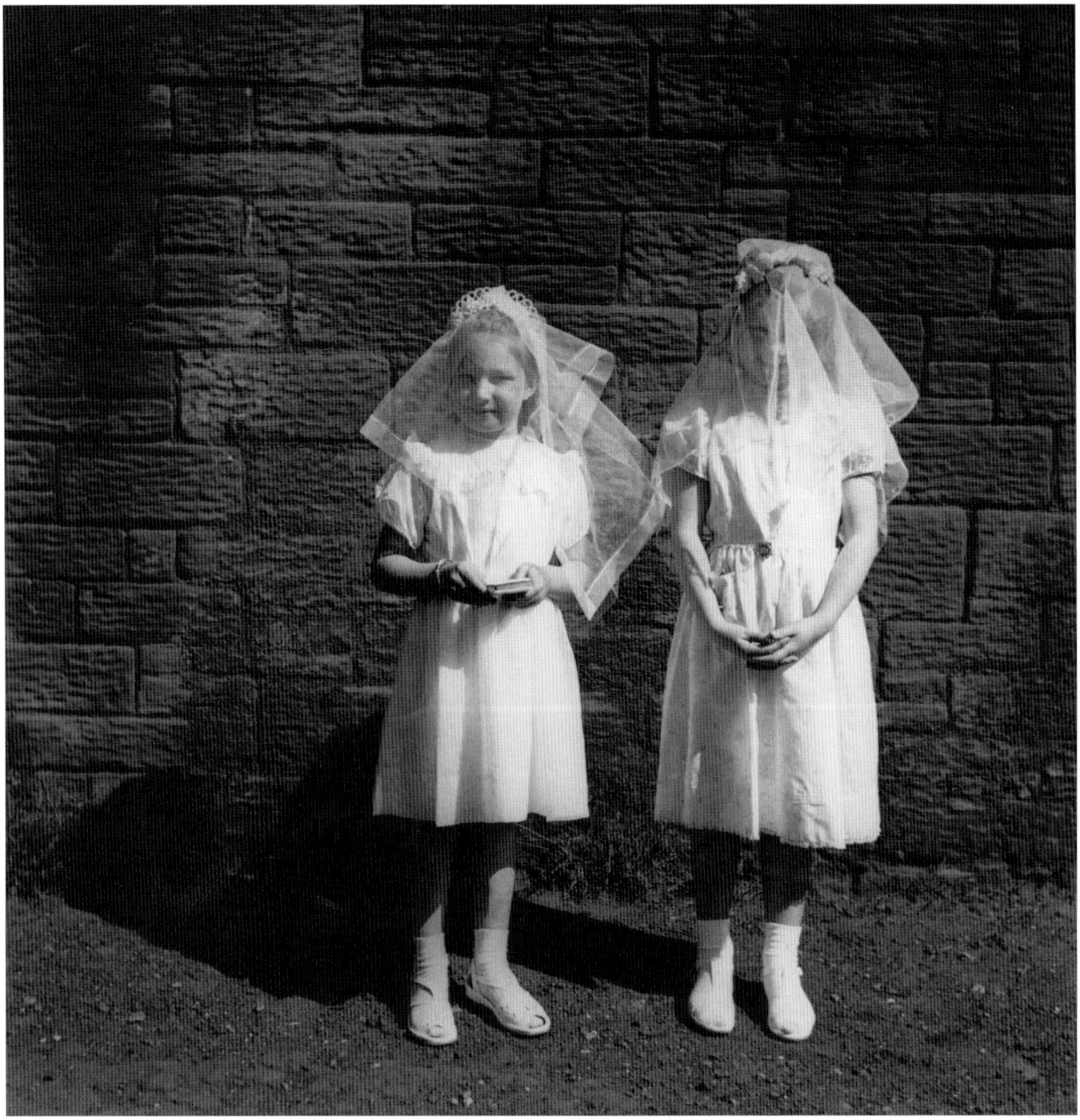

Confirmation Sunday, St Michael's Church 1957.

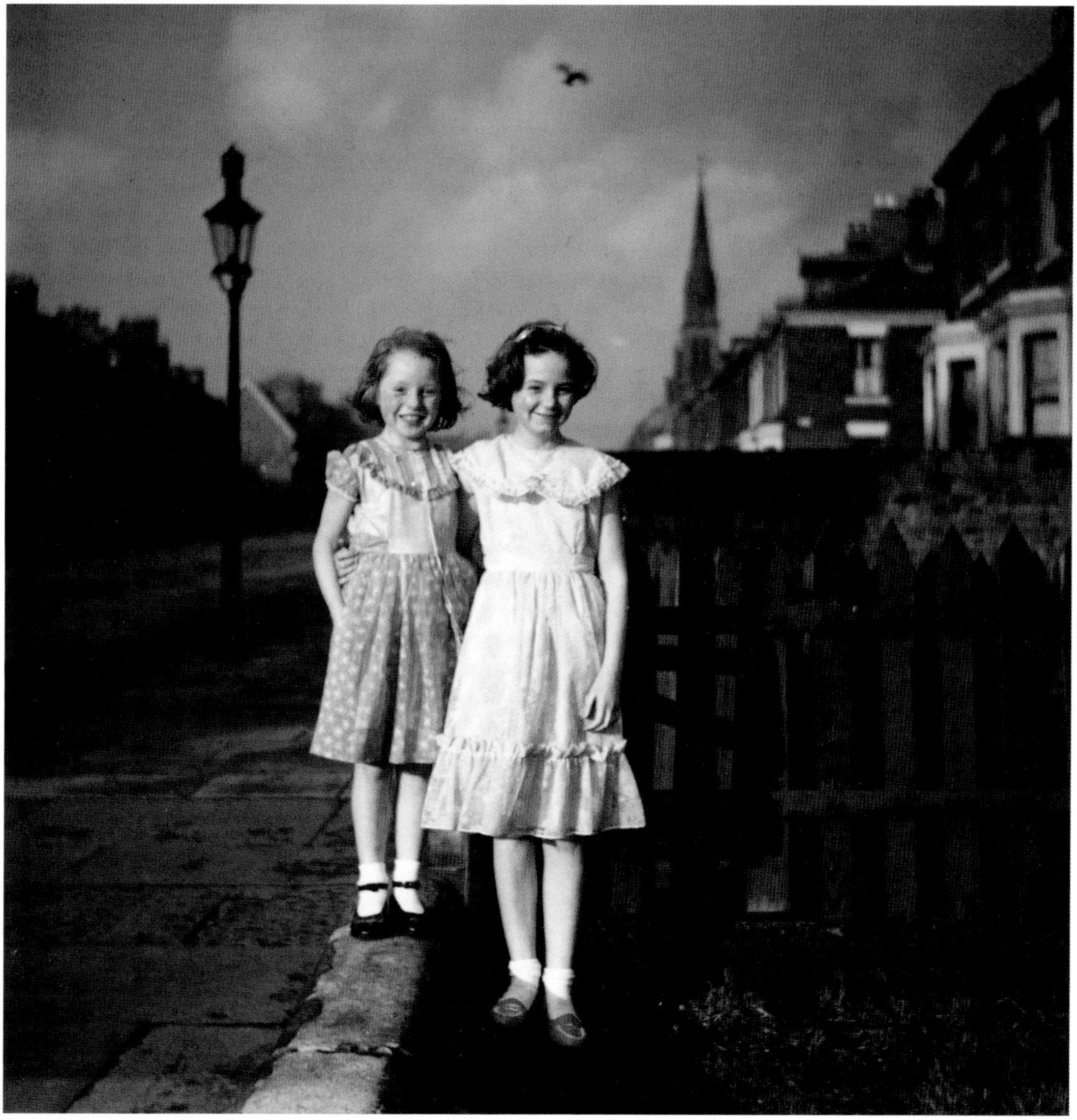

Pat Norman on the right, with her cousin Val Wilson. Park Road, 1959.

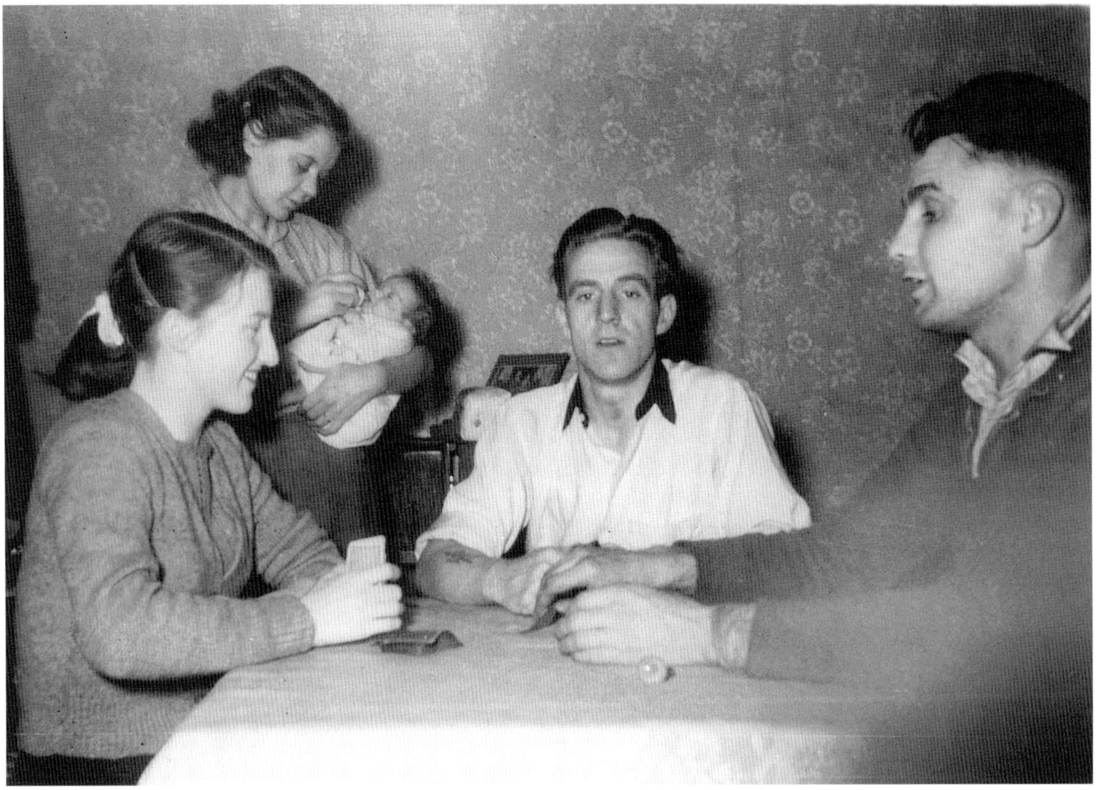

Nancy Little with husband (centre) and baby. 1956.

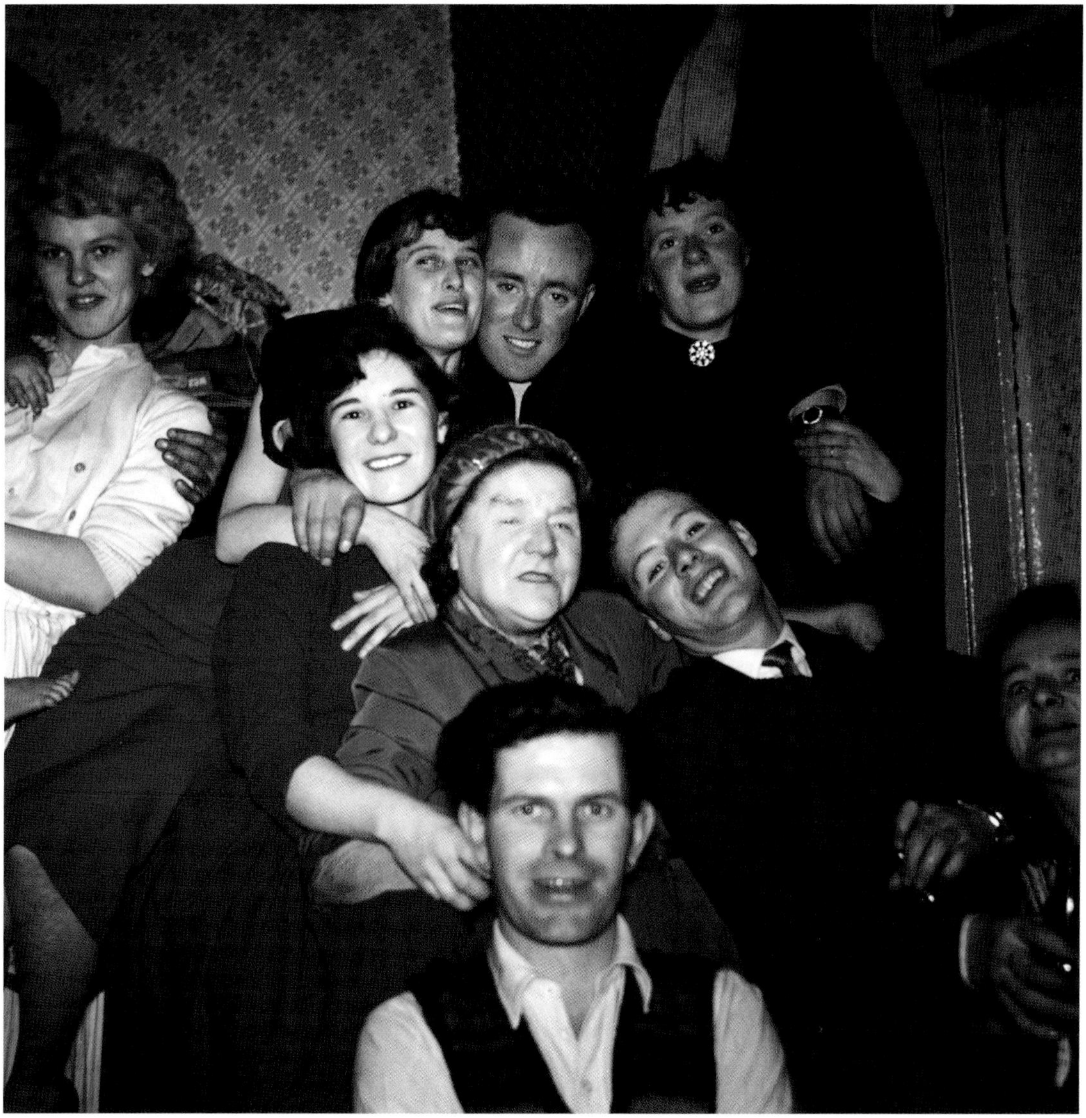

A family party. New Year's Eve 1959.

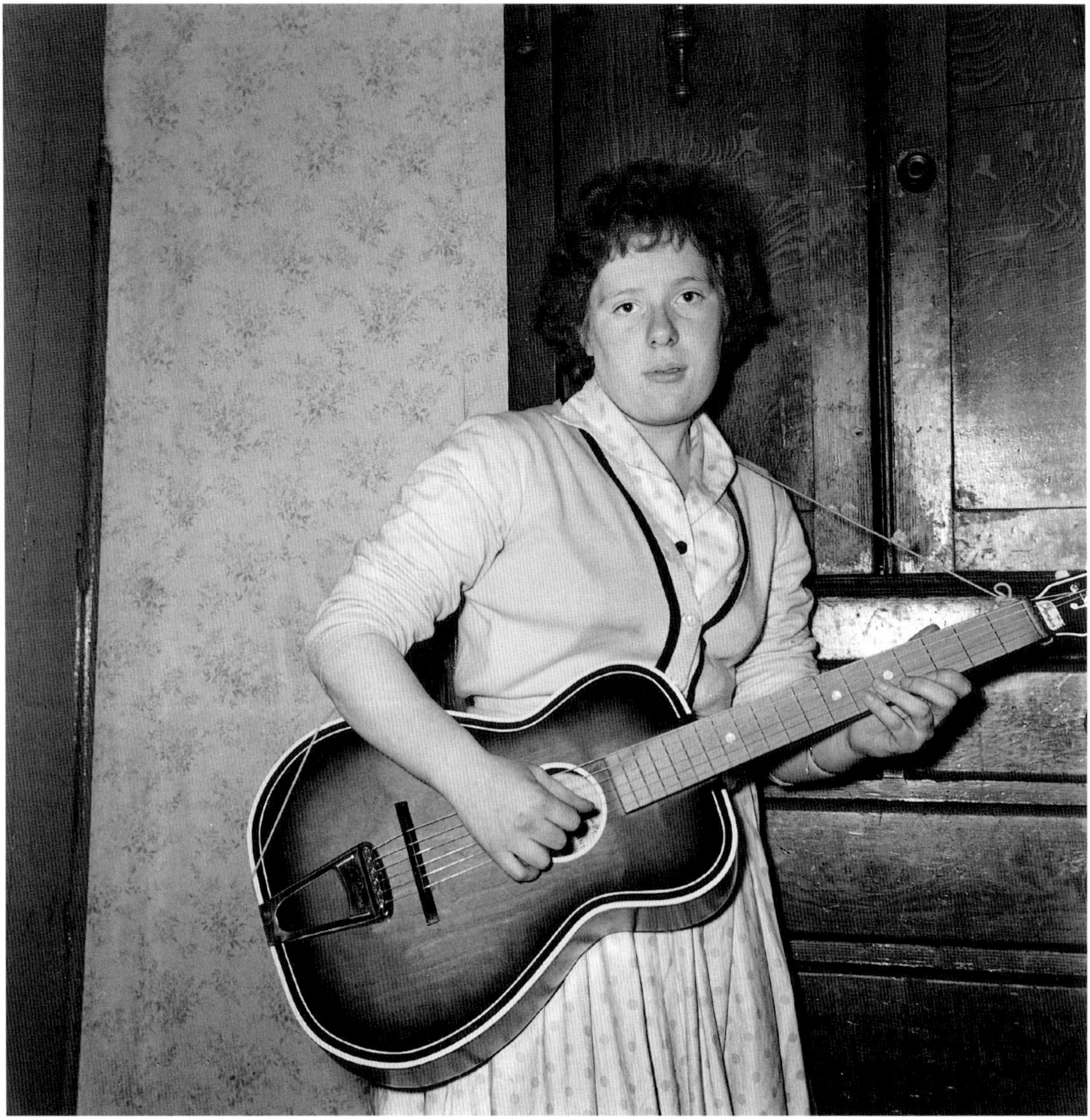

Edith Jardine.

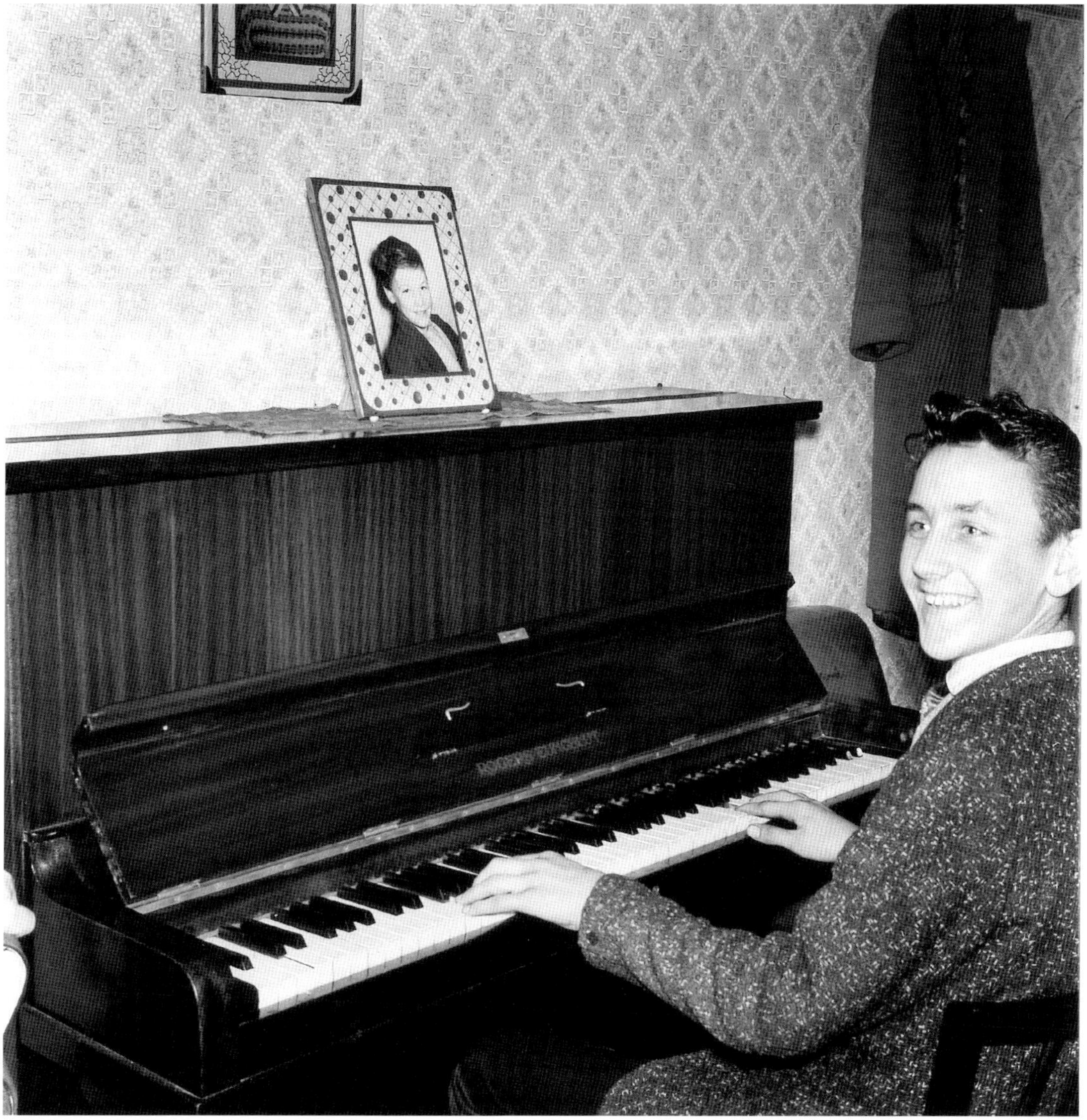

Charlie Airey, Delaval Road, 1958.

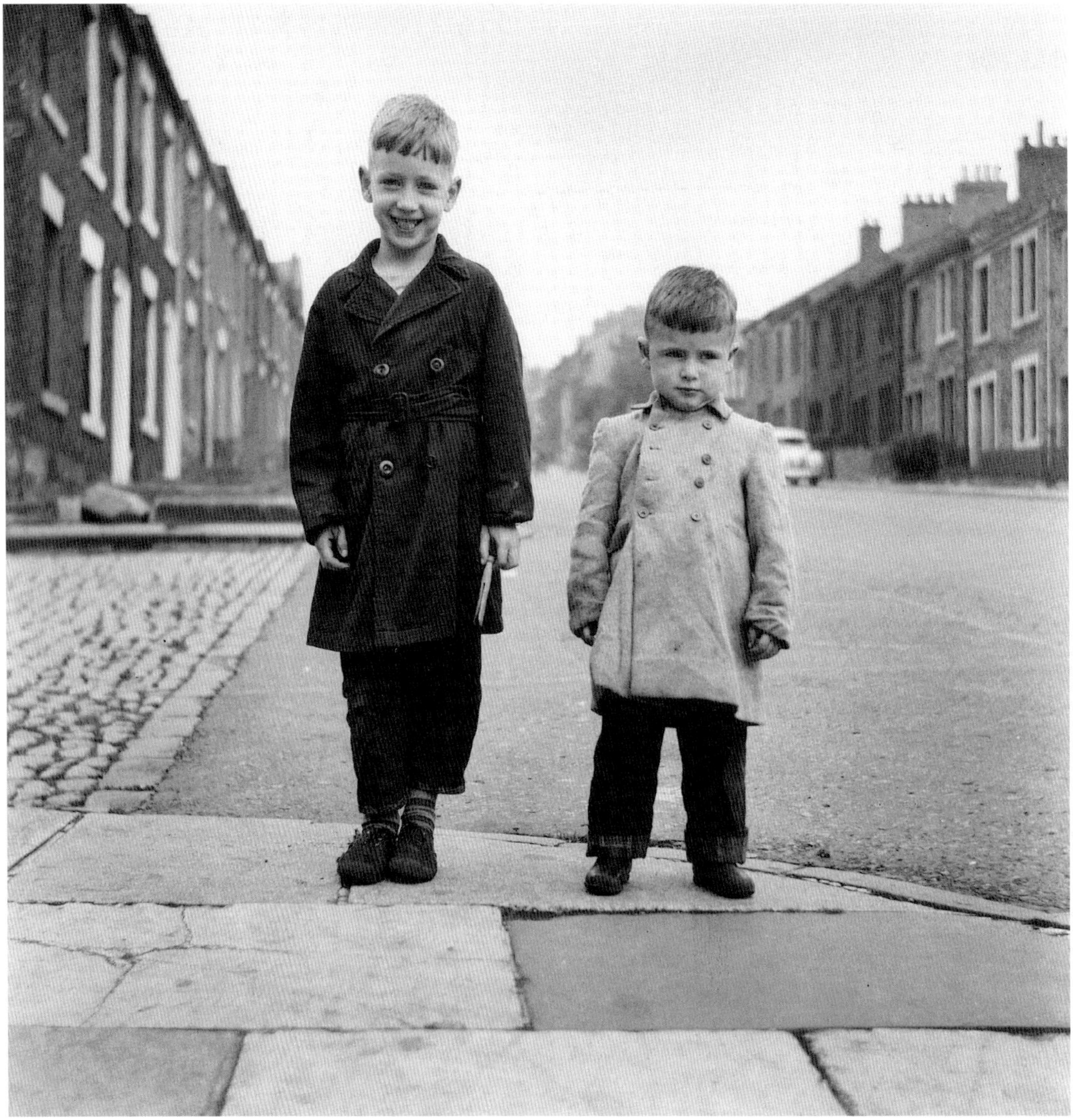

Stuart and Andrew Beveridge.

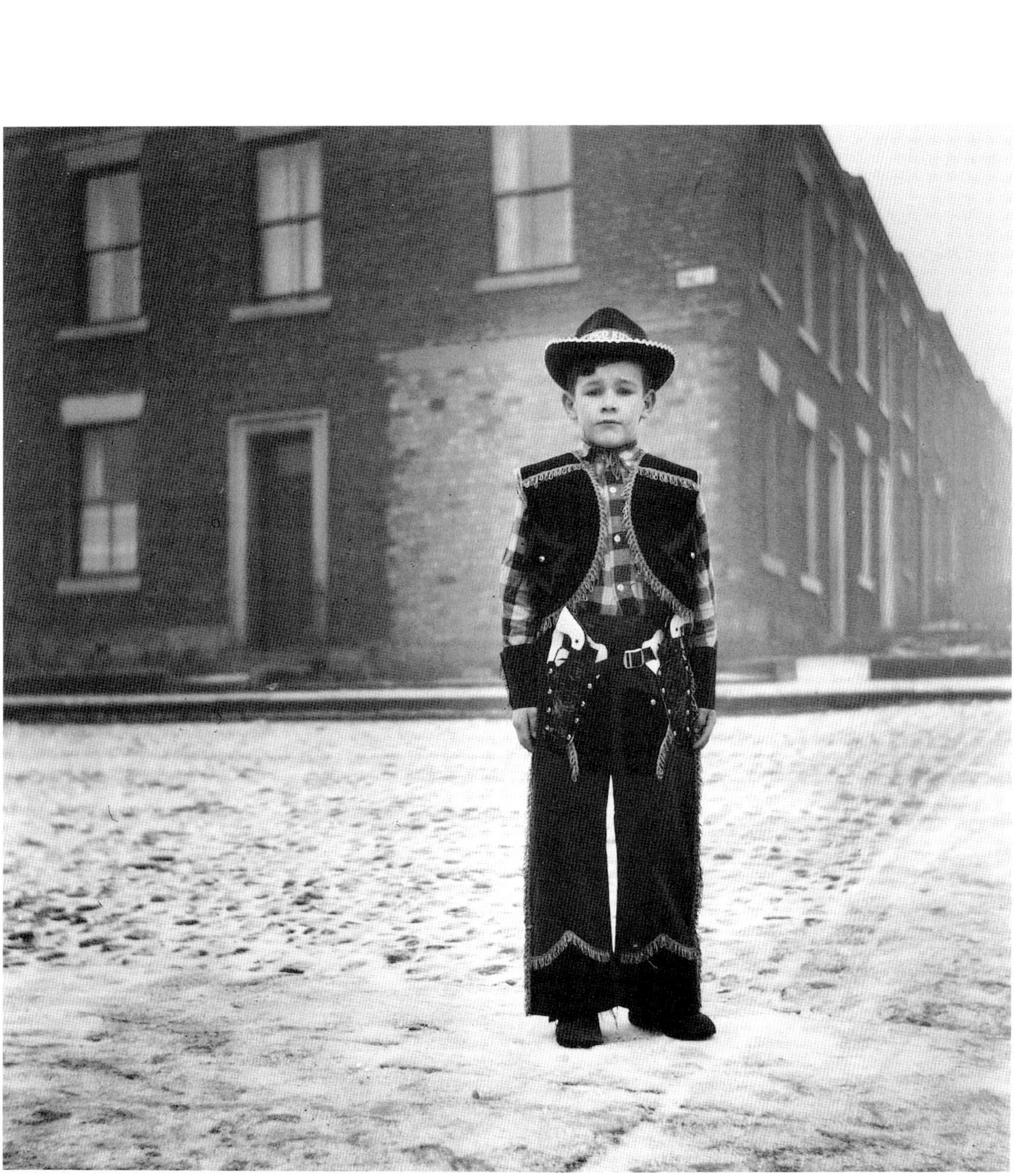

Stephen Charlton, 2 January 1958.

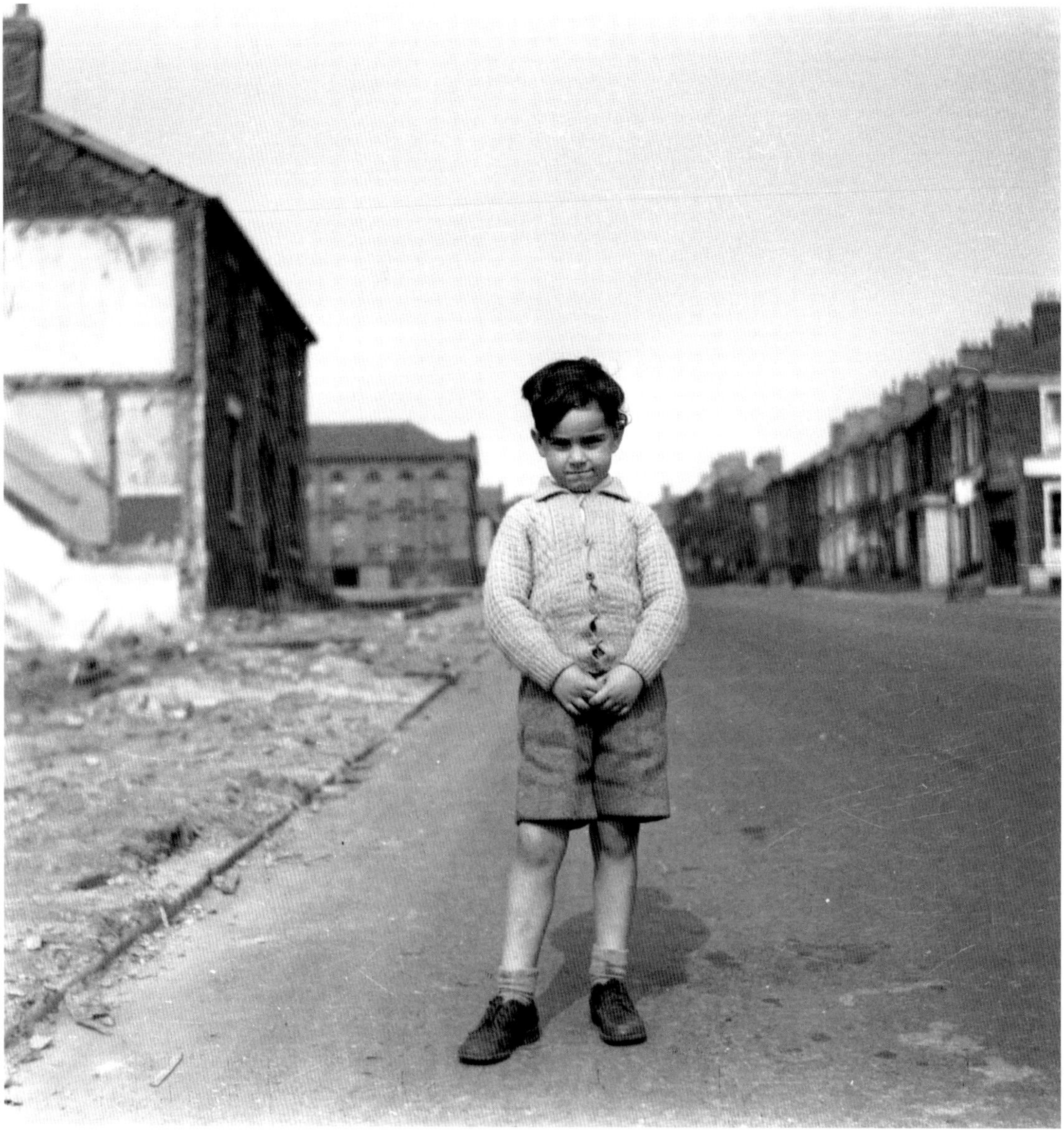

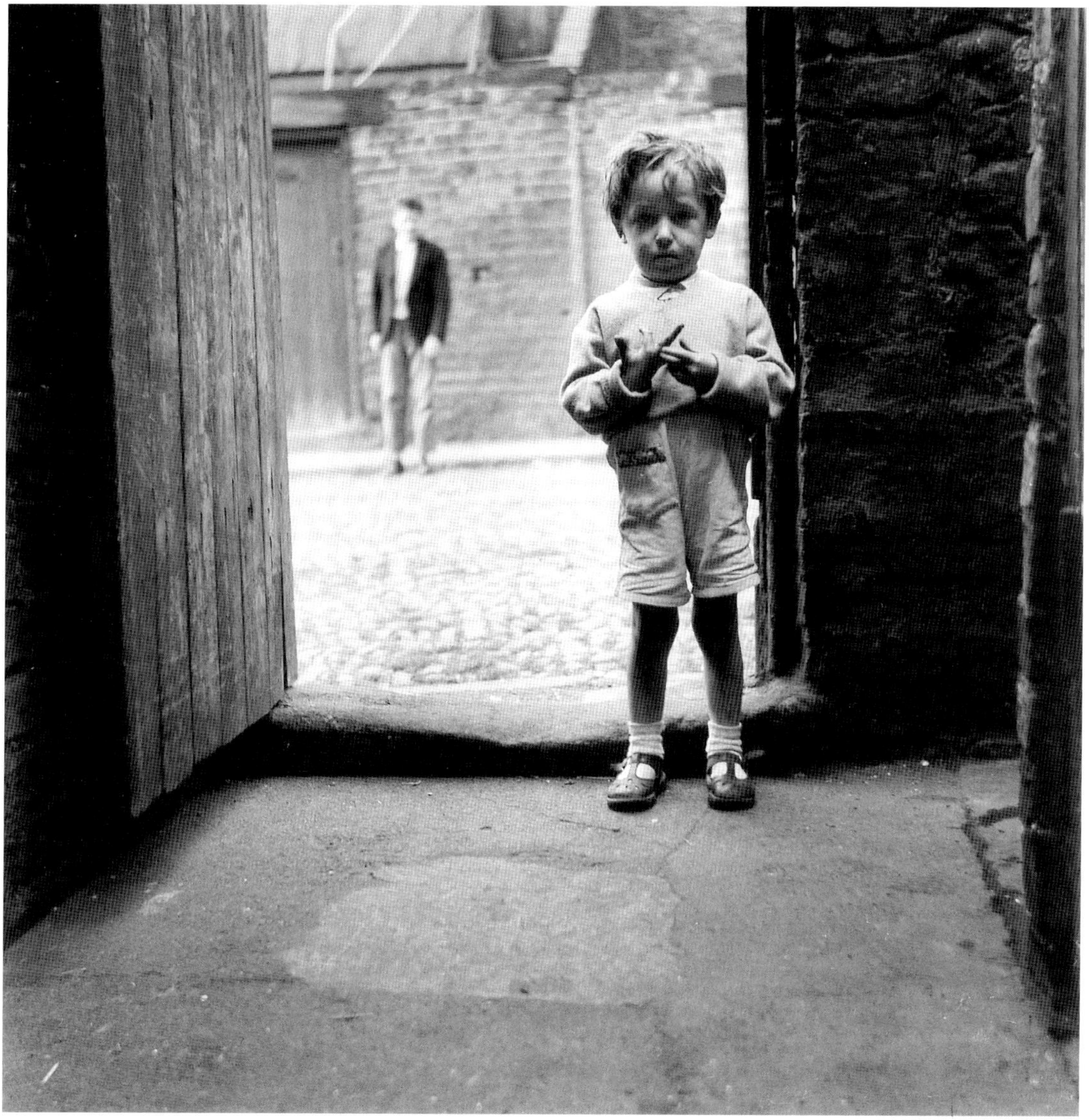

Back yard, 1956.

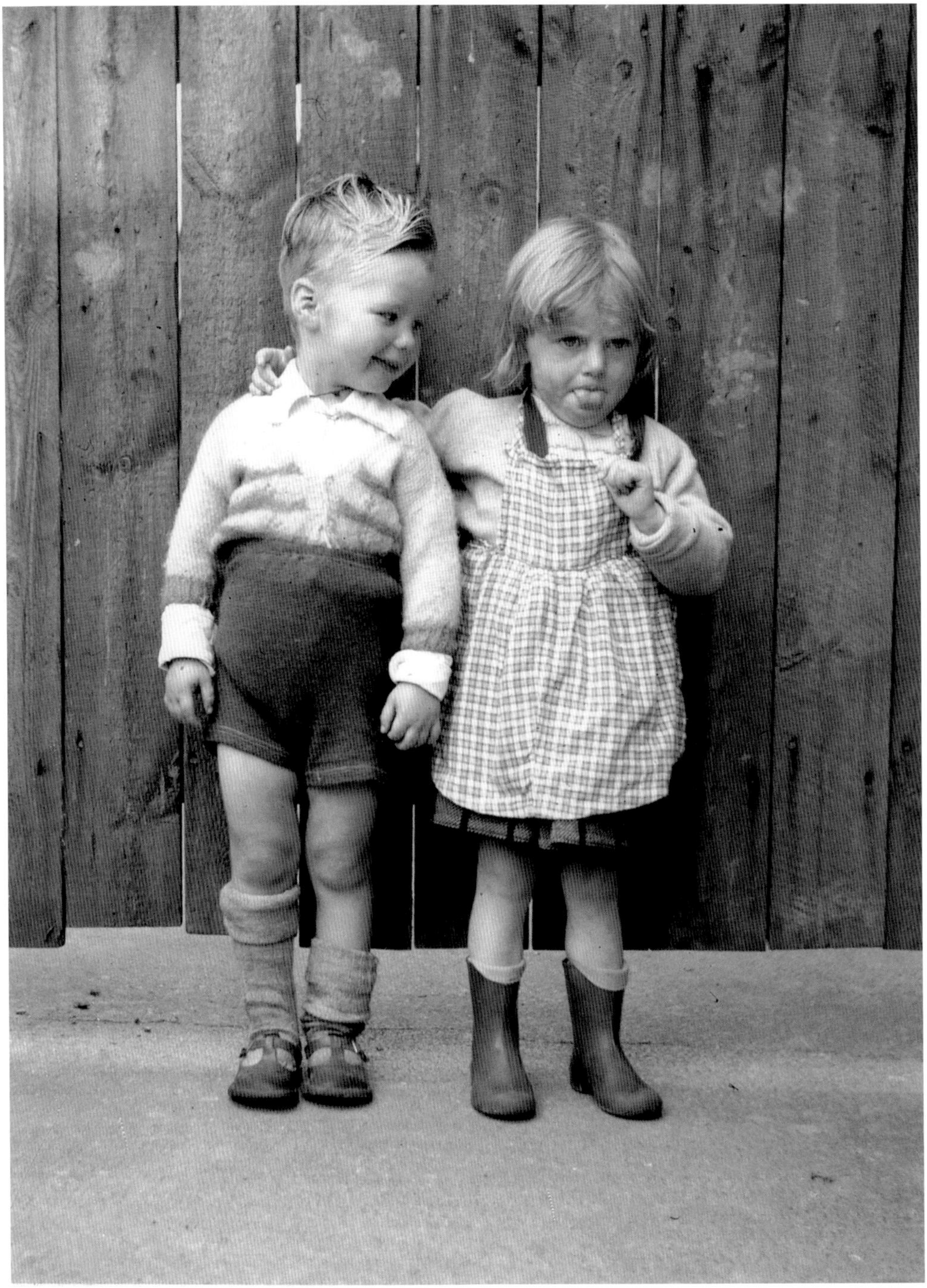

Robert Foster and Linda Gladders, 1957.

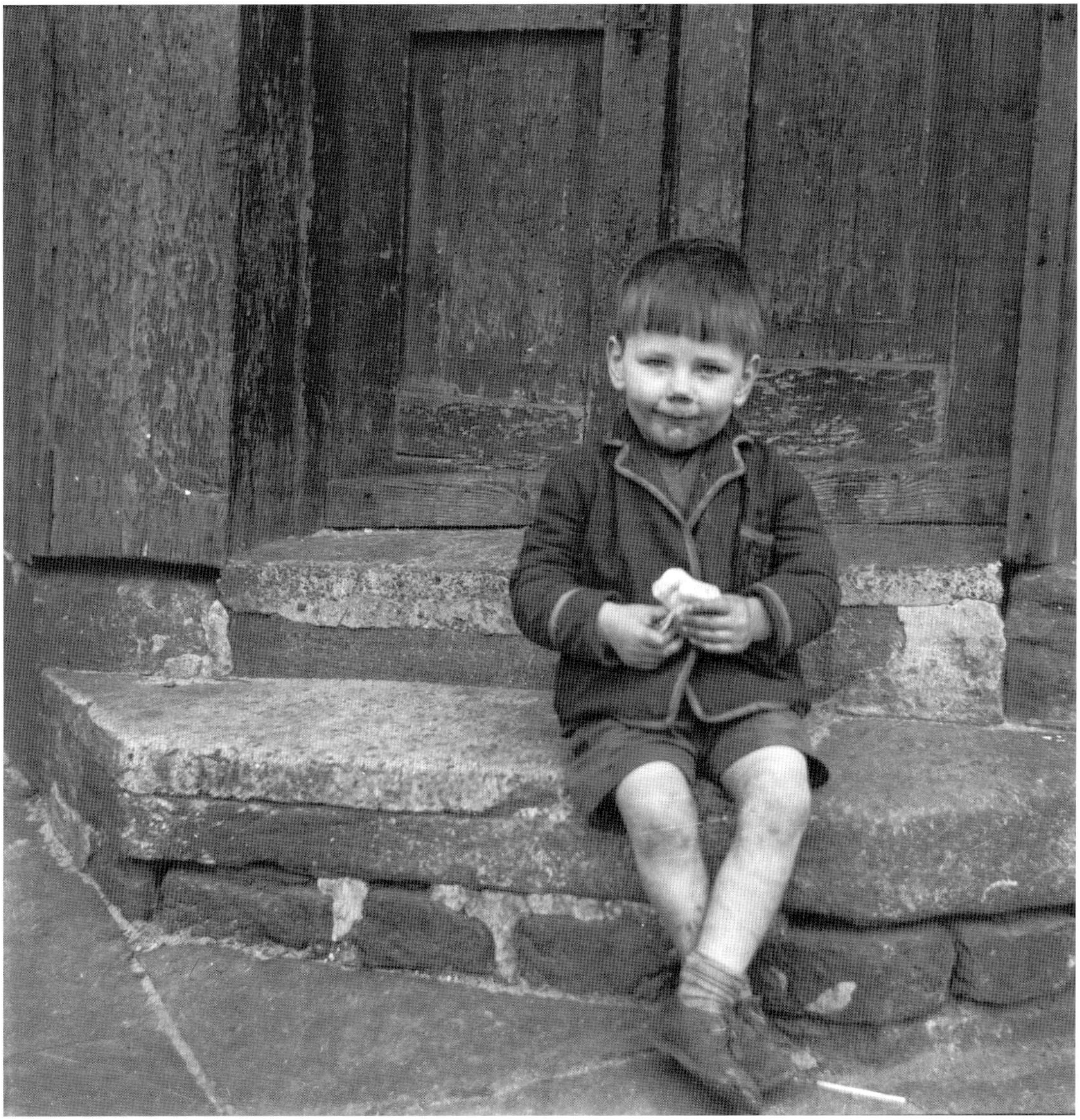

Ralph Liddle c1958.

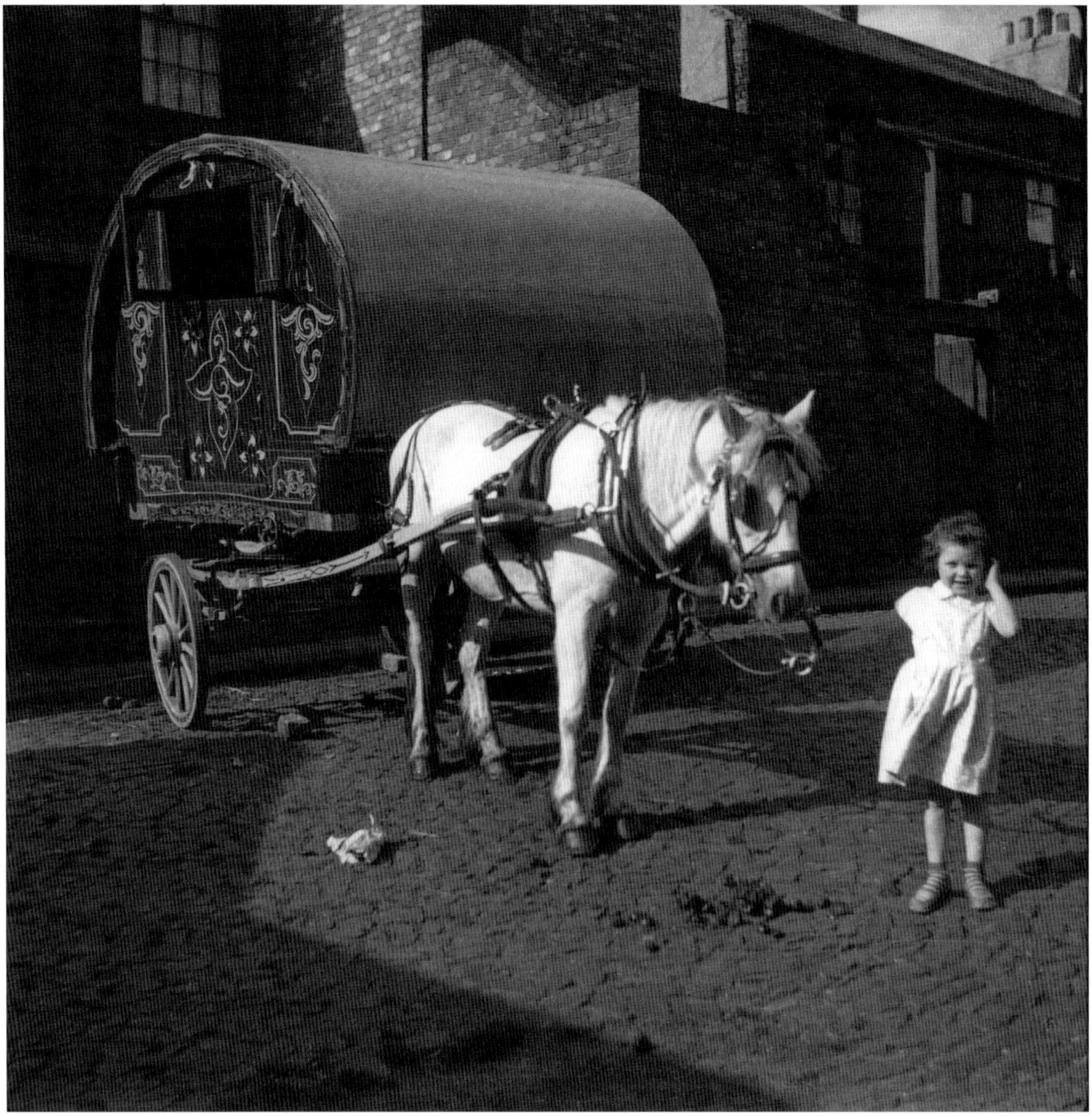

Maureen Liddle with her father Jock's horse and caravan in a back lane behind Scotswood Road. April 1957.

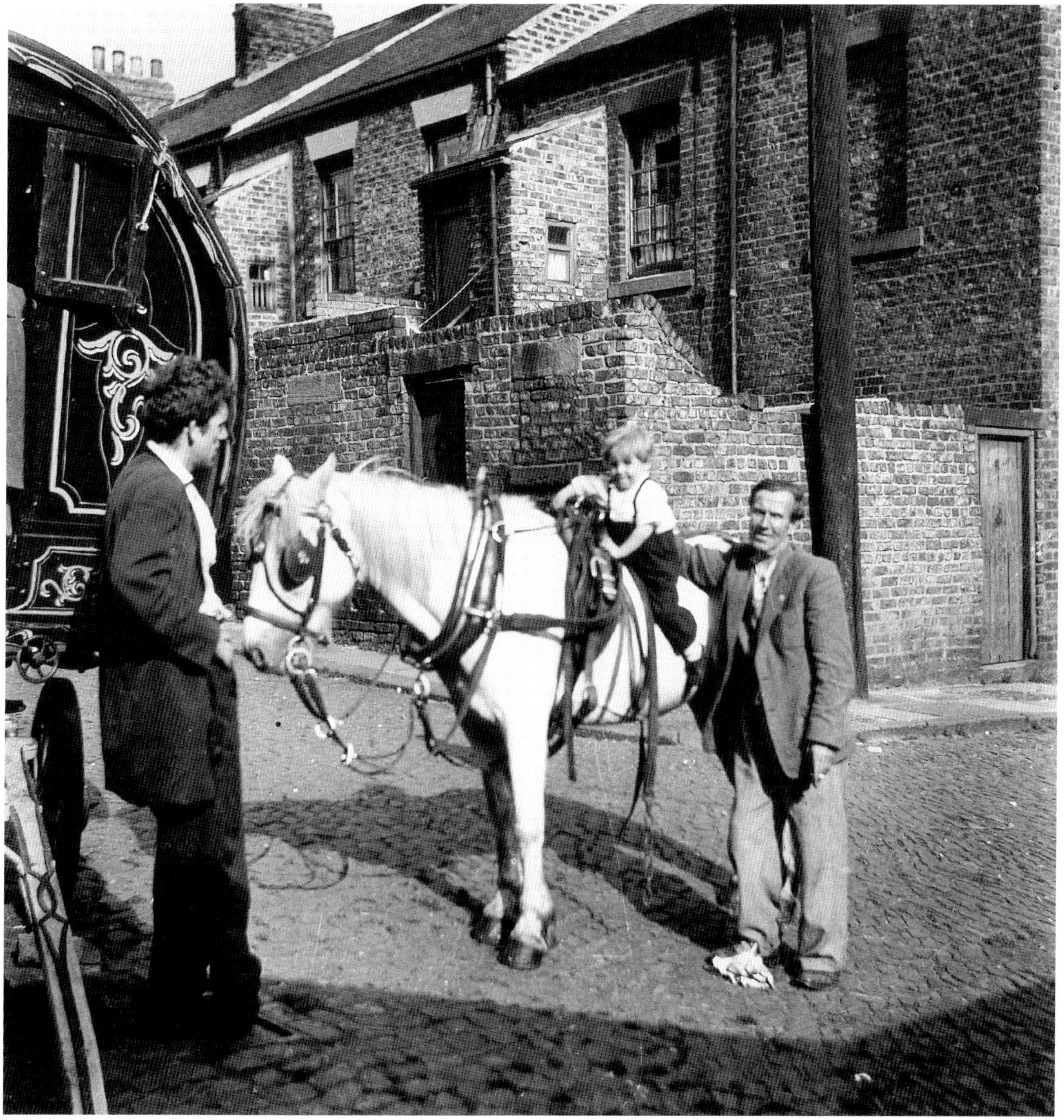

Hawkers in back lane between Scotswood Road and Penn Street, April 1957.

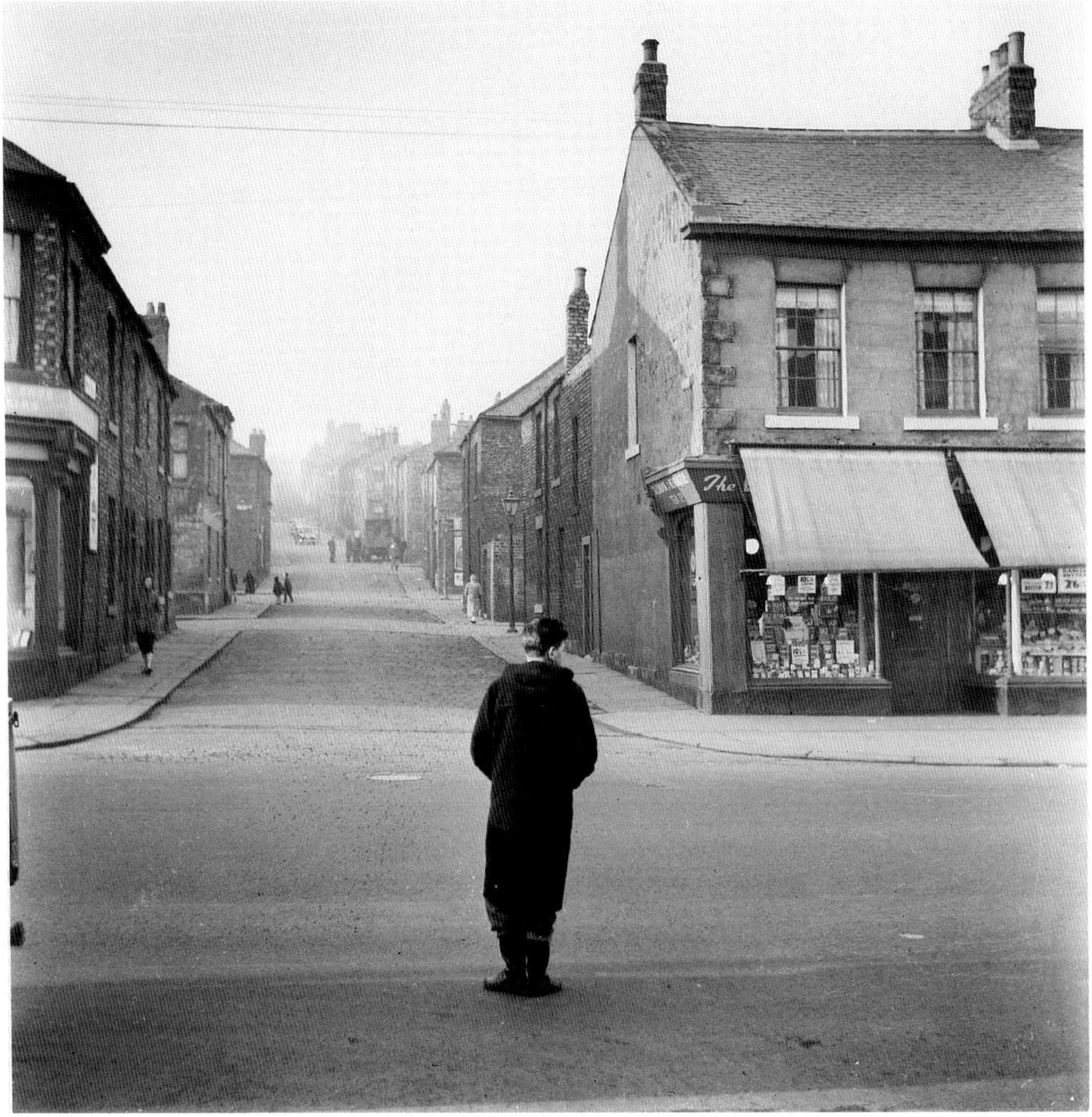

View up Suffolk Street from Scotswood Road, looking towards Pine and Sycamore Street, 1958.

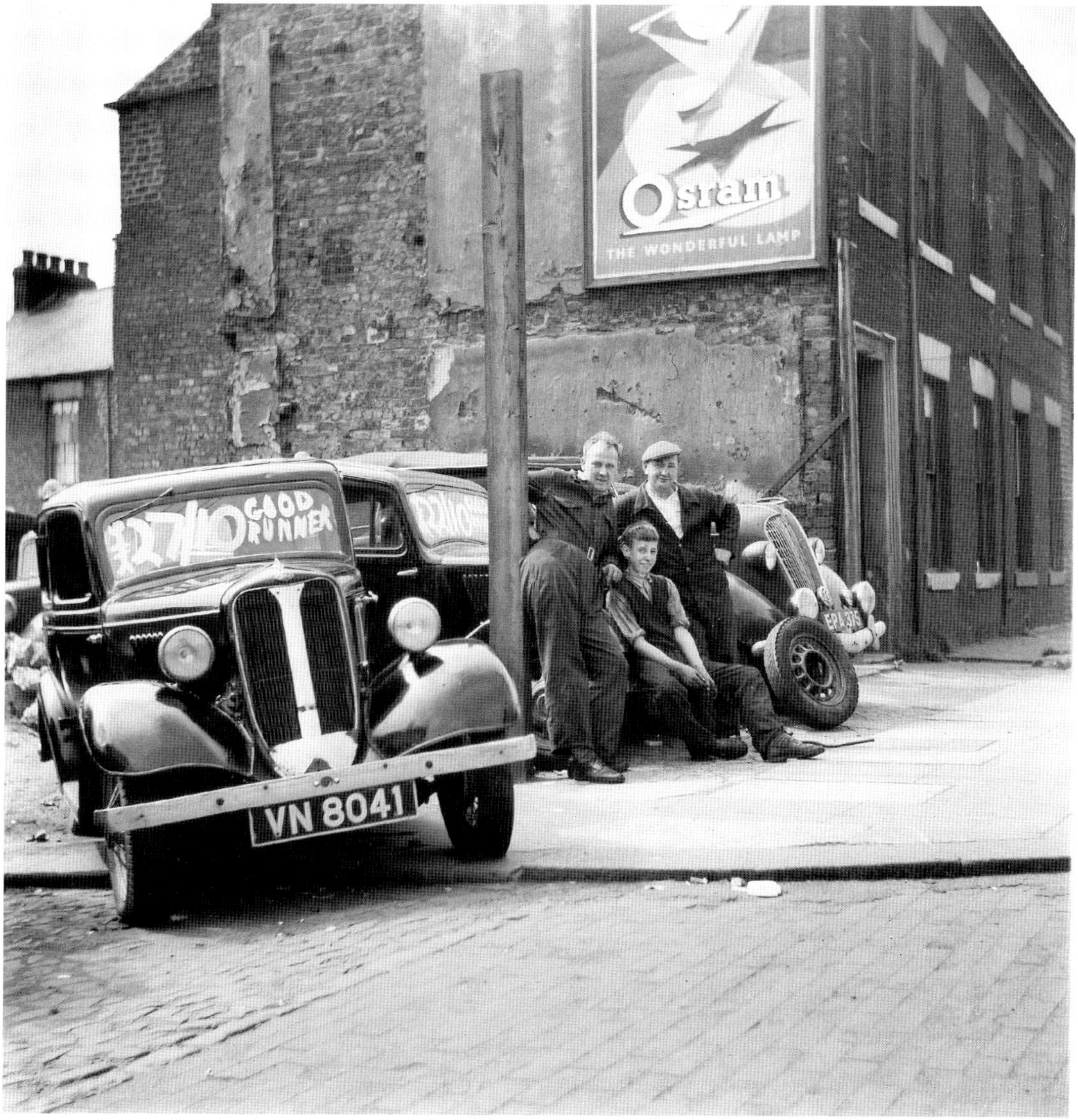

Used car site, Water Street Scotswood Road, Maurice Wilson & workmen. 1958.

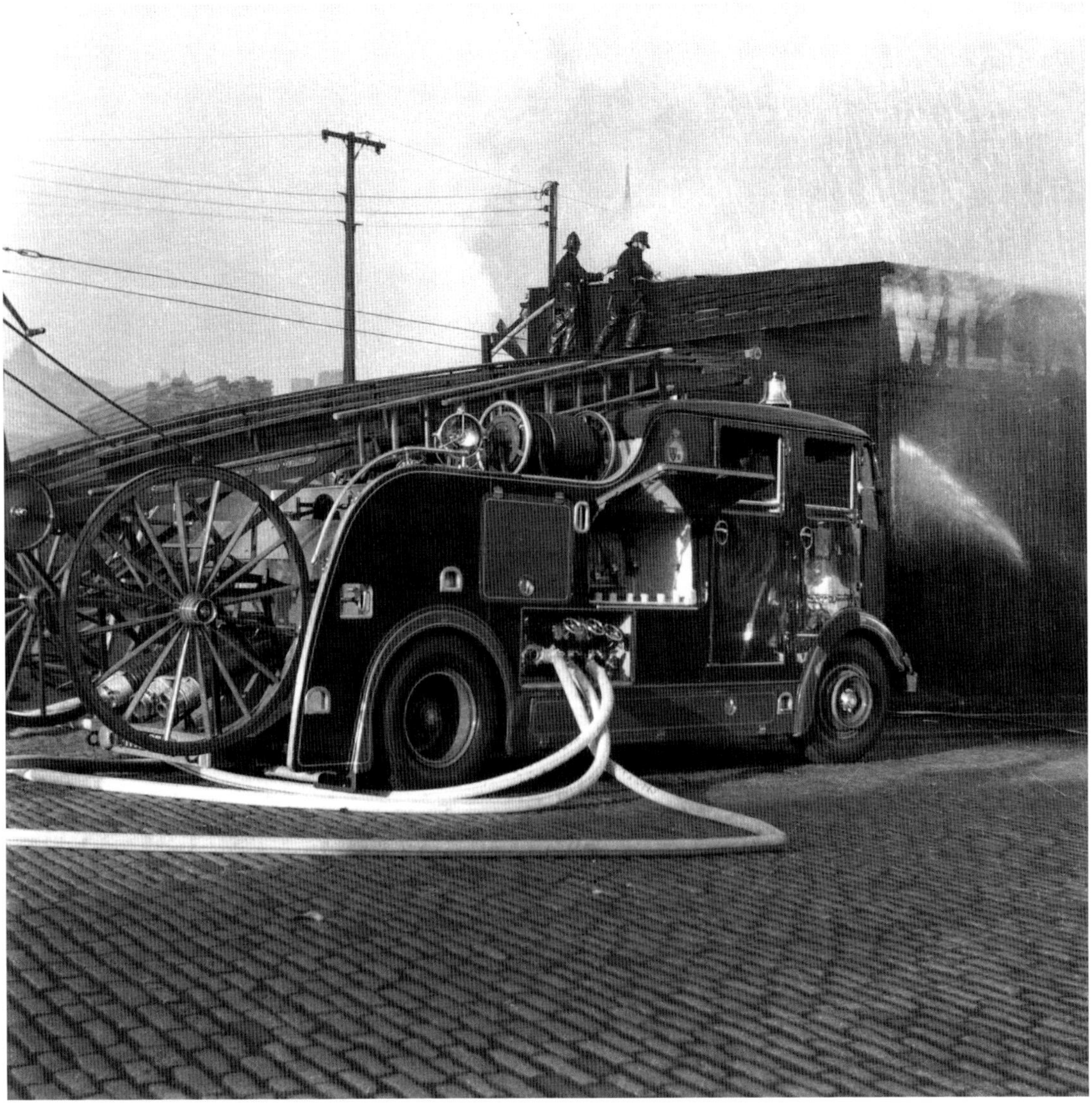

A fire at Bell's timber yard on the corner of Railway Street, 1959.

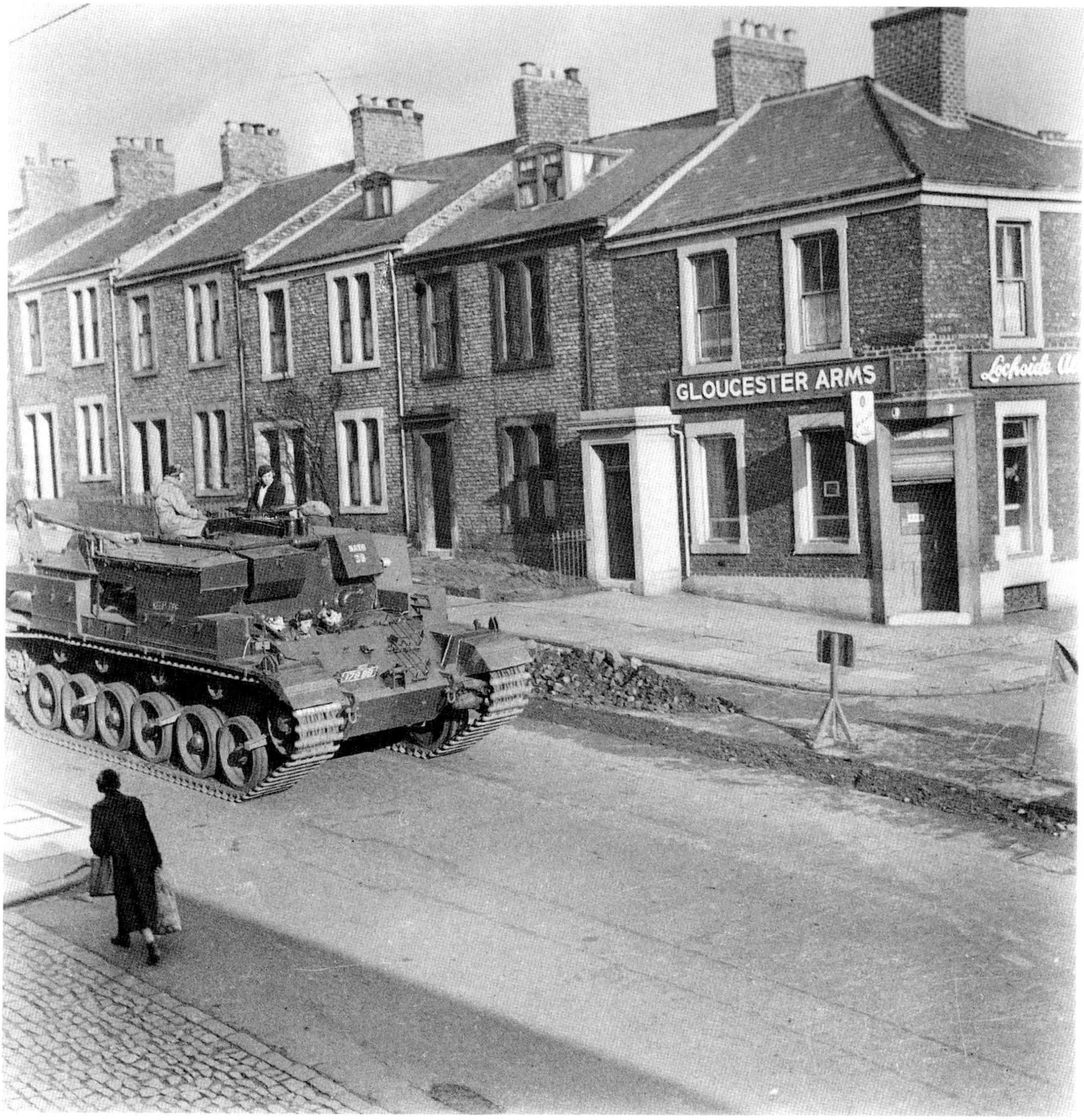

Tank, Gloucester Arms, January 1957.

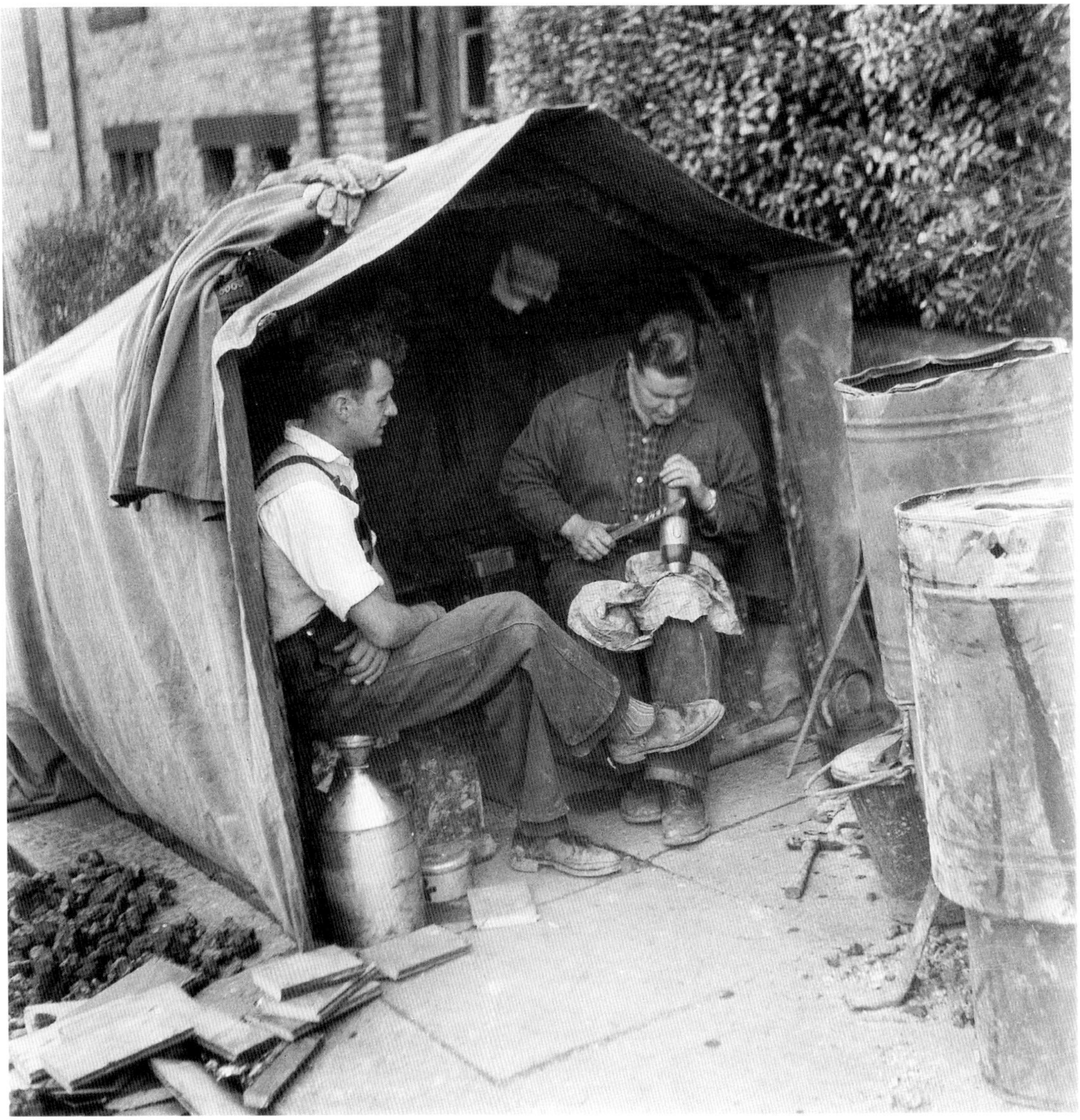

Electricians in Delaval Road during demolition for continuation westwards of Whitehouse Road, 1961.

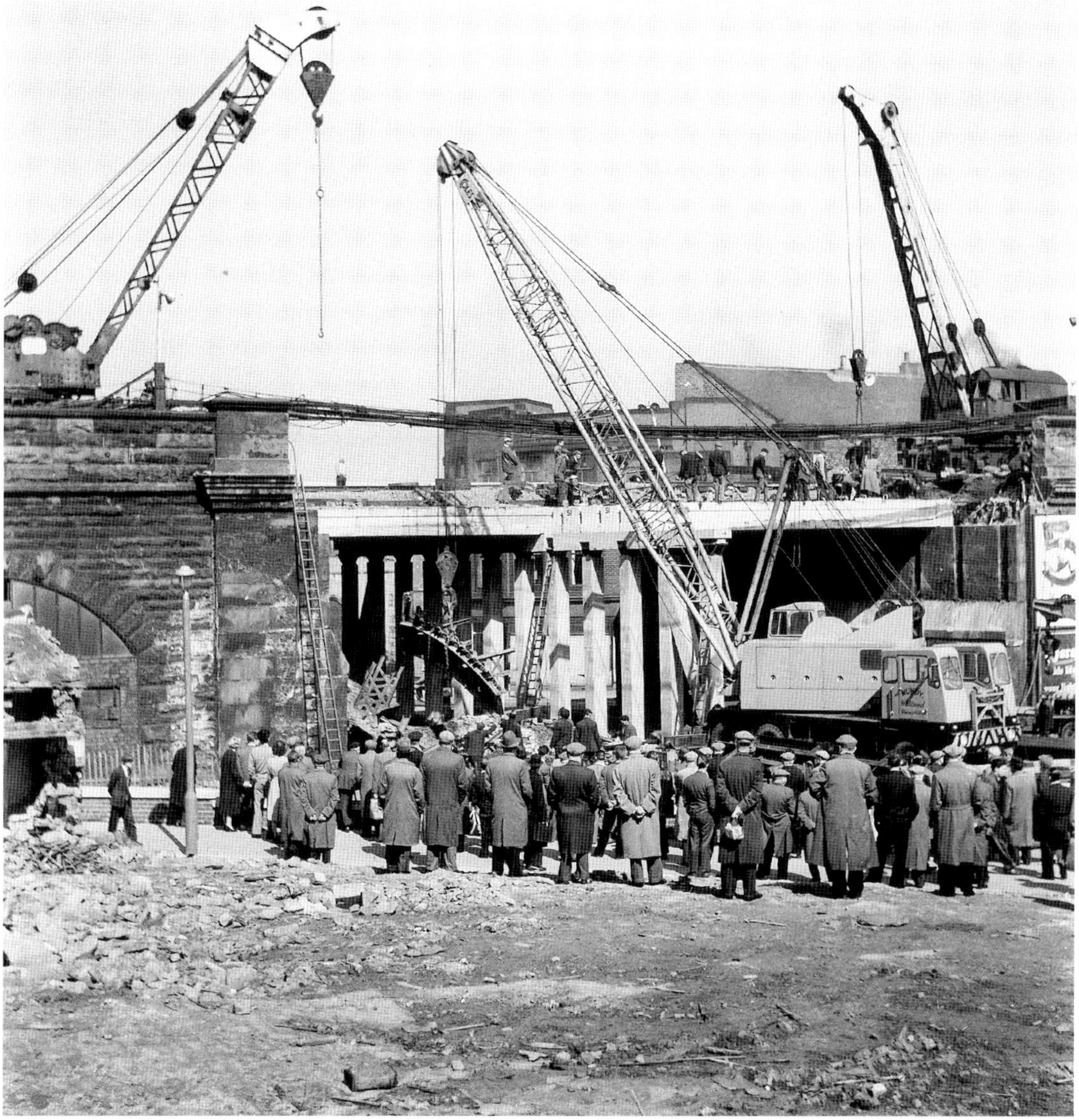

Railway bridge, Gateshead High Street, 1960.

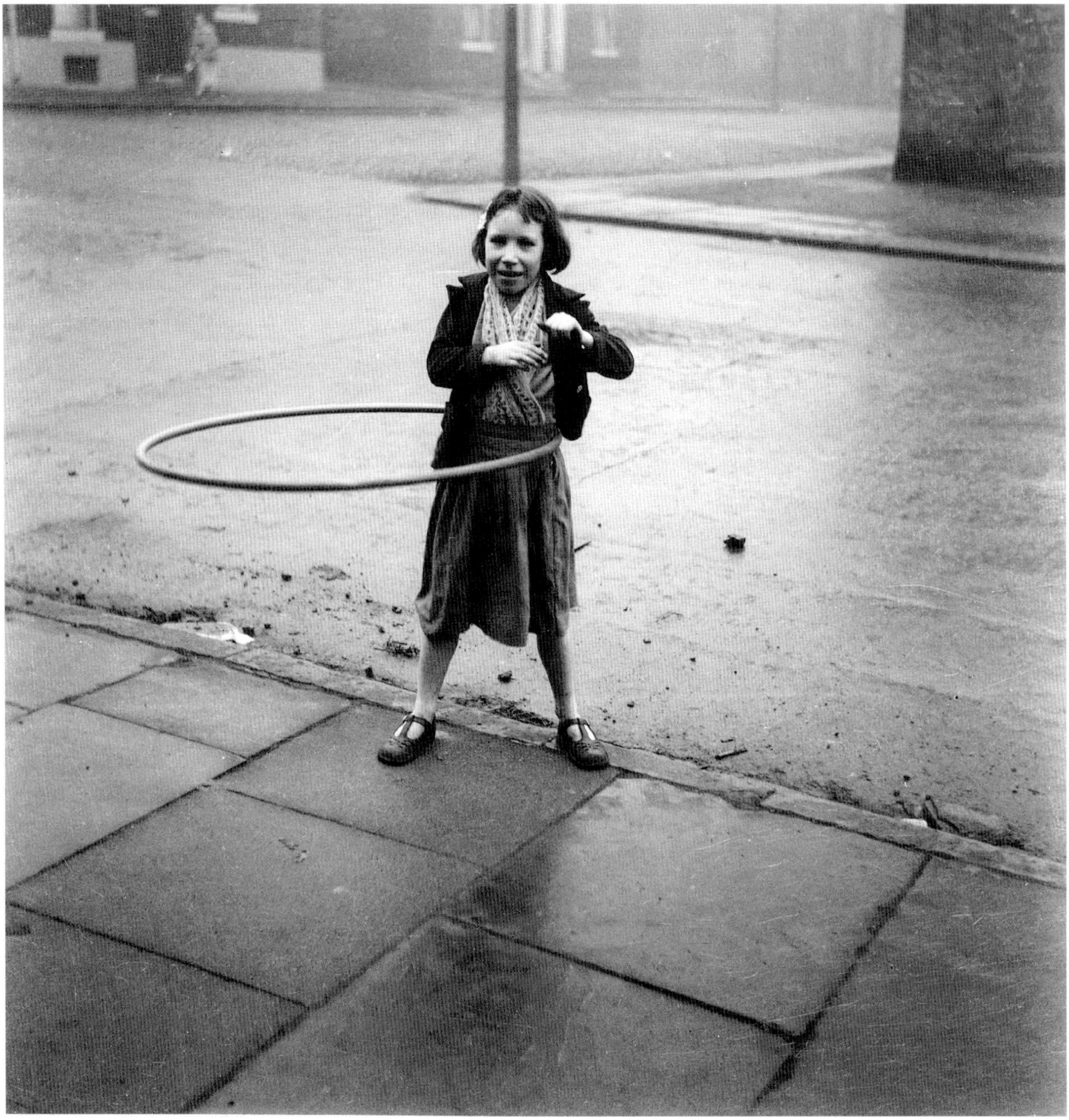

Anne Prendergast outside the Gloucester pub, Gloucester Street, 1957.

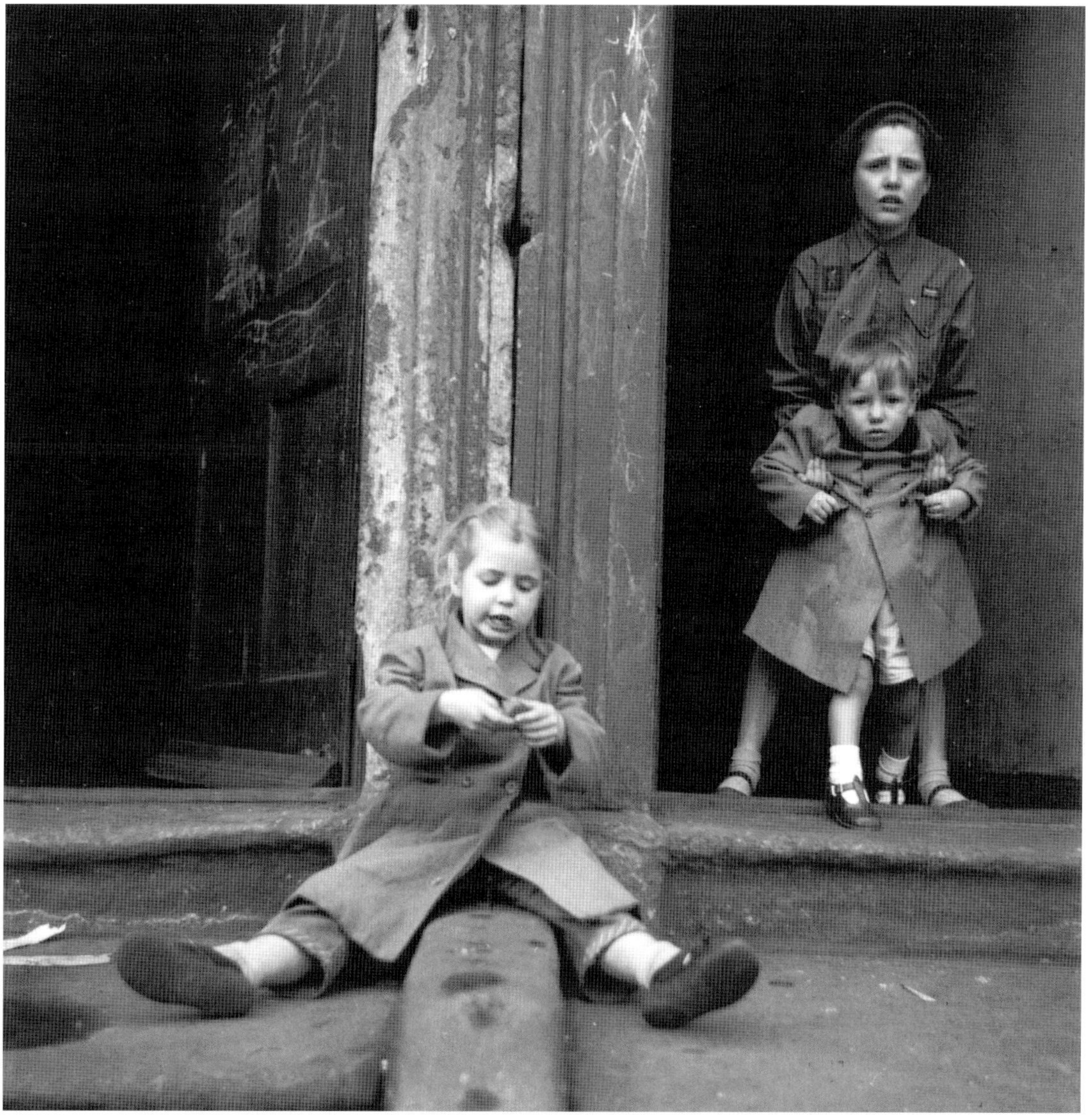

Dorothy, Carol and Arthur Bransby, 26 July 1958.

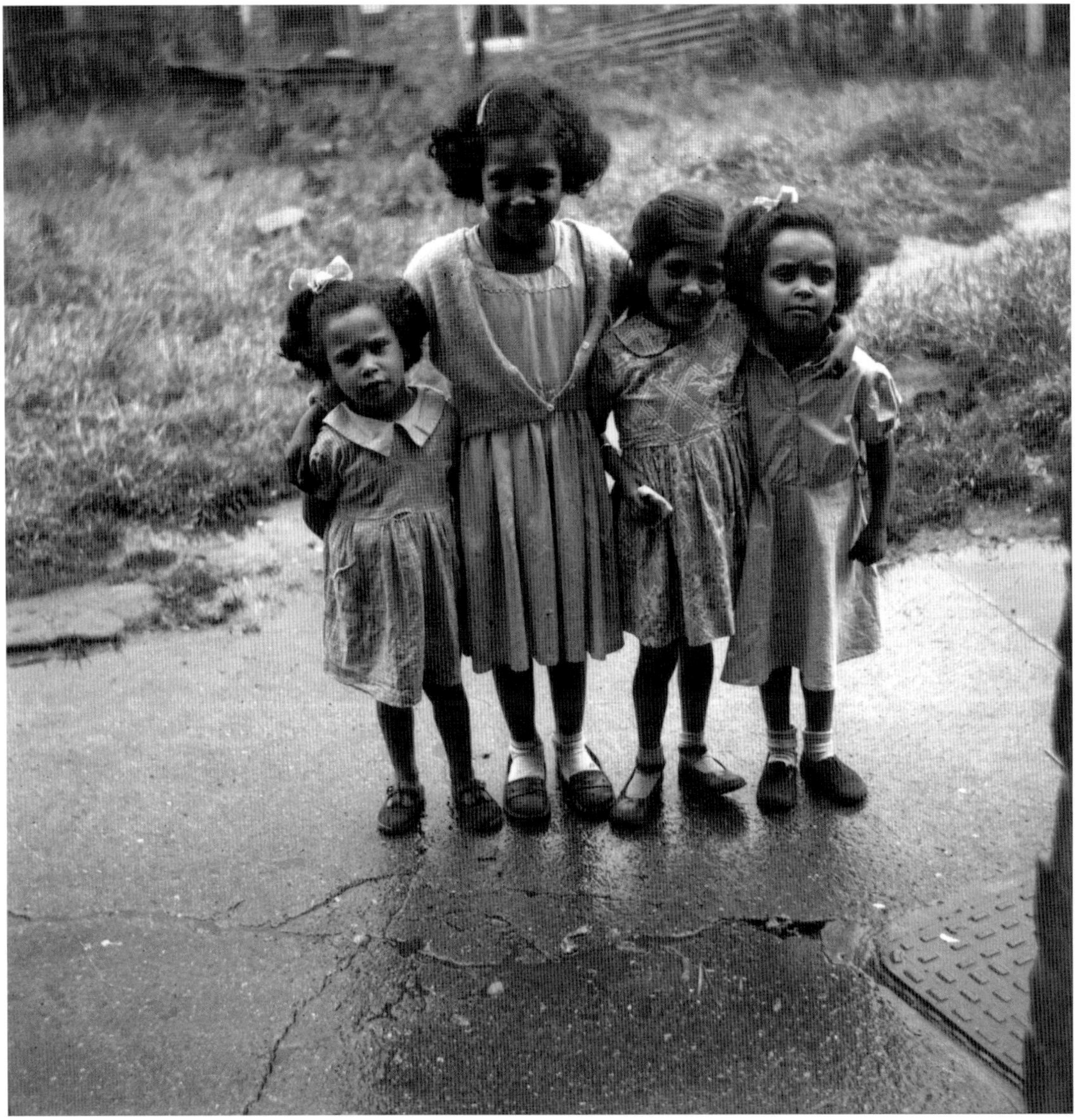

The Avilez children in their back garden at 48 Forest Road, July 1958.

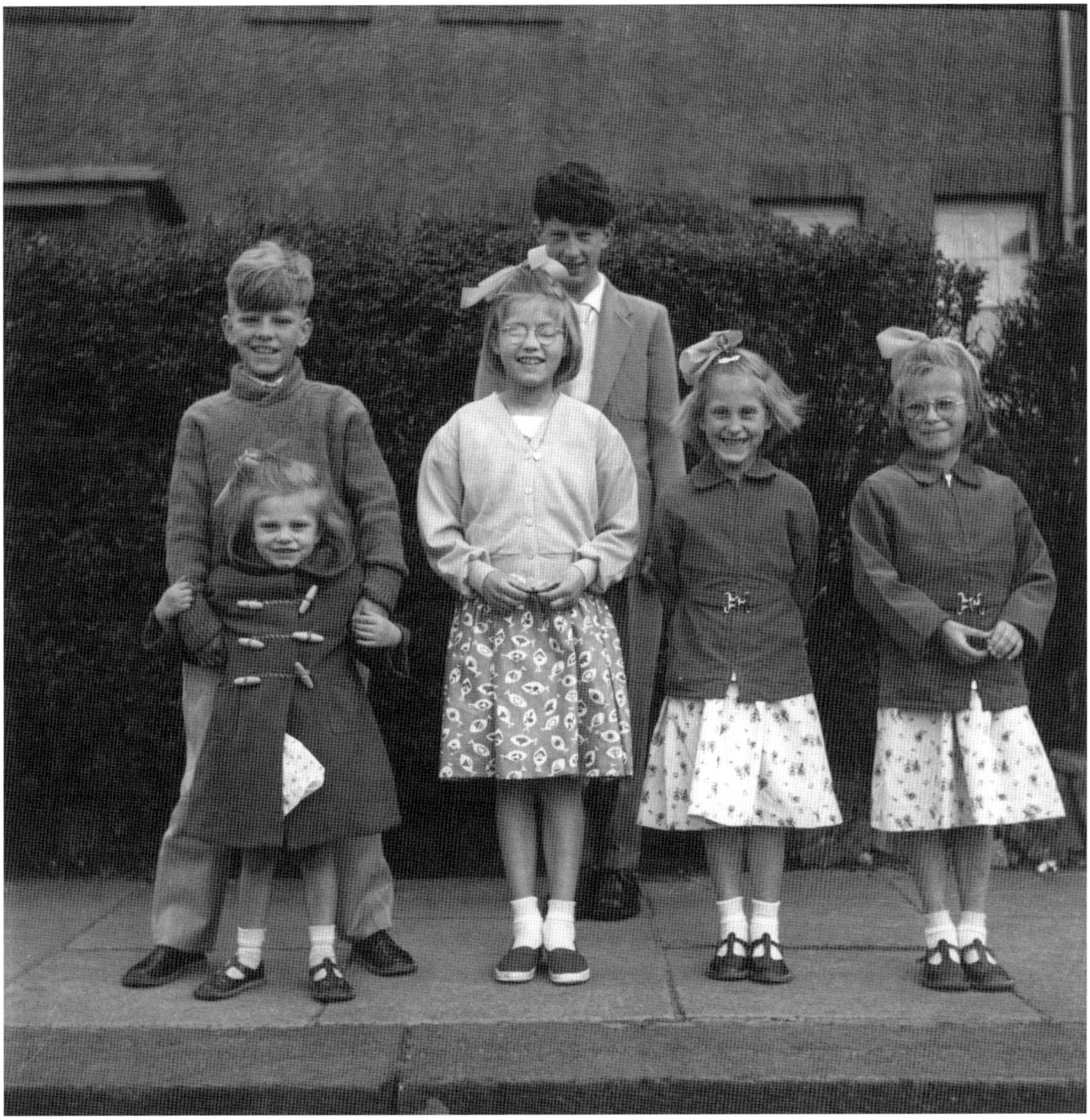

The Cruse children, Whitsun Sunday 1958.

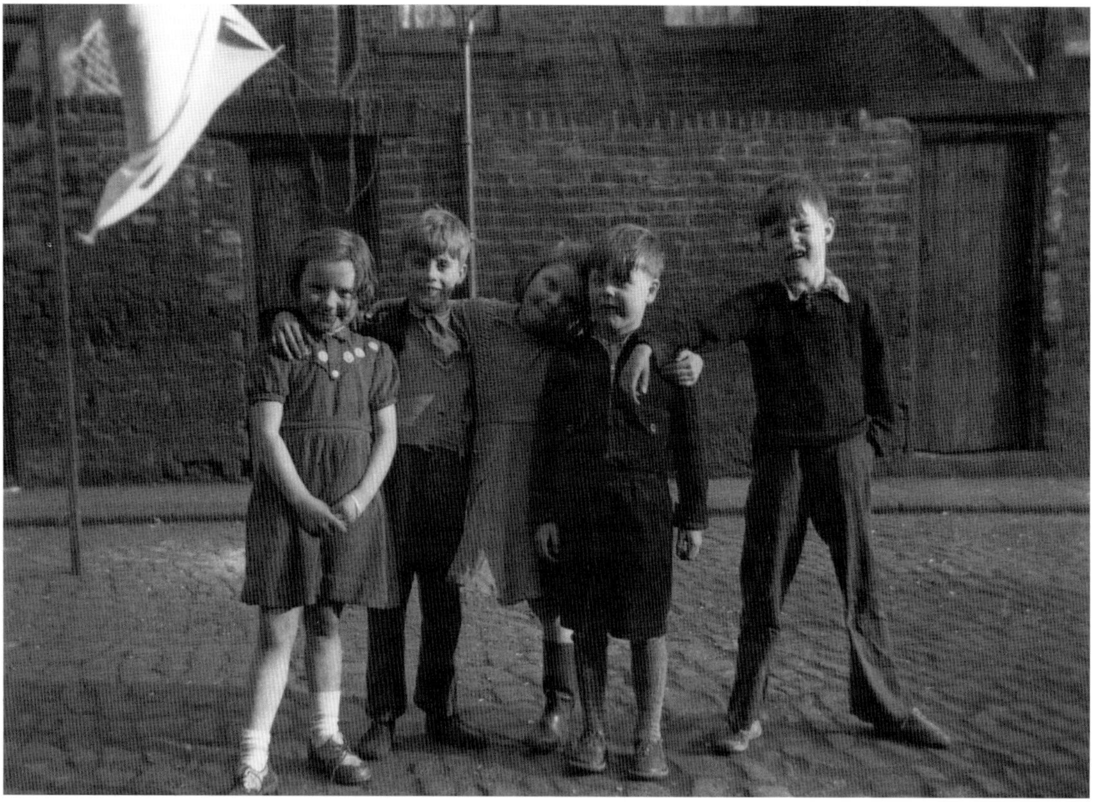

Angela Pearce and friends, Scotswood Road back lane, 1956.

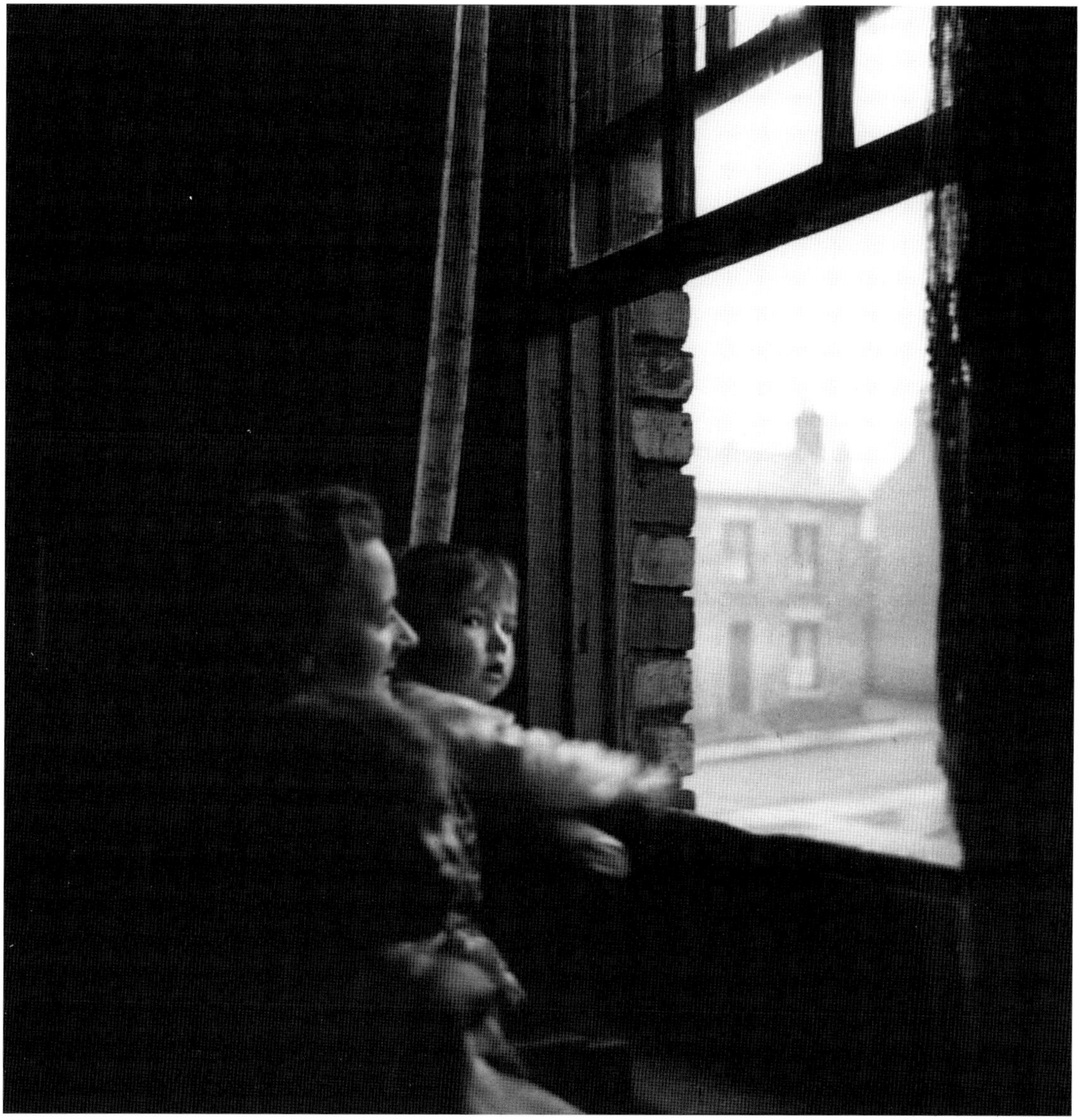

Mother and children, 1957.

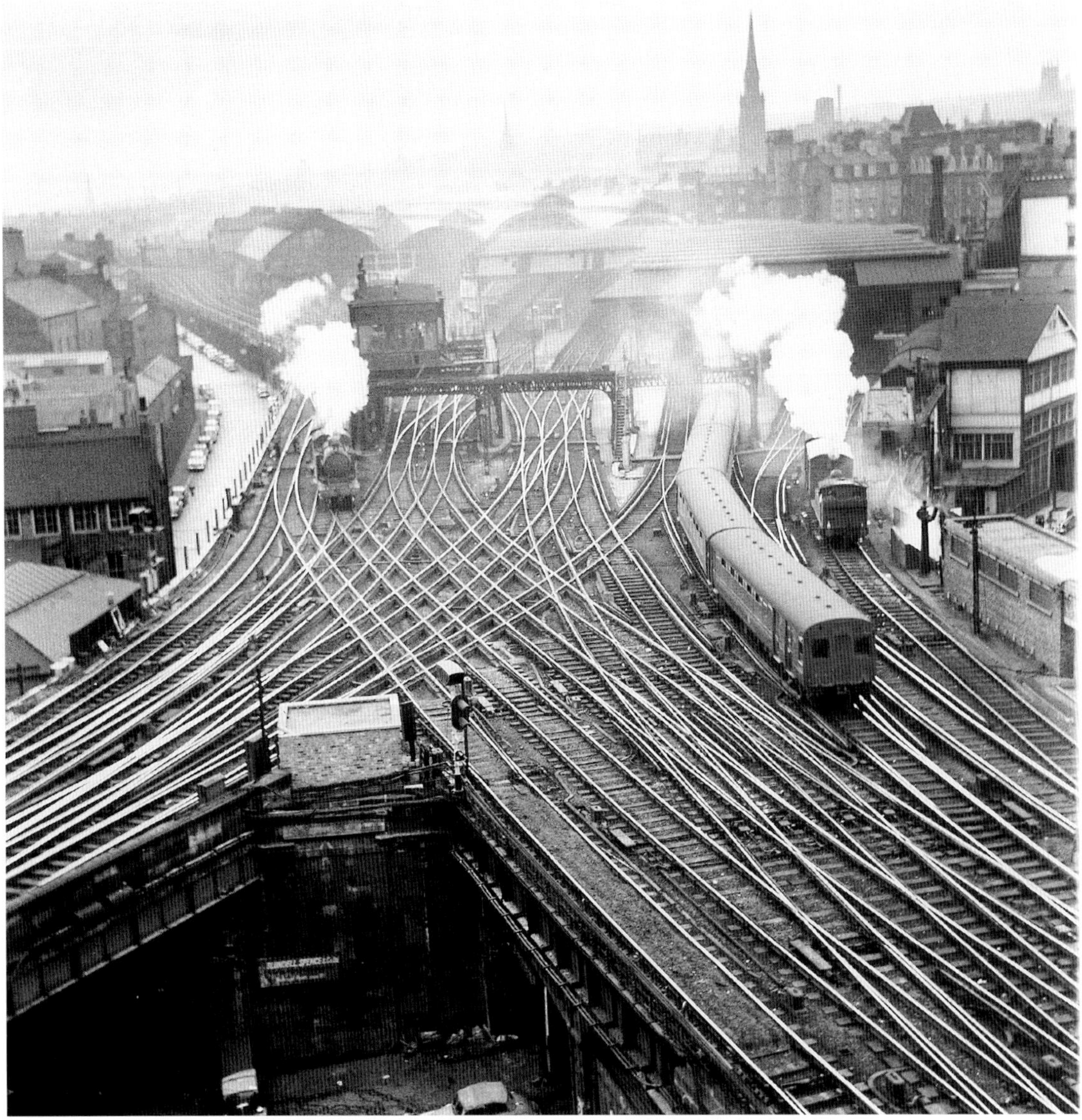

Central Station from the top of the Castle Keep, 1957.

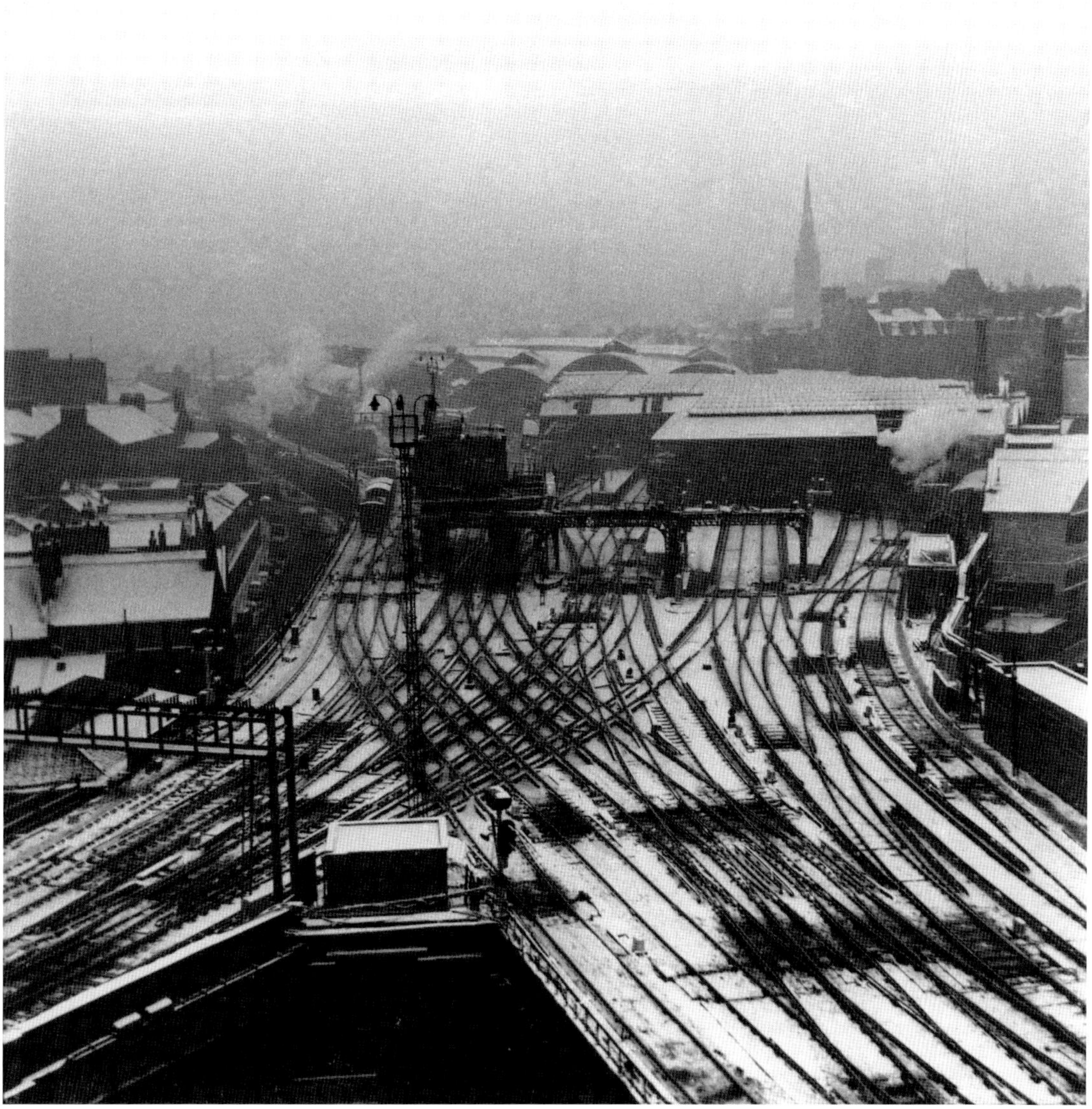

Central Station from the top of the Castle Keep, 1958.

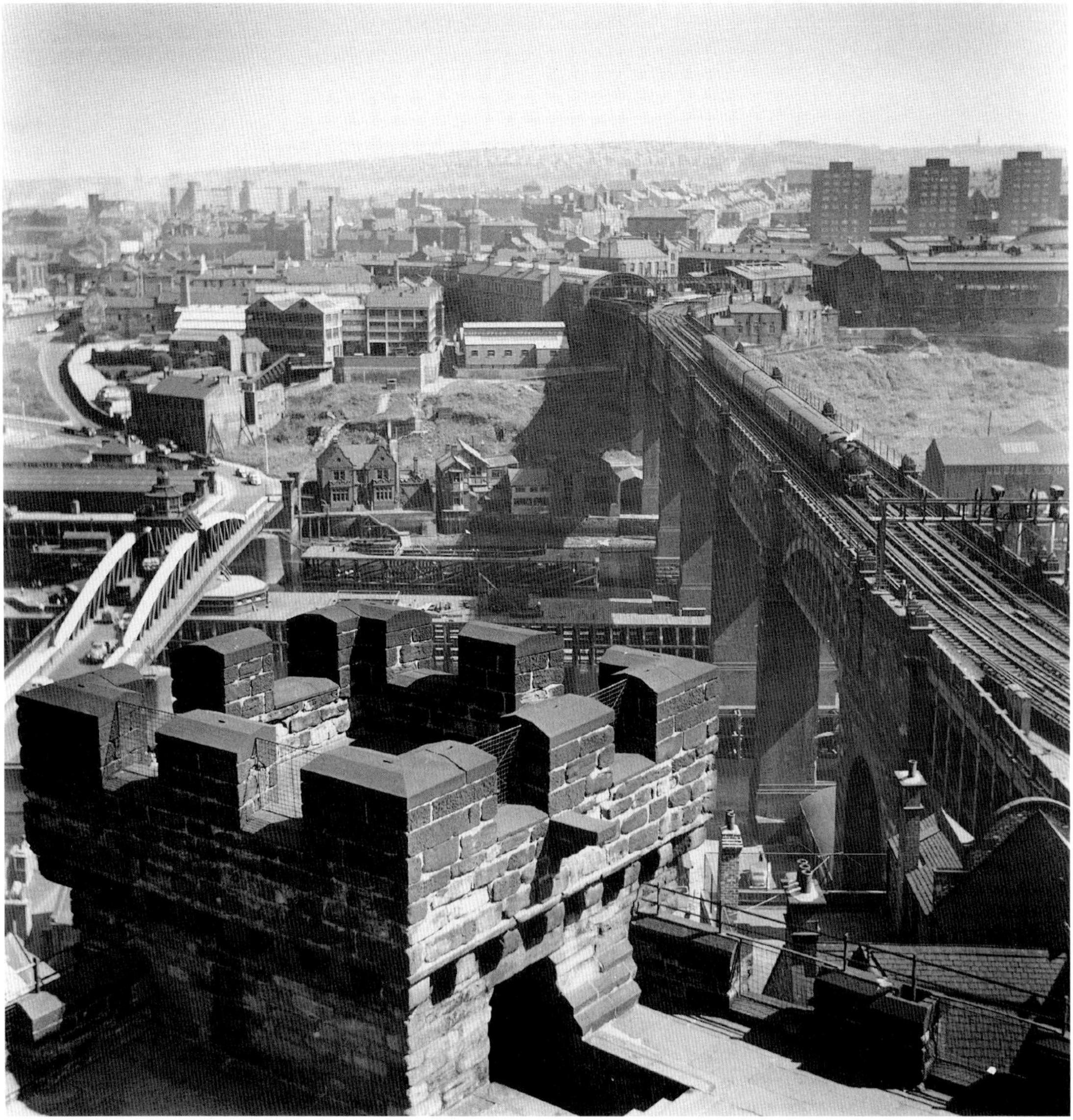

Castle turret, June 1957.

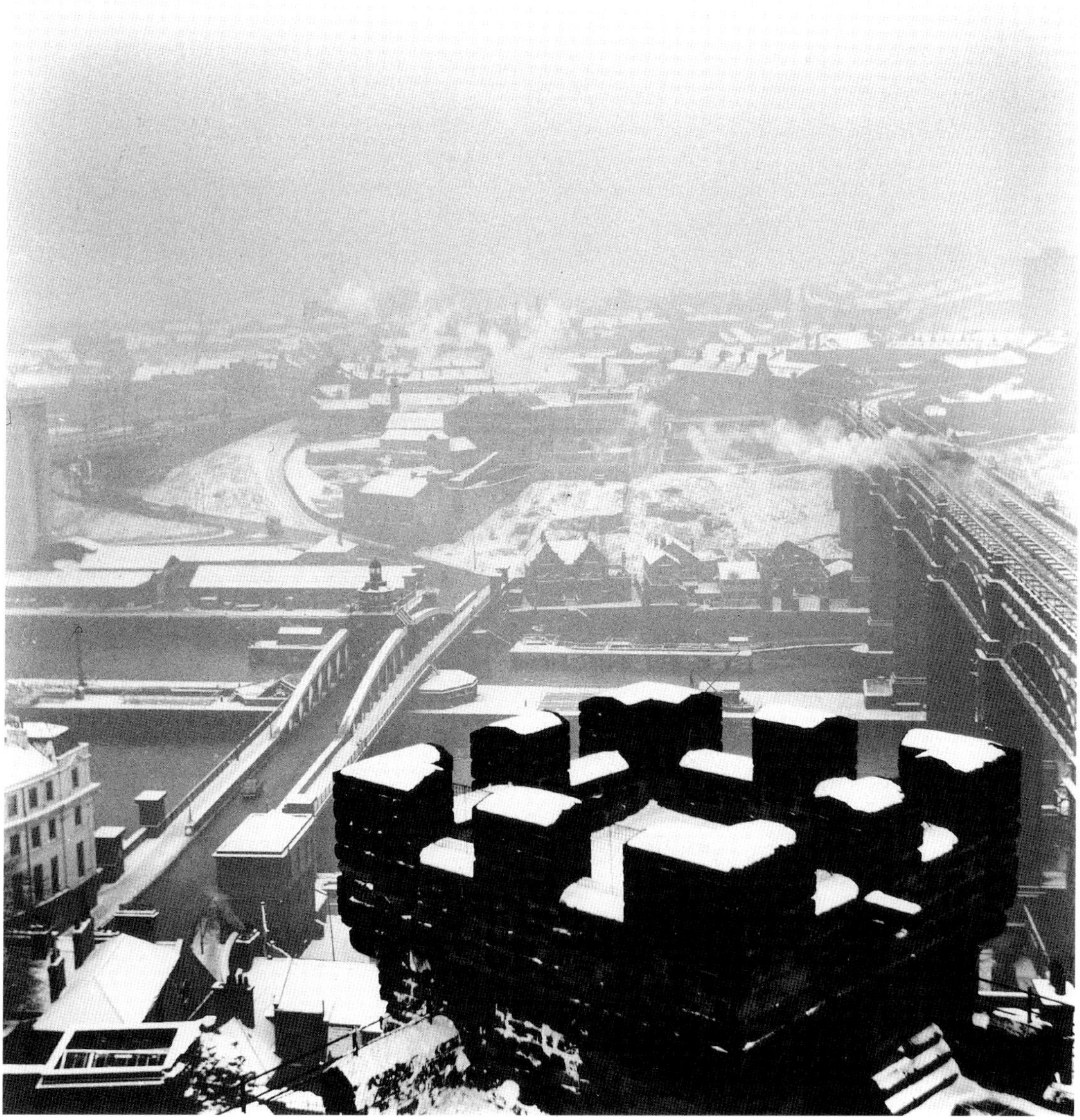

Castle turret, February 1958.

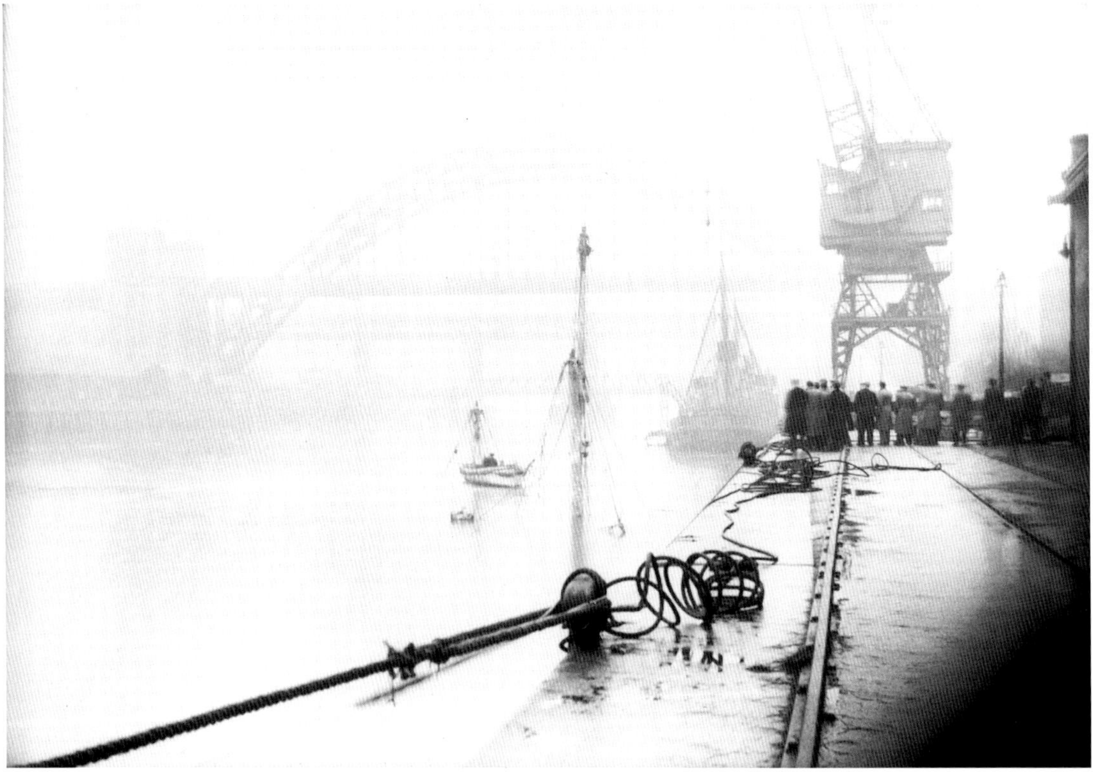

Quayside. 6 February, 1956.

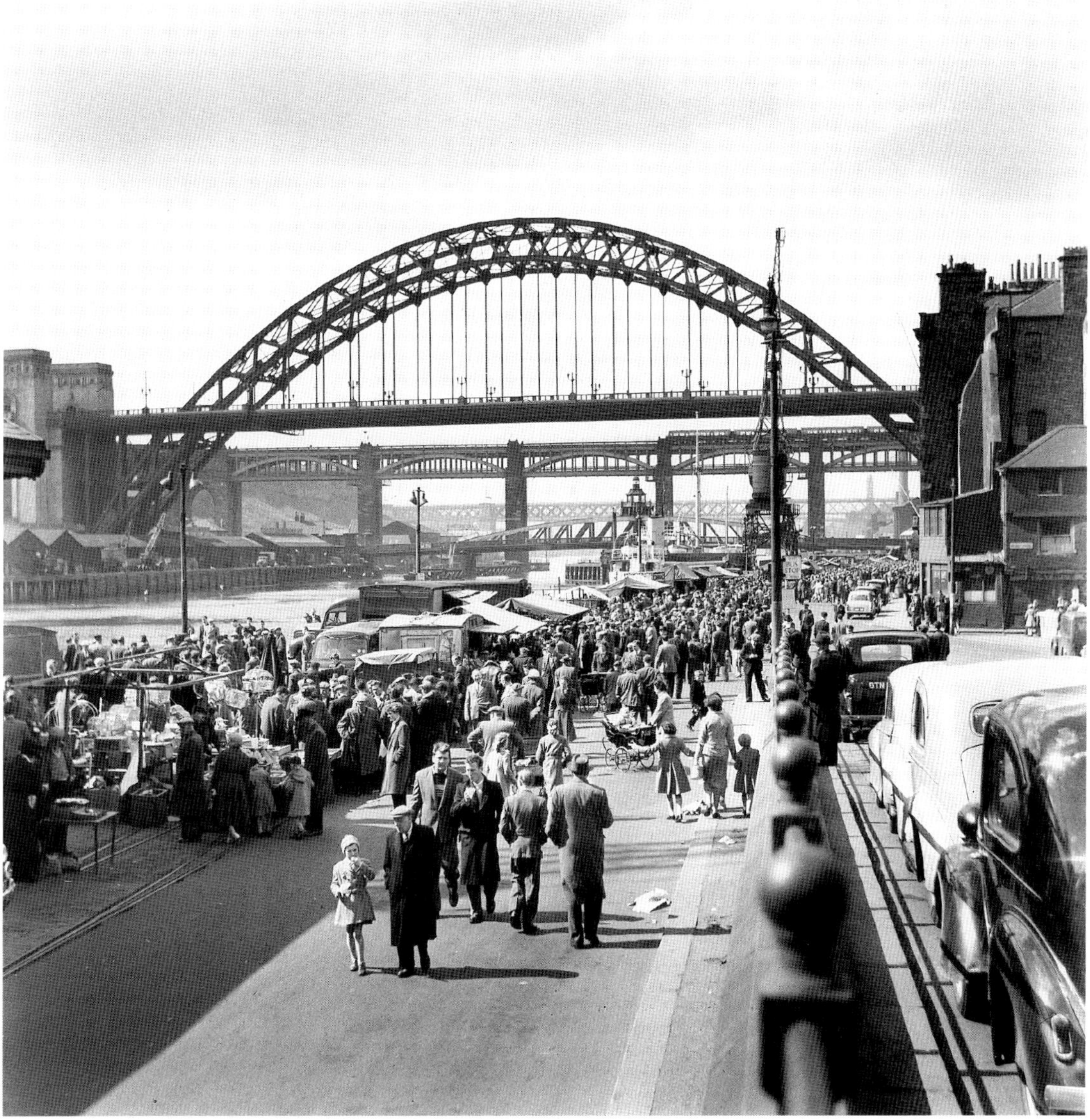

Quayside, St George's Day 1958.

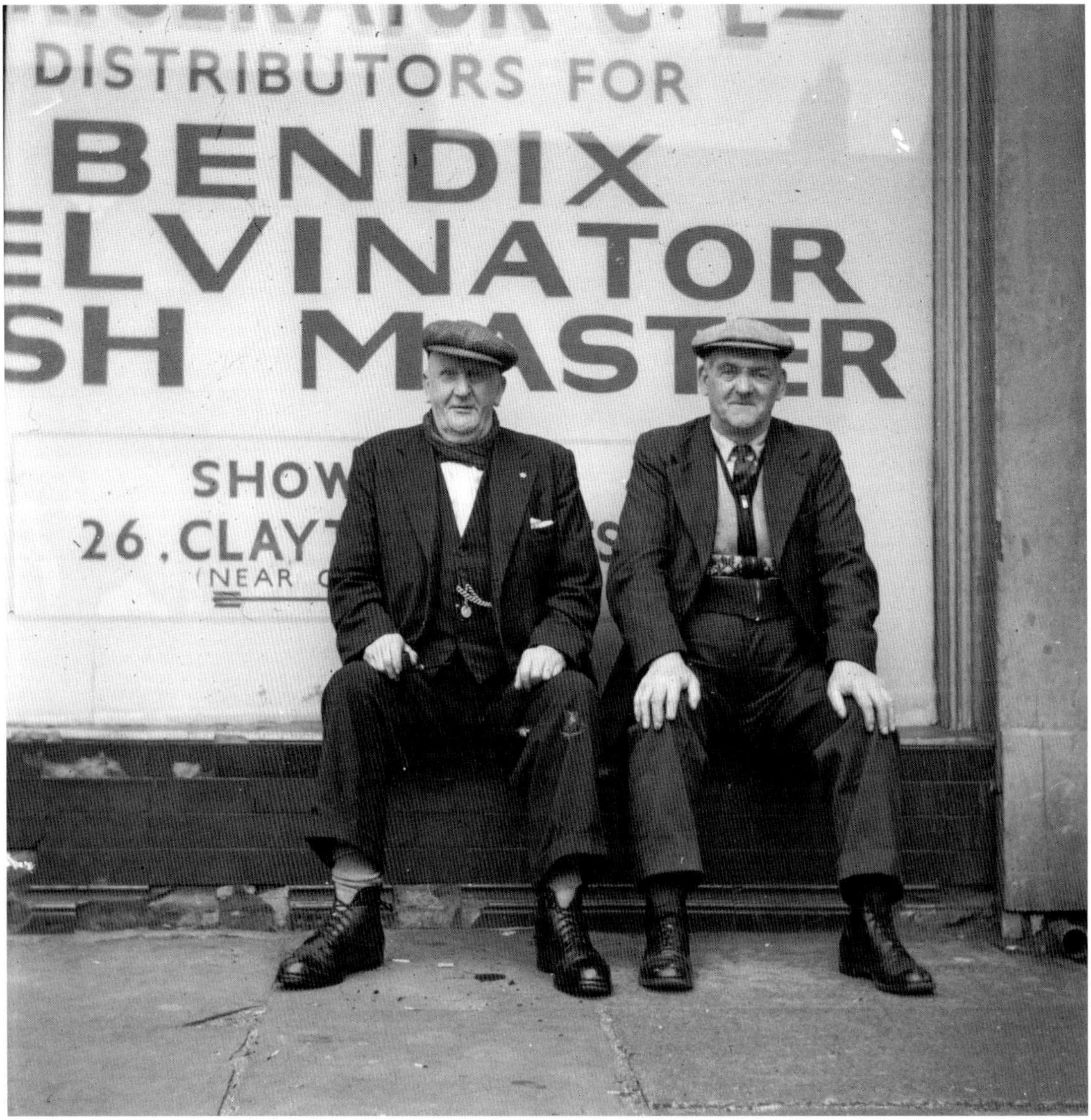

Jimmy the Cooper and Mr Bryson, 1958.

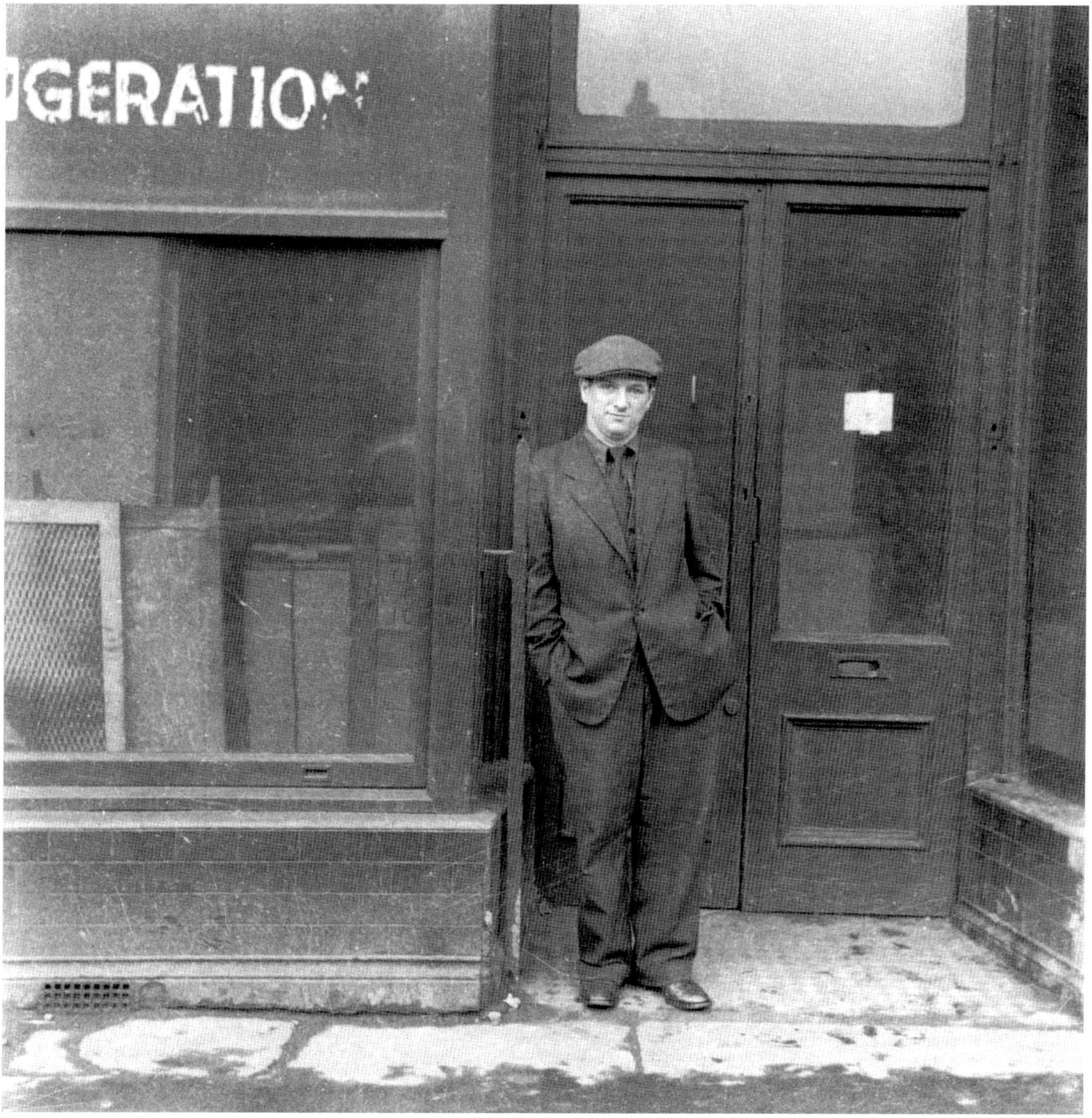

Gatters McEldery. c1957.

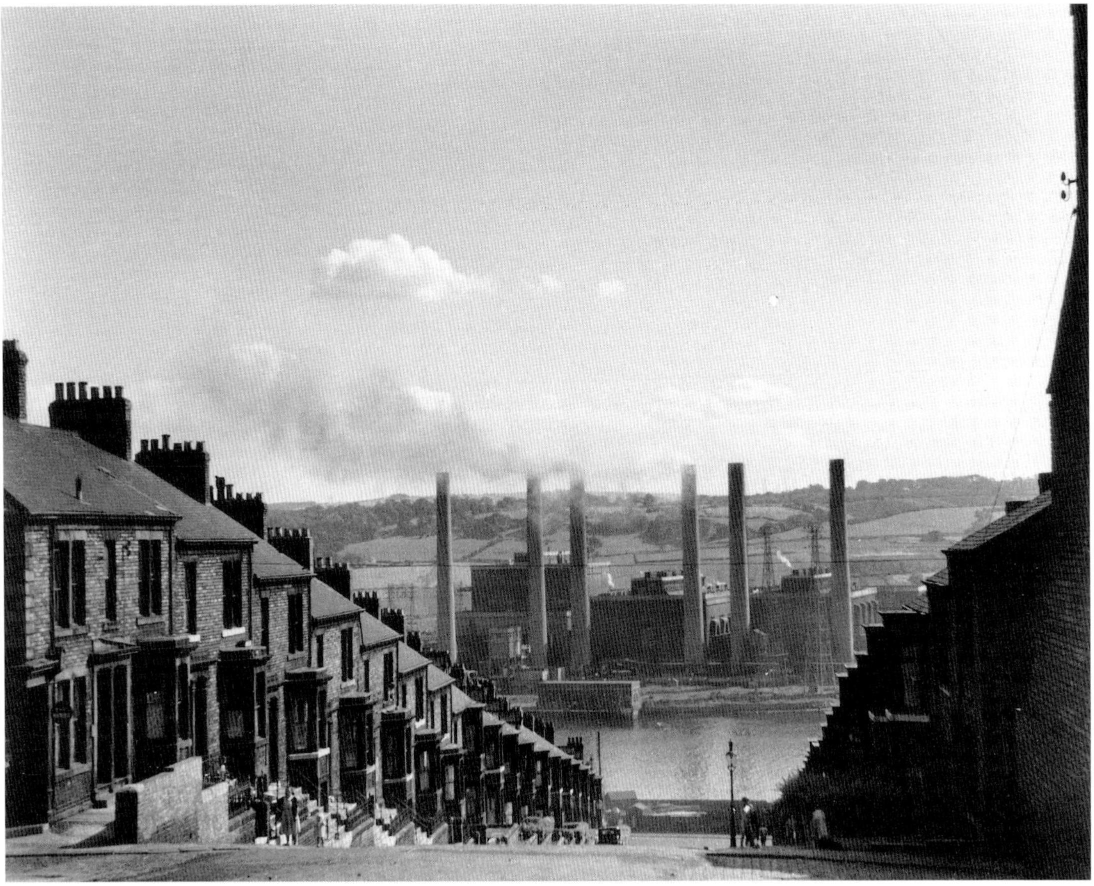

View down Clara Street to Dunston Power Station from Buddle Road. November, 1955.

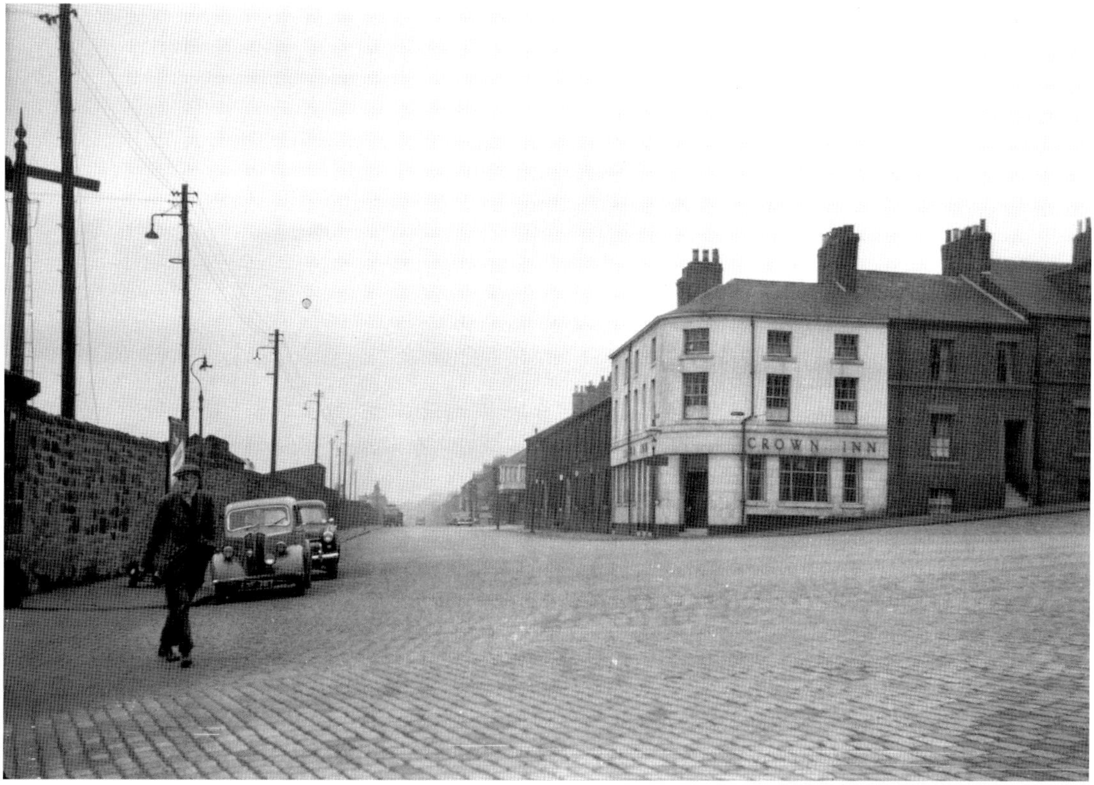

Junction of Ord Street and Railway Street.

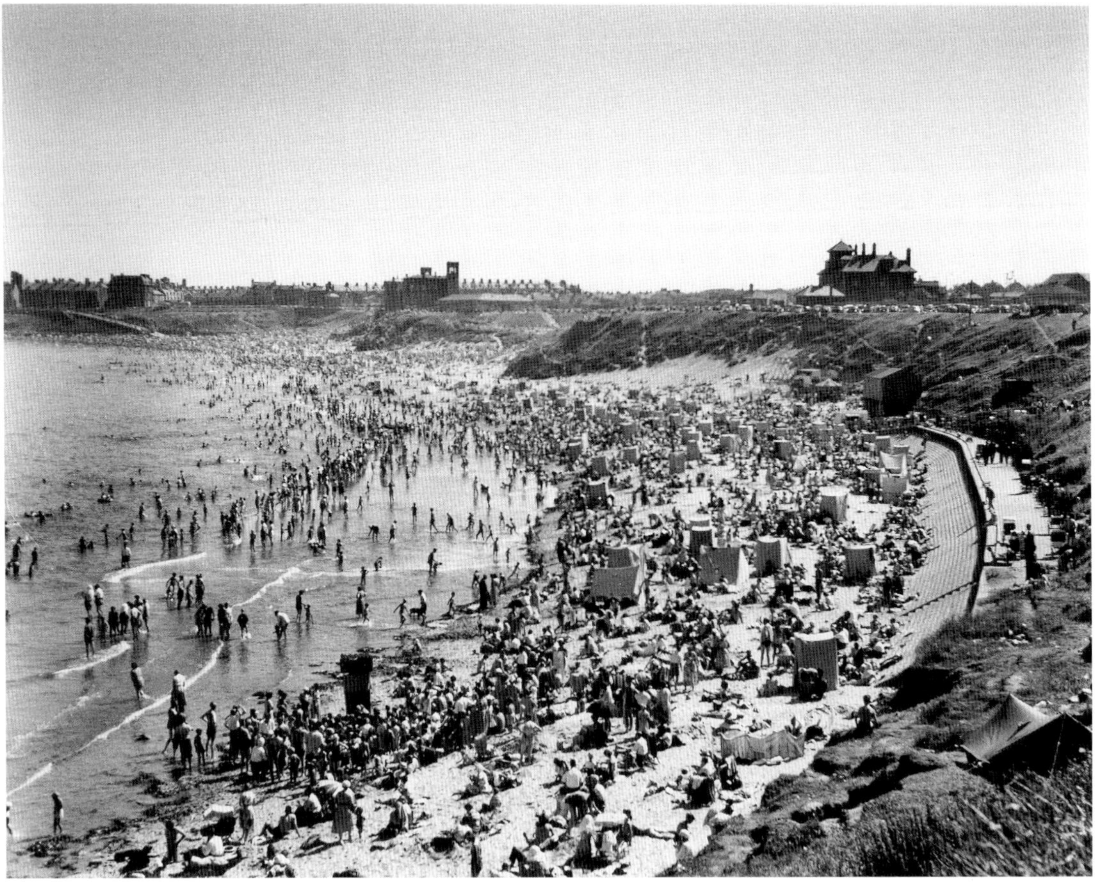

The Long Sands, Tynemouth, August Bank Holiday, 1955.

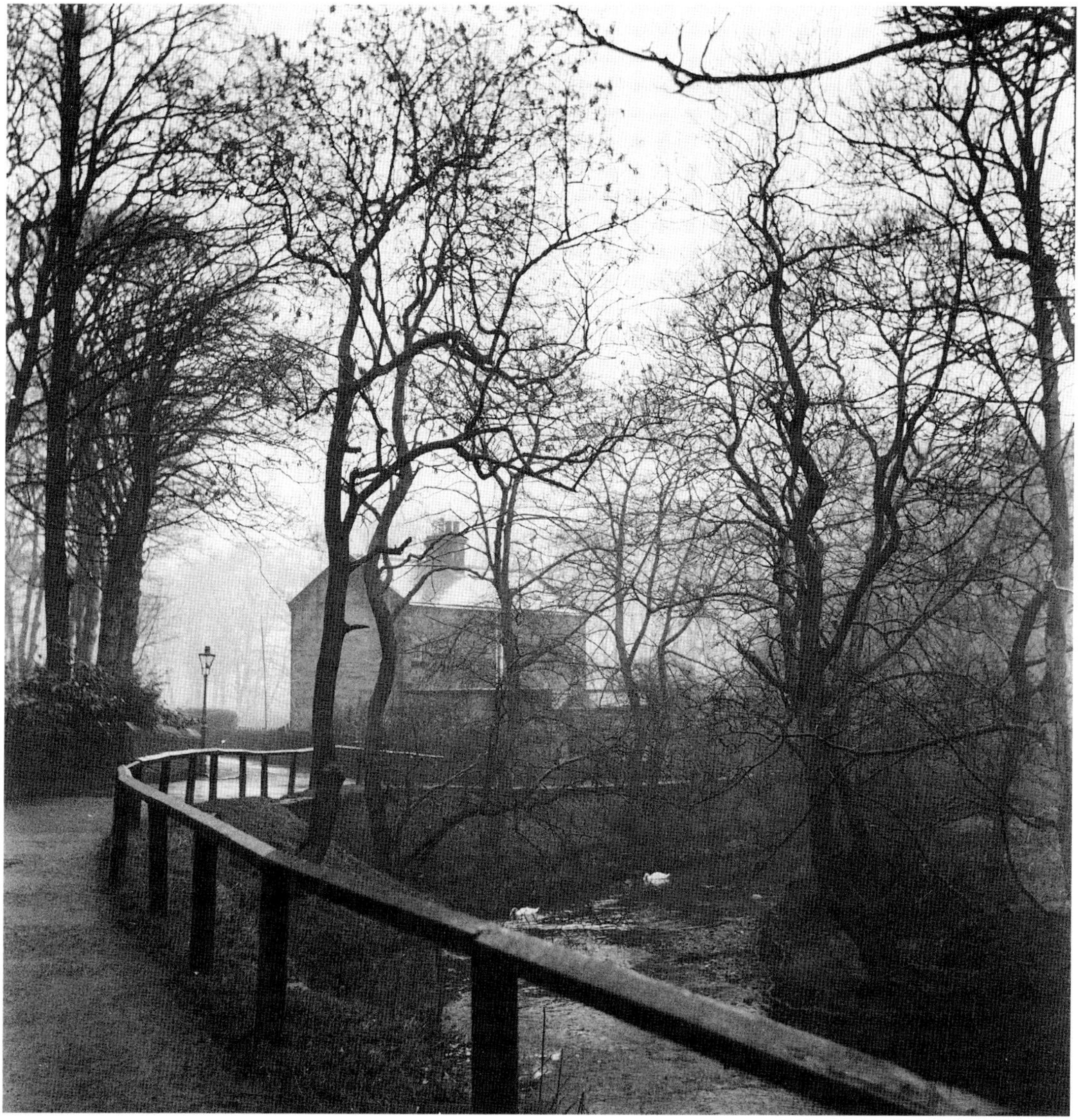

Jesmond Dene, 1957.

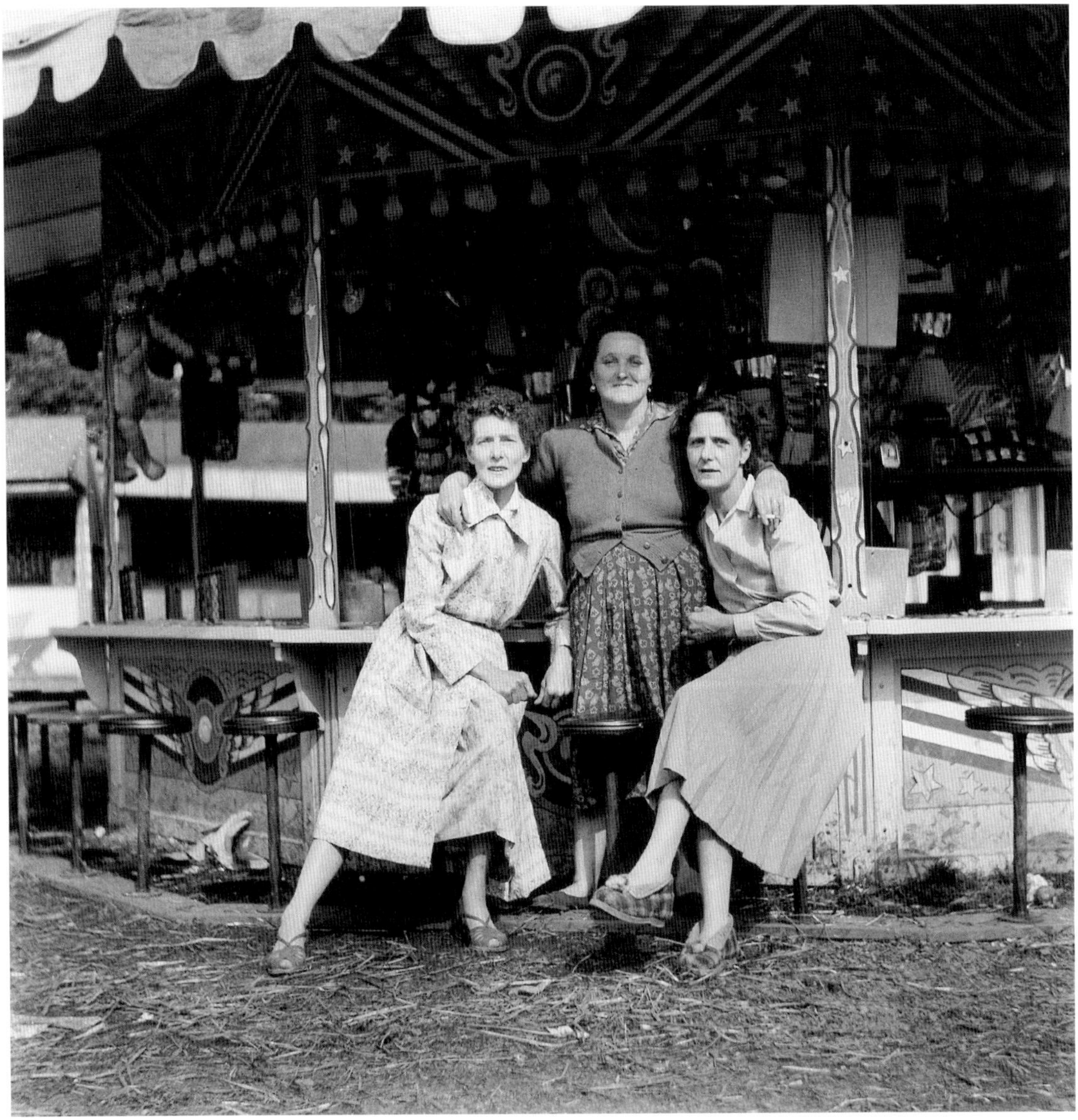

Yolande Gladders on Vic's Housey-Housey Stall 30 June, 1958.

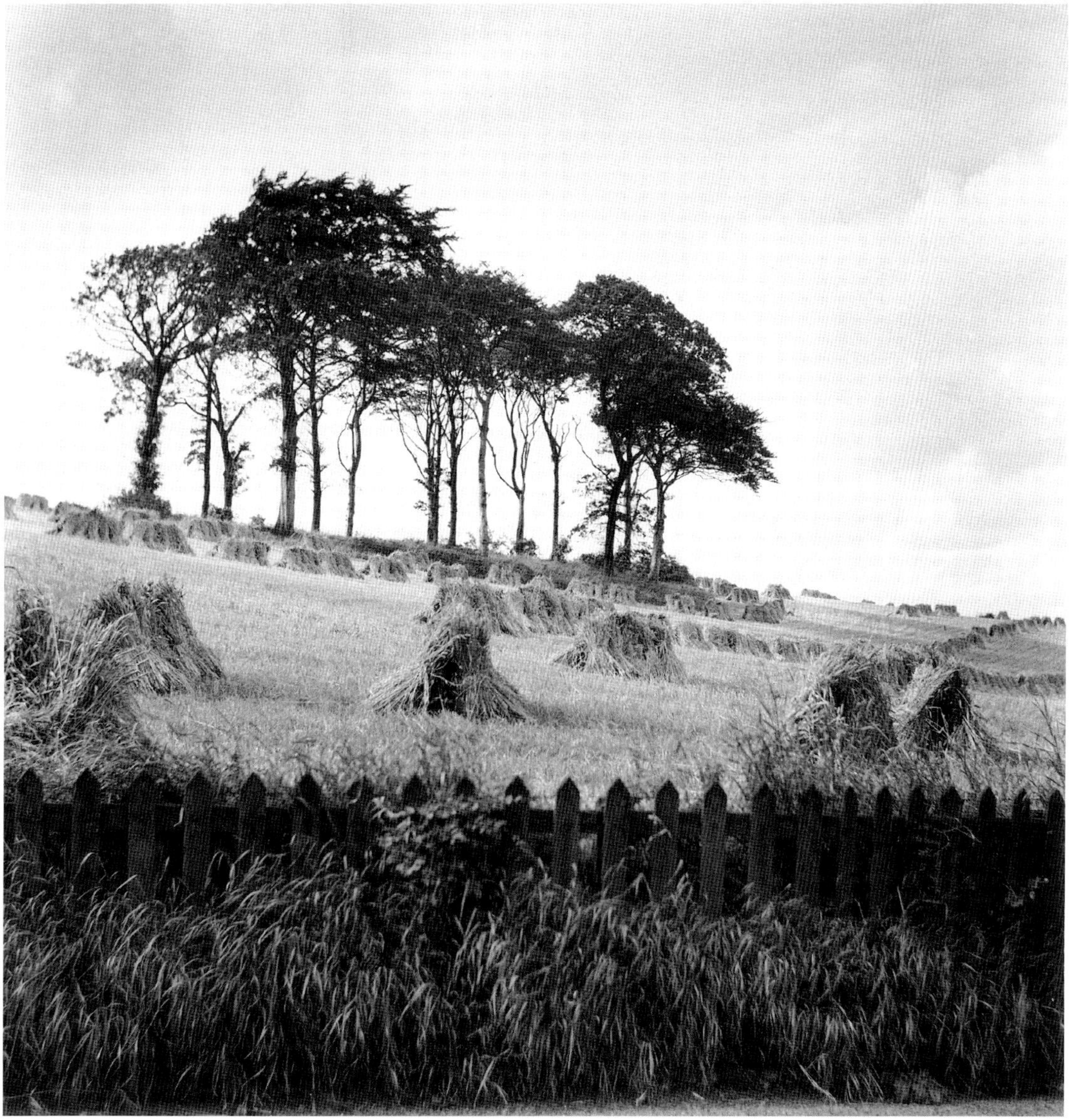

The road to East Herrington, 7 September 1958.

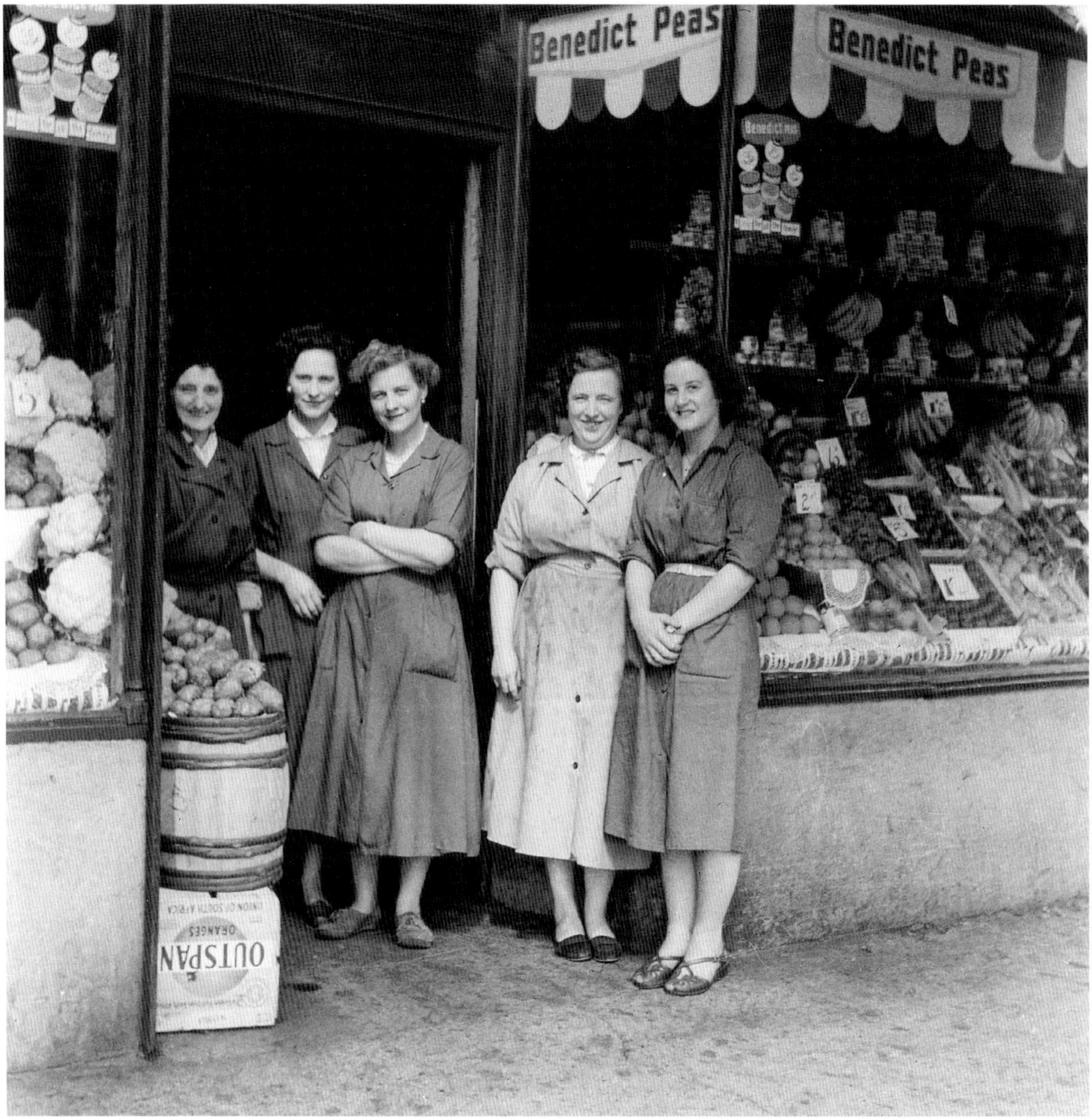

Gibson's fruit and vegetable shop, 1958, Mrs Gibson far left.

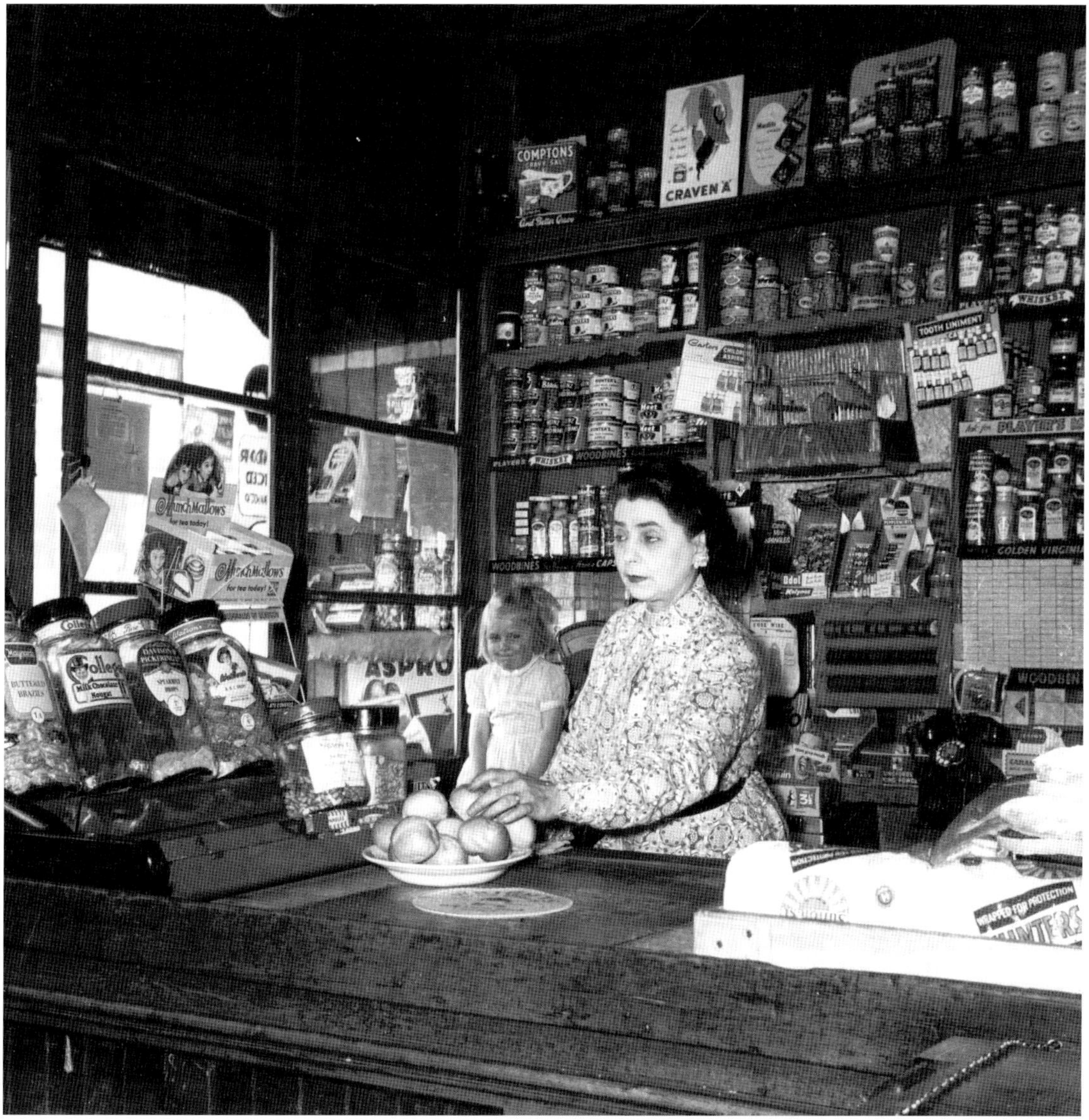

Peggy Moore and granddaughter in Jack Reay's shop on Scotswood Road. April 1957.

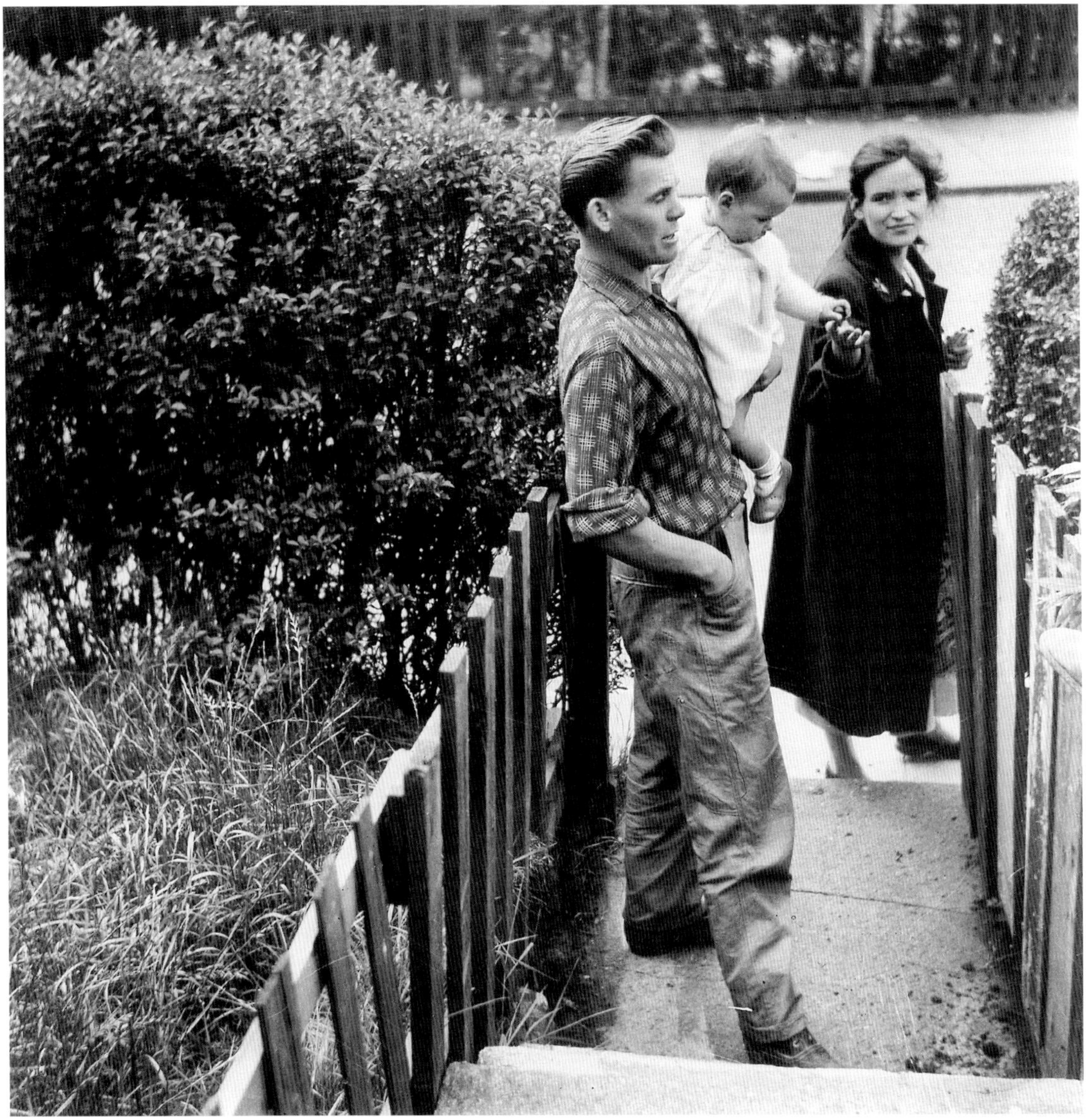

The Waites family, Delaval Road, 1958.

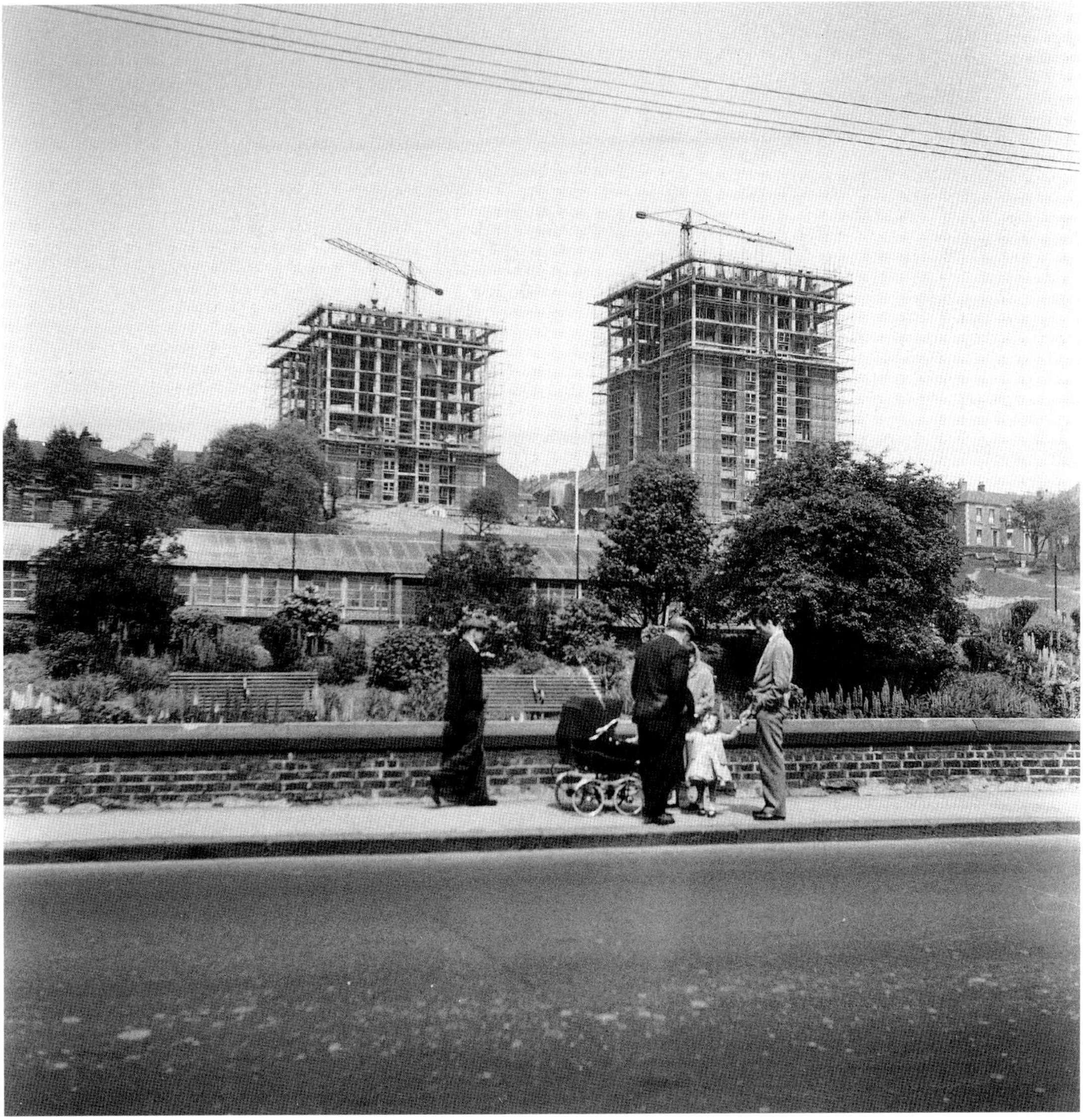

Cruddas Park flats on the site of St Vincent's School Home. May 1960.

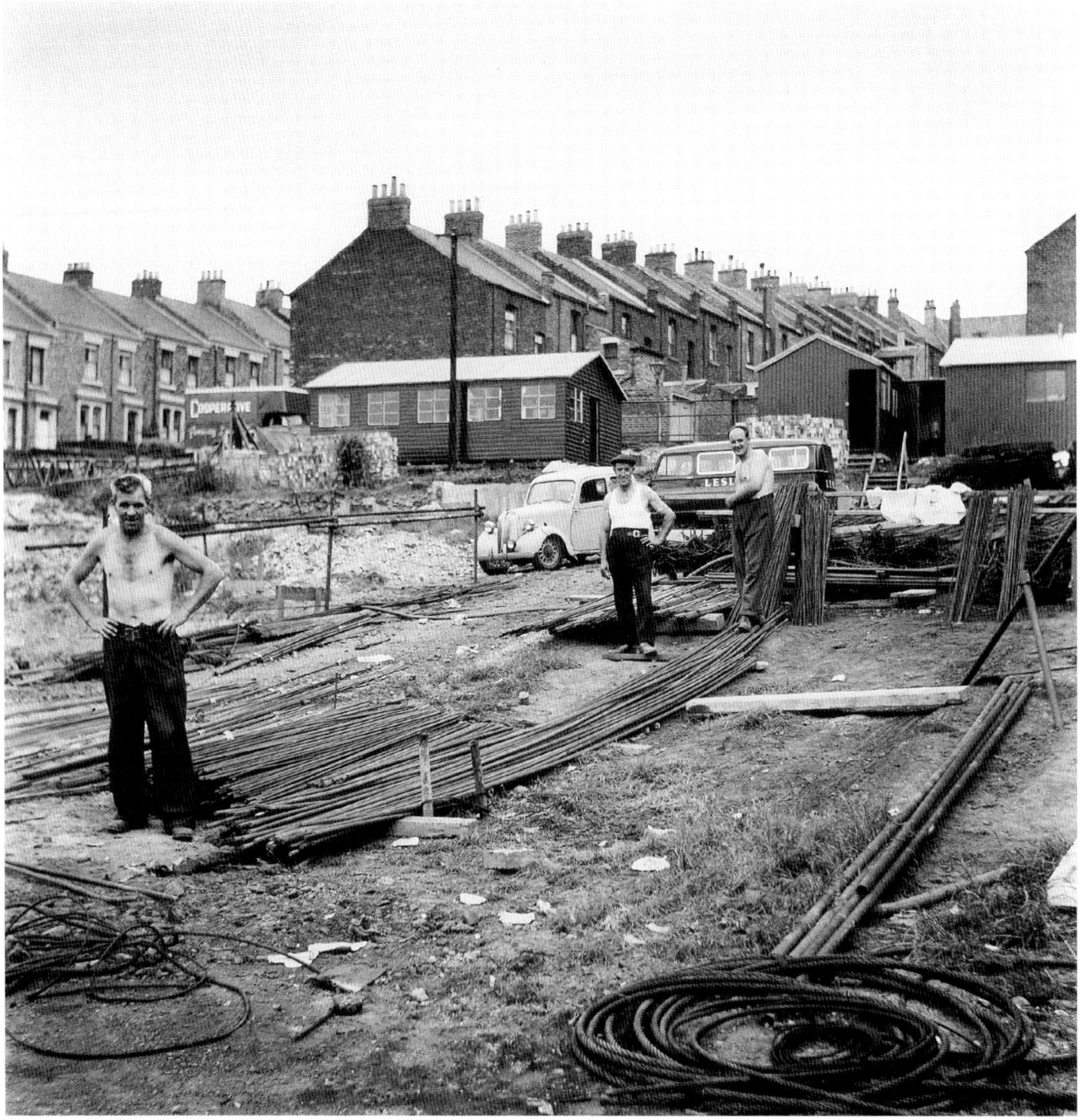

The north-east corner of the site for the Kings Meadow & Houghton Court flats. Budle Street is in the background running up from Wolsingham Street. 1959.

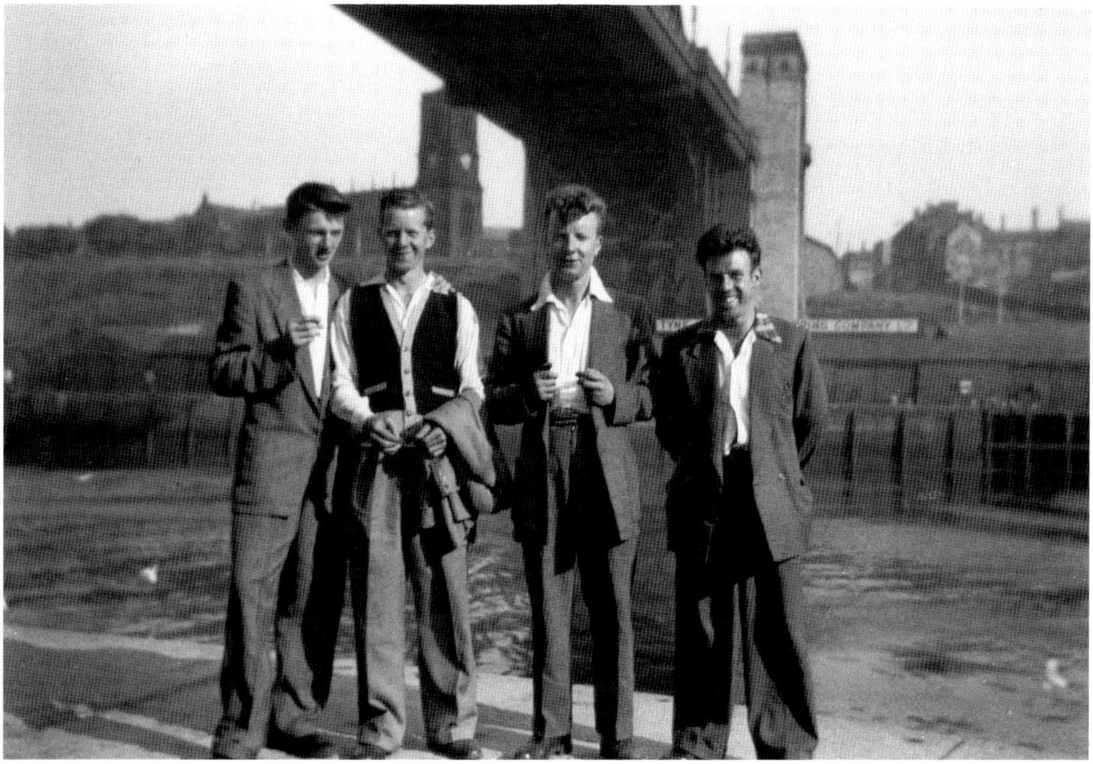

Young men about town. 1957.

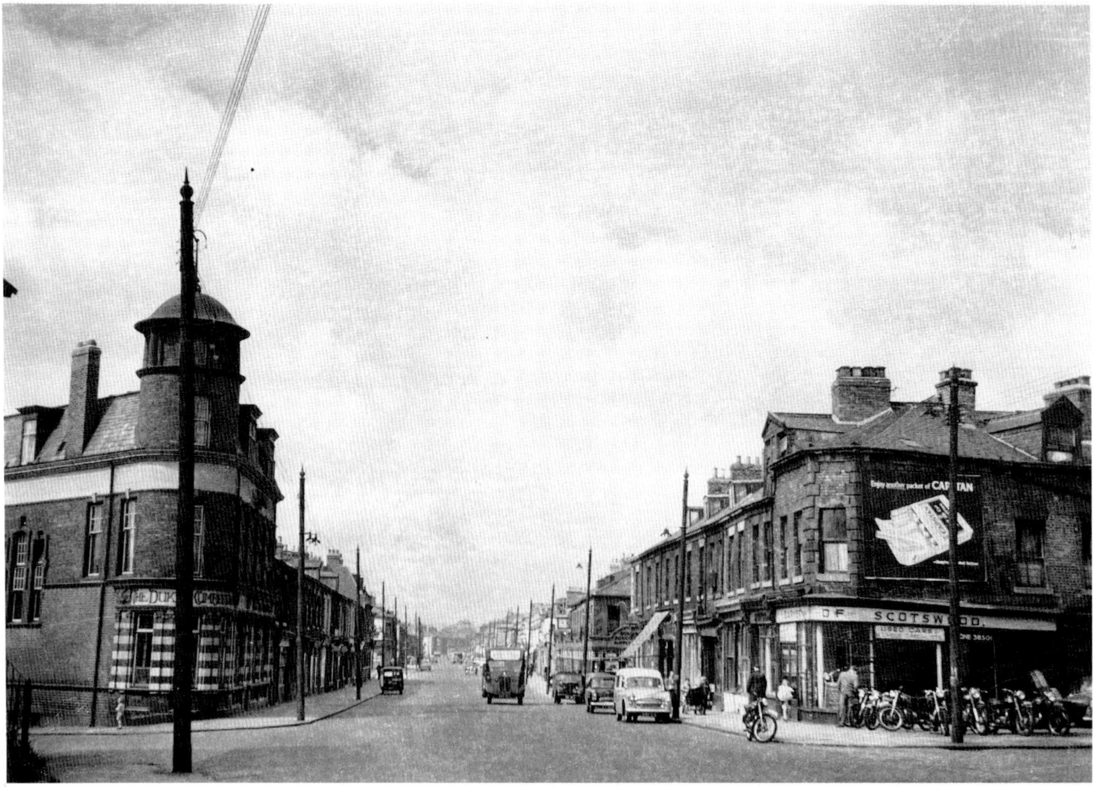

Scotswood Road, 1956.

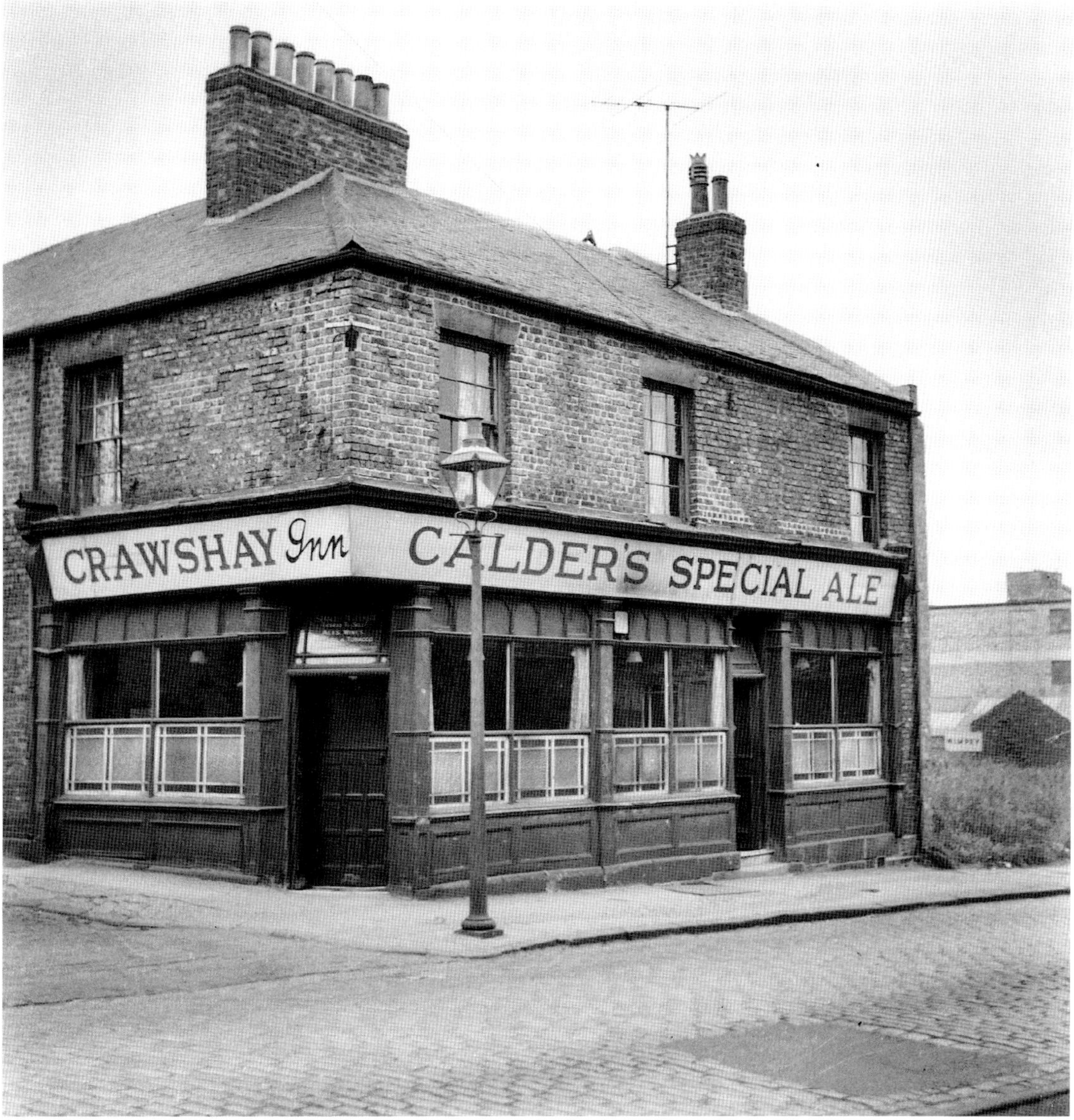

The Crawshay Inn, 12 East Street, Gateshead.

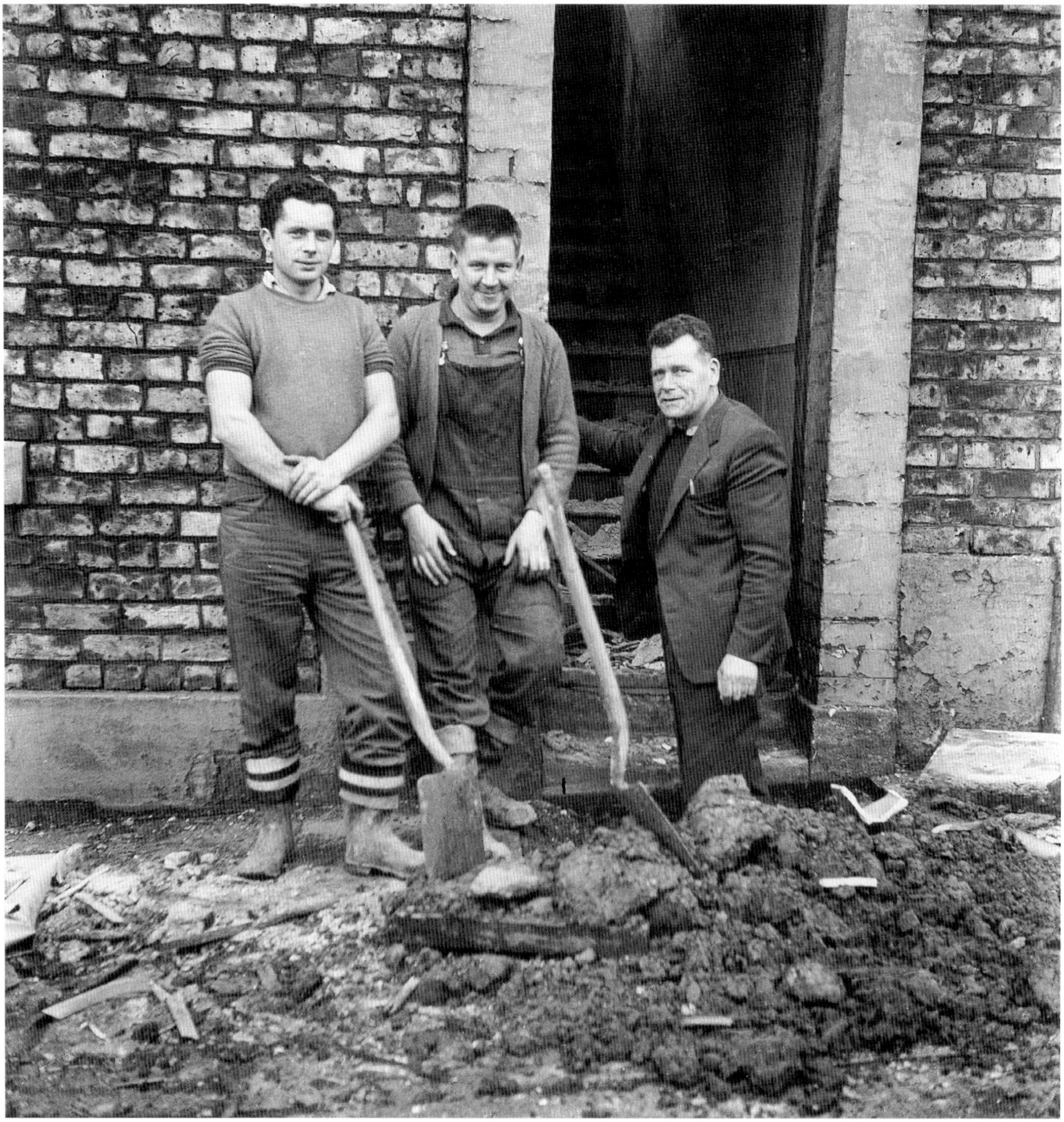

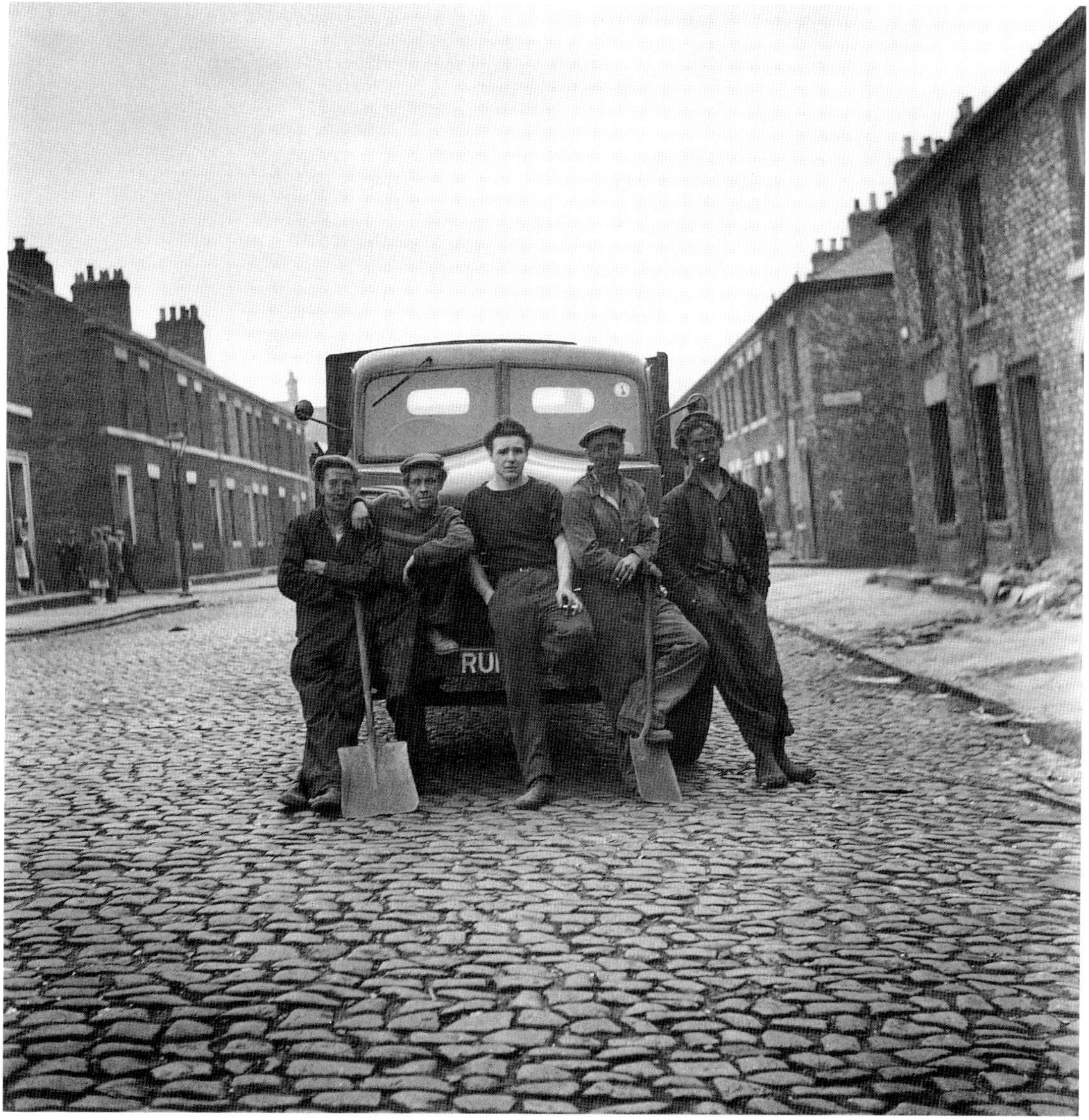

View east along Pine Street showing stripping gang taking wood and slates off empty houses. 24 August 1960.

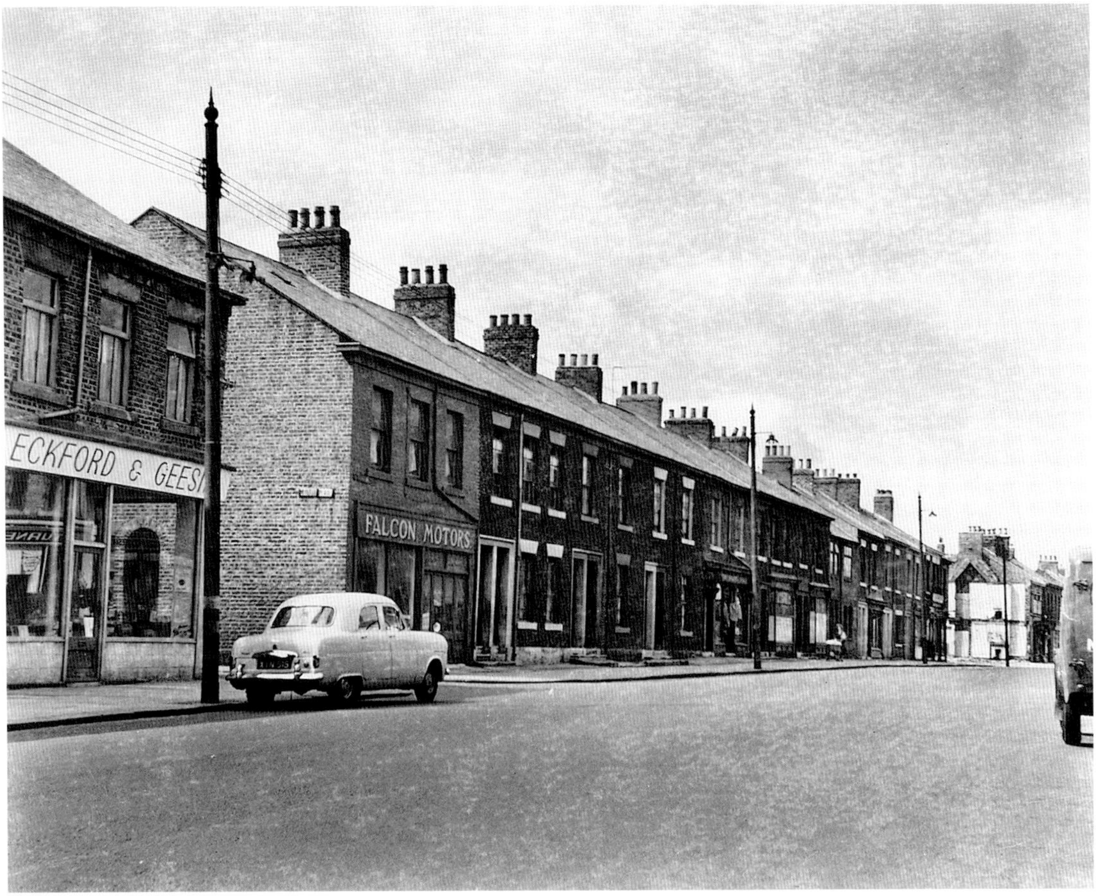

View along Scotswood Road across Myrtle Terrace. Jimmy's house is the fourth door along from the Falcon Motors shop. 1956.

Right, above, Scotswood Road, 1956.
Below, Scotswood Road east from Gloucester Street, 1956.

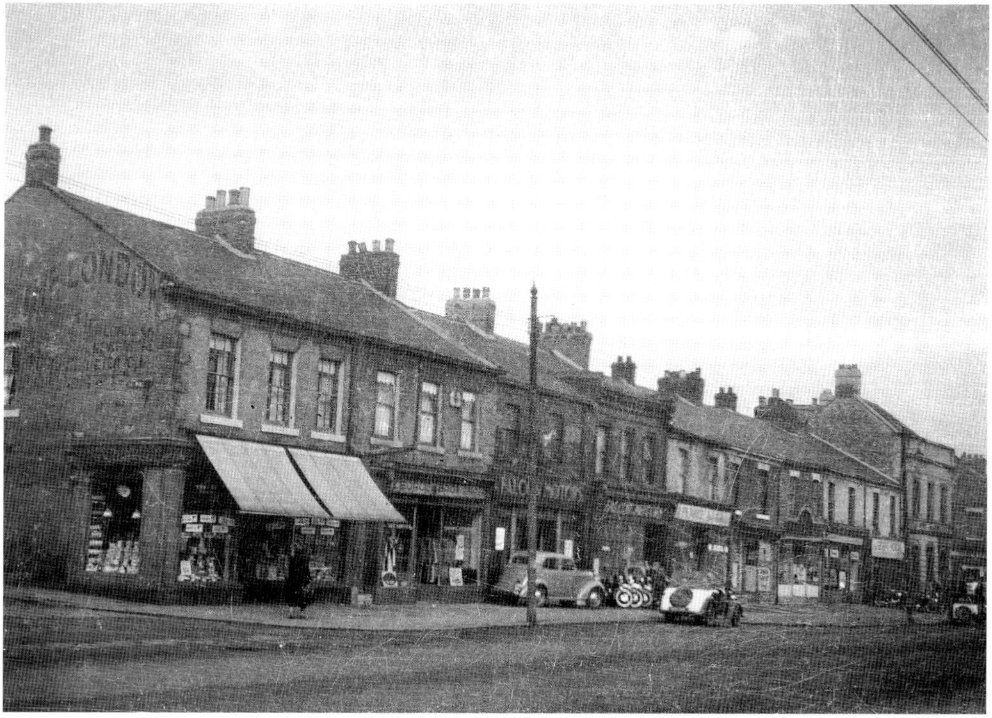

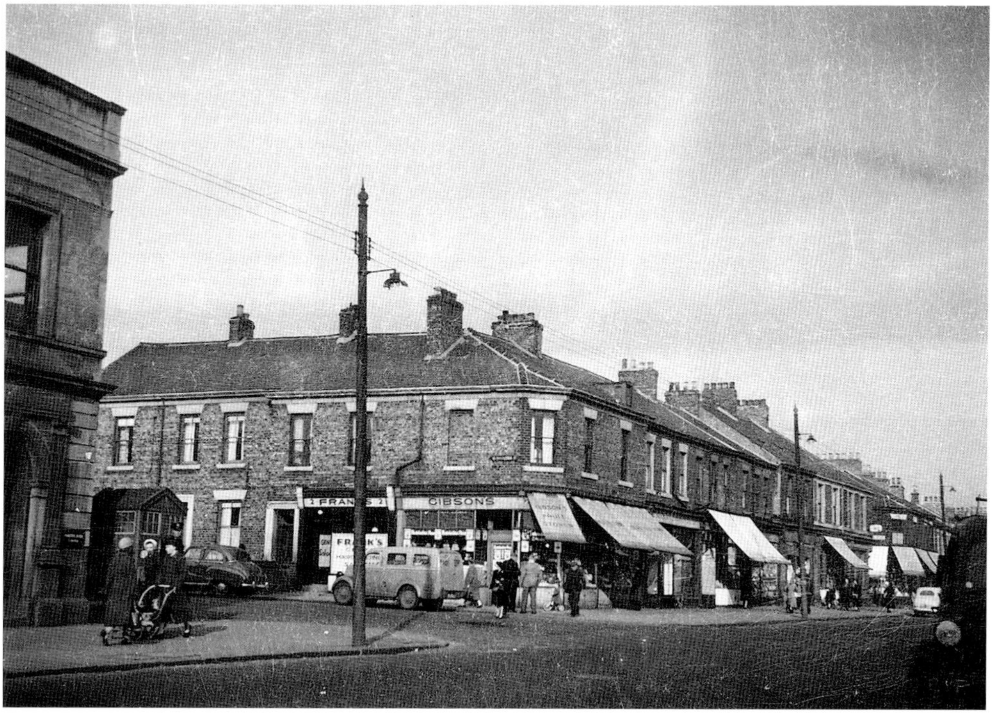
GIBSONS

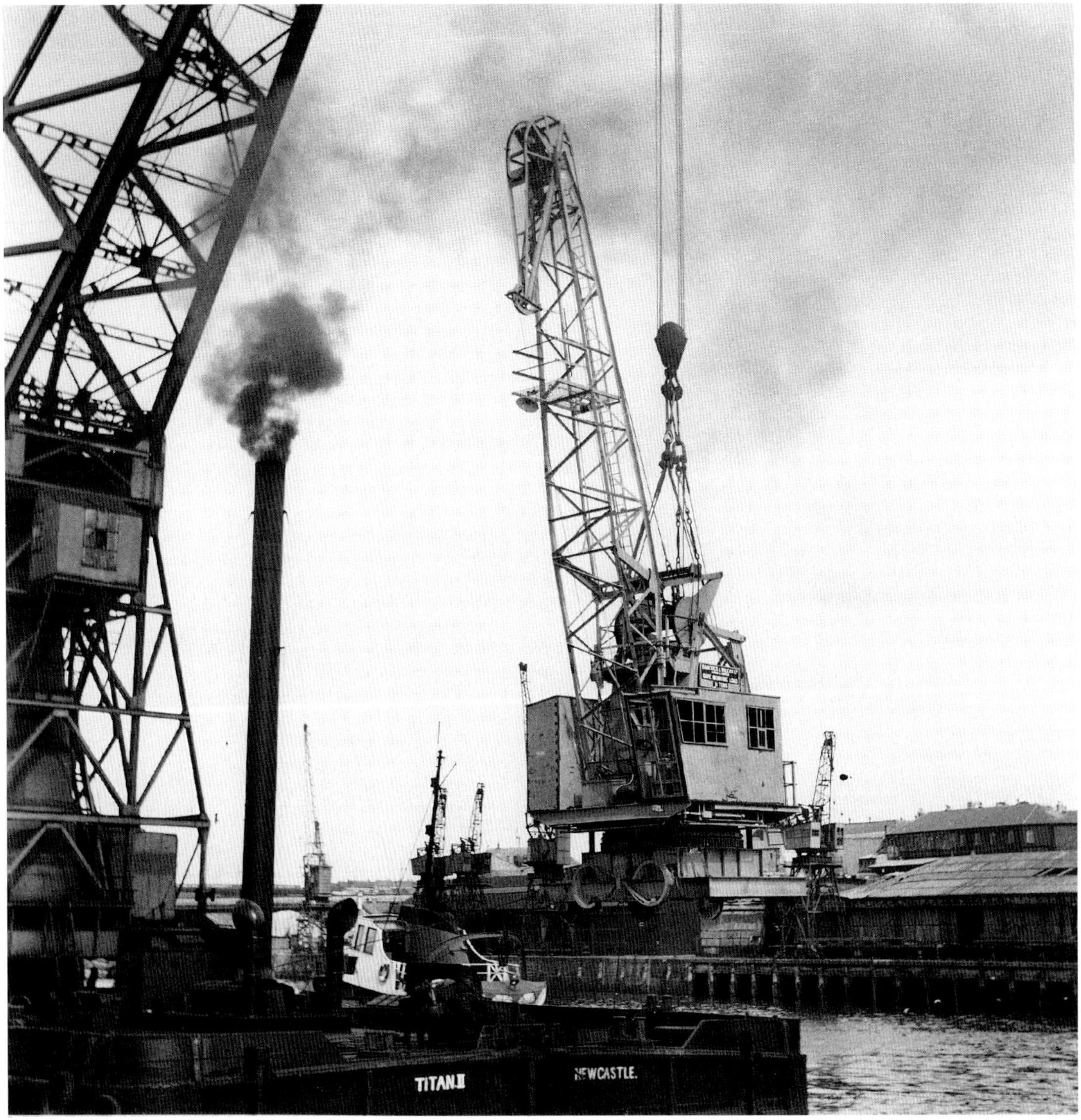

Titan II crane removing a smaller crane over River Tyne to cement loading wharf, summer, 1959.

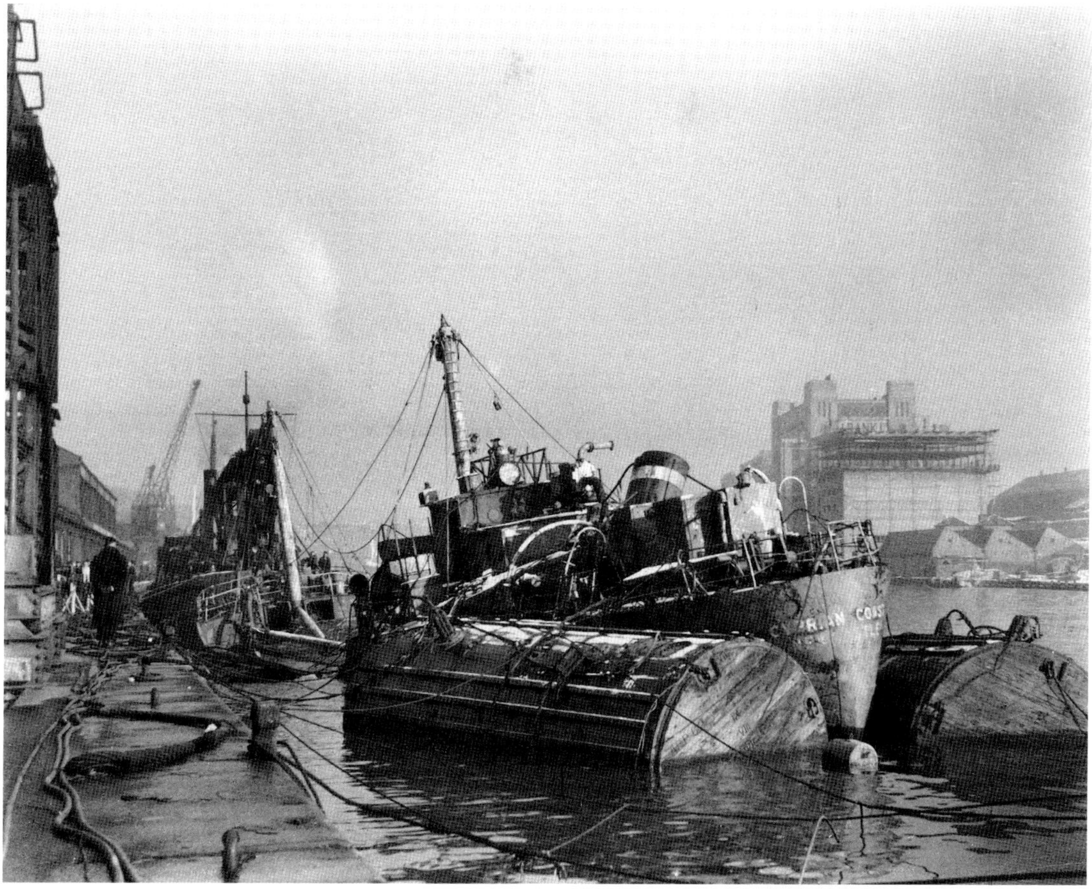

9 February 1956, the wreck of the Cyprian Coast refloated in the Tyne.

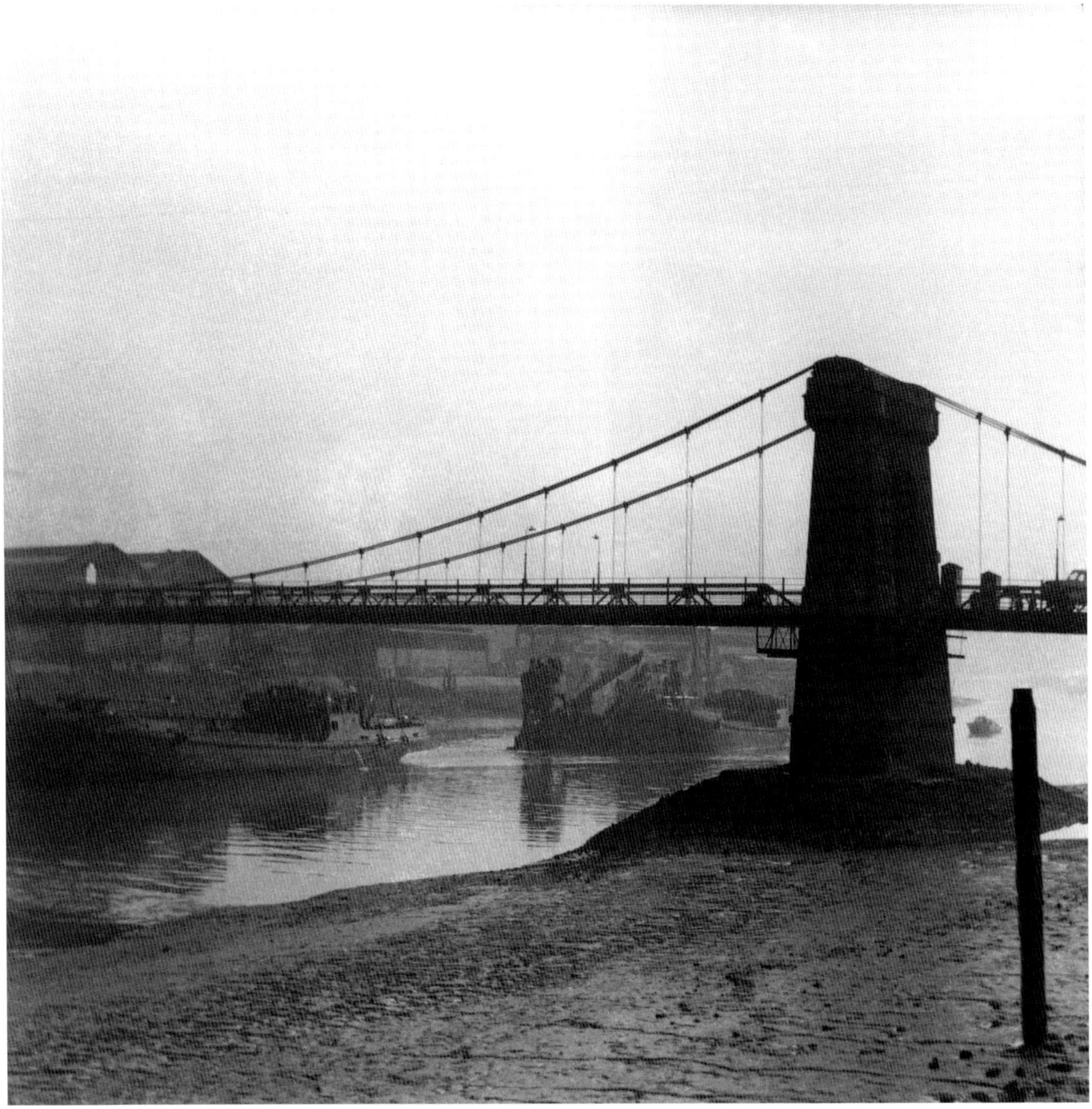

'The 1831 Scotswood Bridge at low tide. I took it from the South side on Sunday morning to include the Vickers' Scotswood factory. Below is the Bessie Surtees, on its way back to Stella power station after discharging ash out at sea. Next to it, a dredger.'

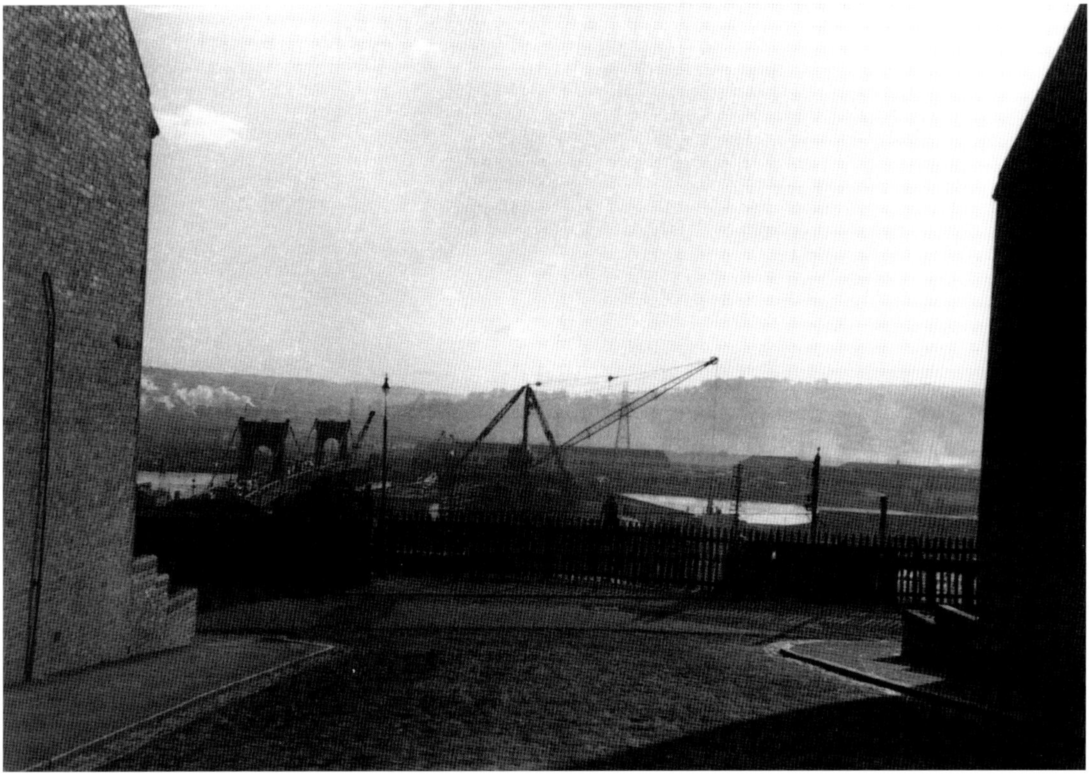

'Old Scotswood bridge, 1964. Opposite the Ord Arms at the end of the road, the Scotswood Suspension Bridge. Construction began on the new bridge on 30 August 1965. This is from St Margaret's Road.'

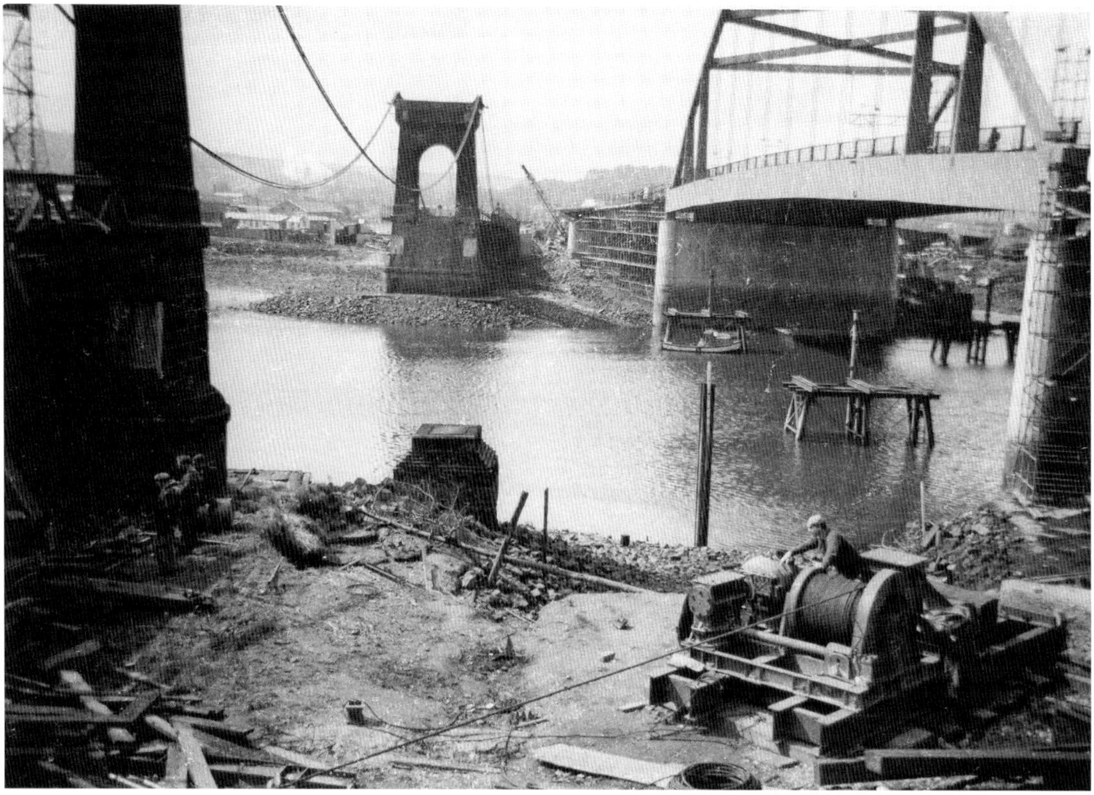

'Winch for hauling cables across river at Old Scotswood Bridge. After they are cut off at south side they are cut on north & drawn out for scrap.'

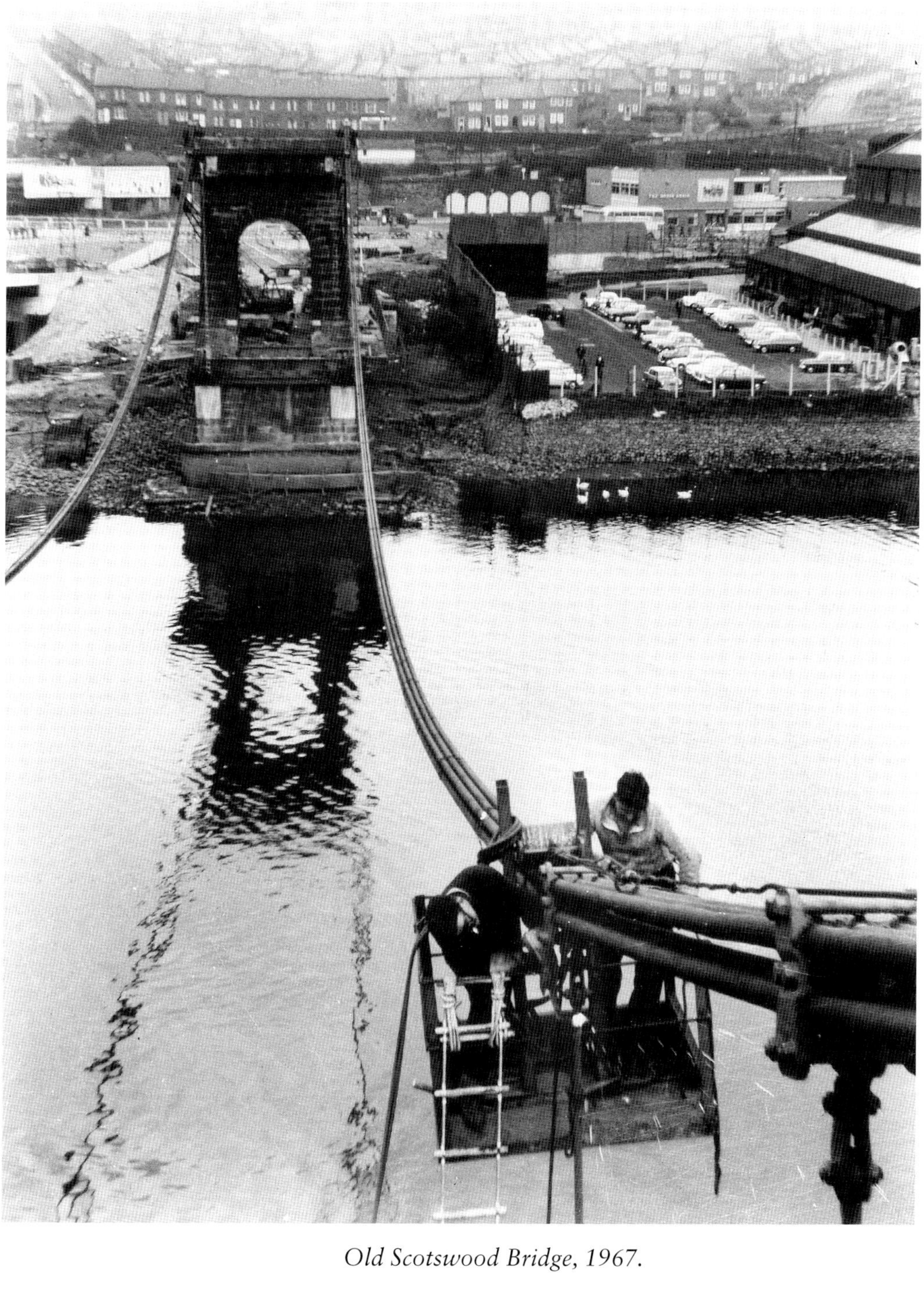

Old Scotswood Bridge, 1967.

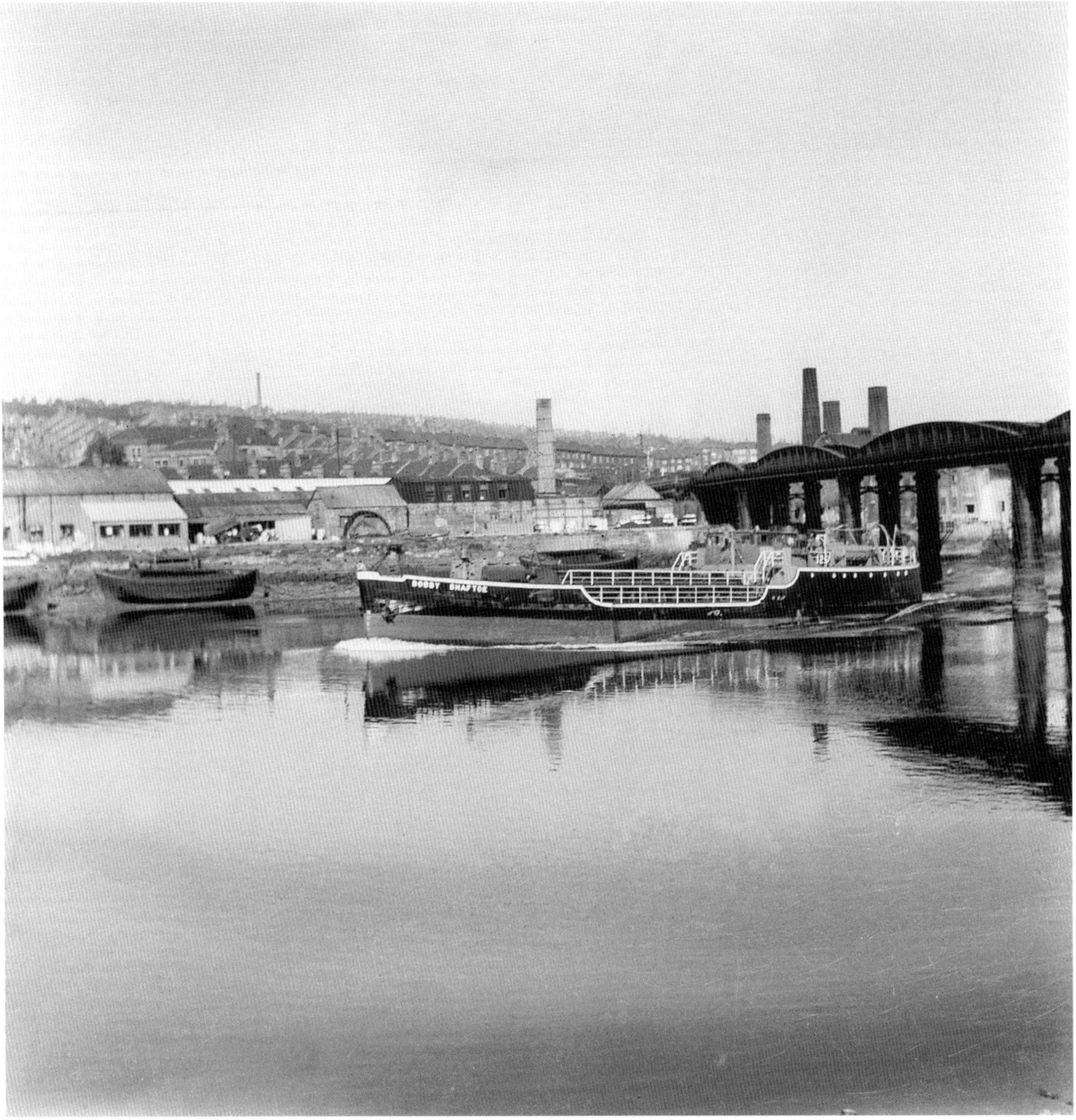

'View North across Tyne W. of London and North East Railway Bridge. The chimneys belonged to Adamzez the famous toilet makers. The Bobbie Shaftoe and its sister ships took ashes from Stella Power Station to be dumped at sea.'

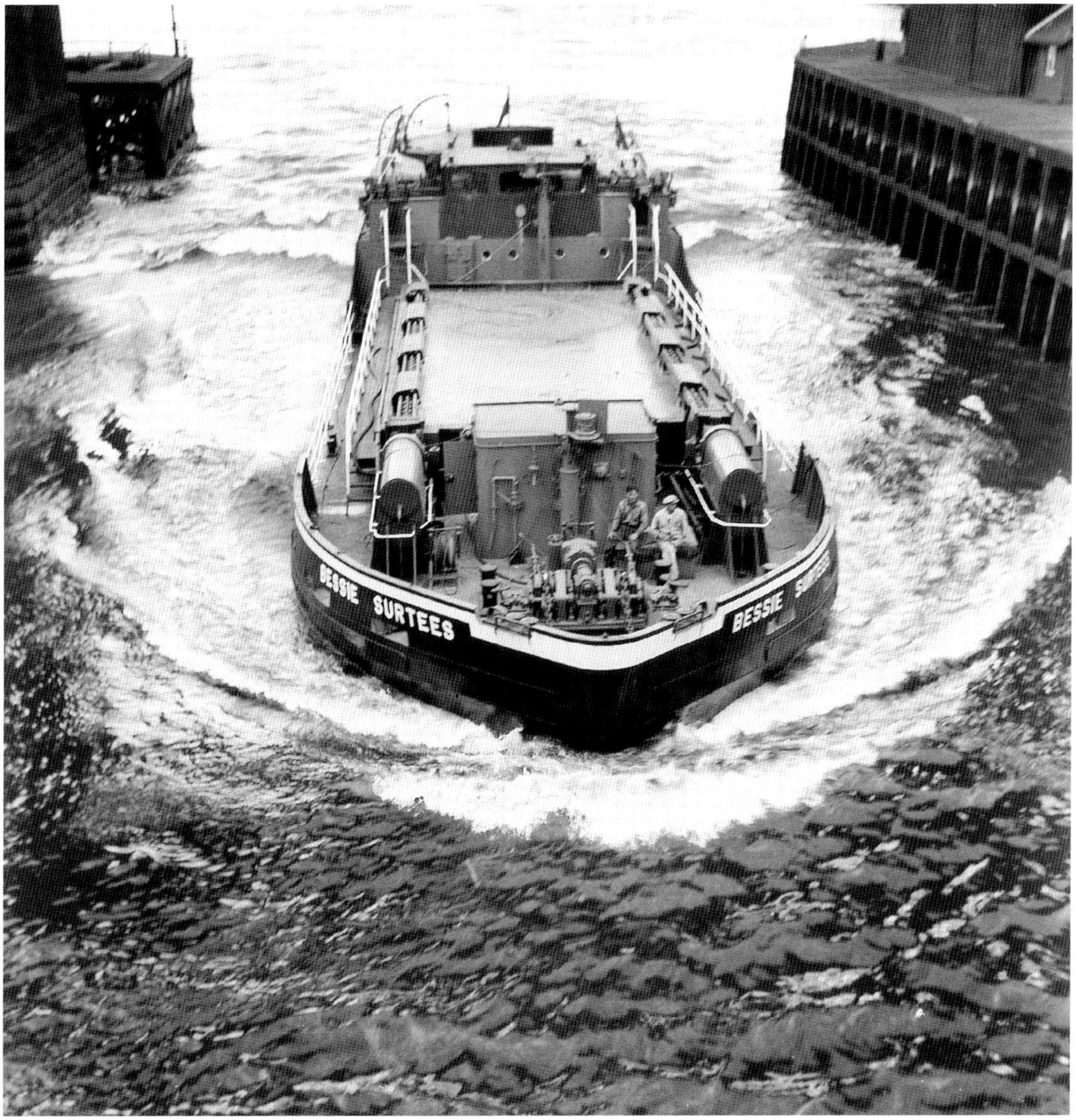

The Bessie Surtees, about to pass under the Swing Bridge, 12 July 1958.

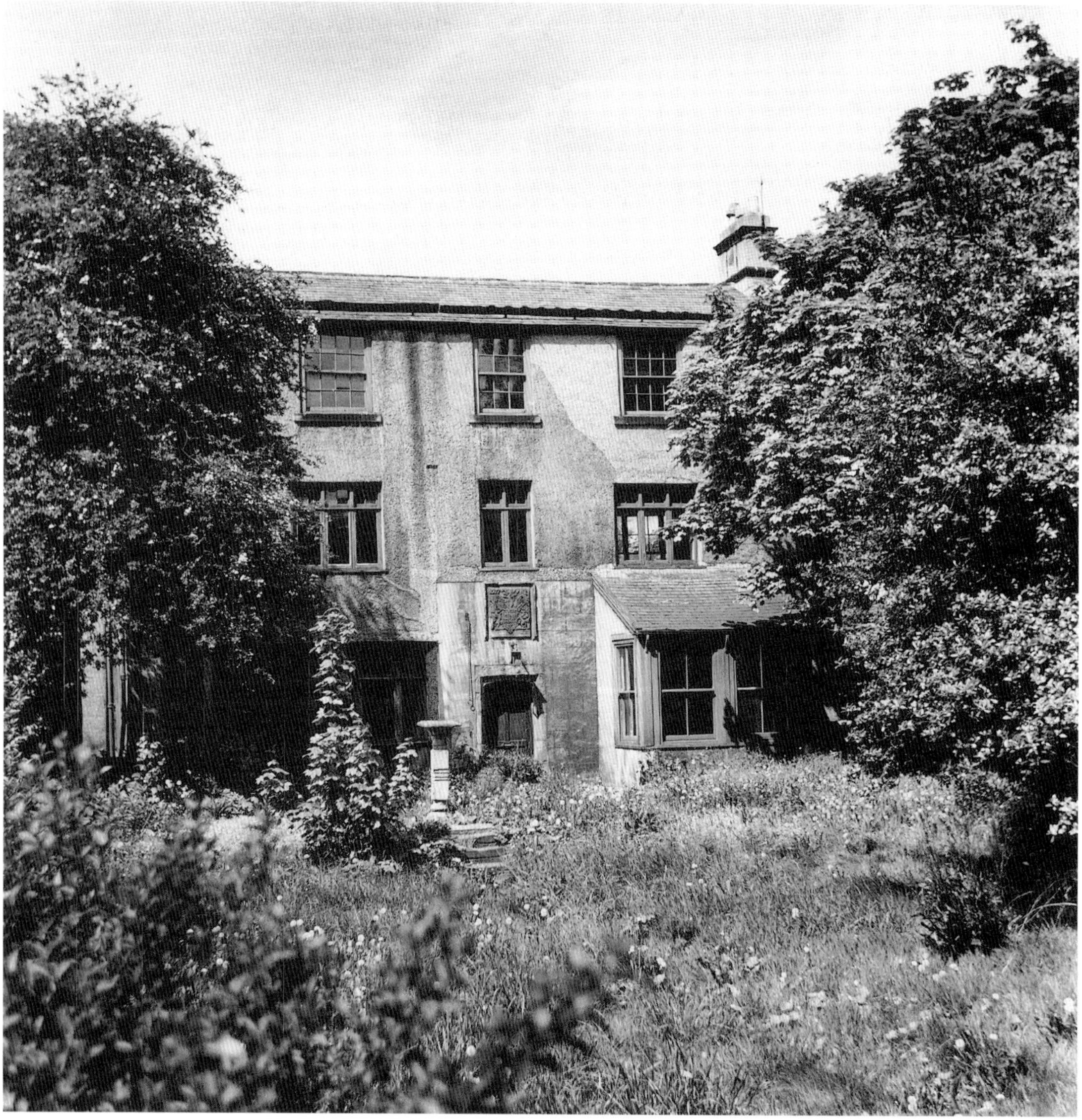

Stotes Hall, Jesmond, 1957.

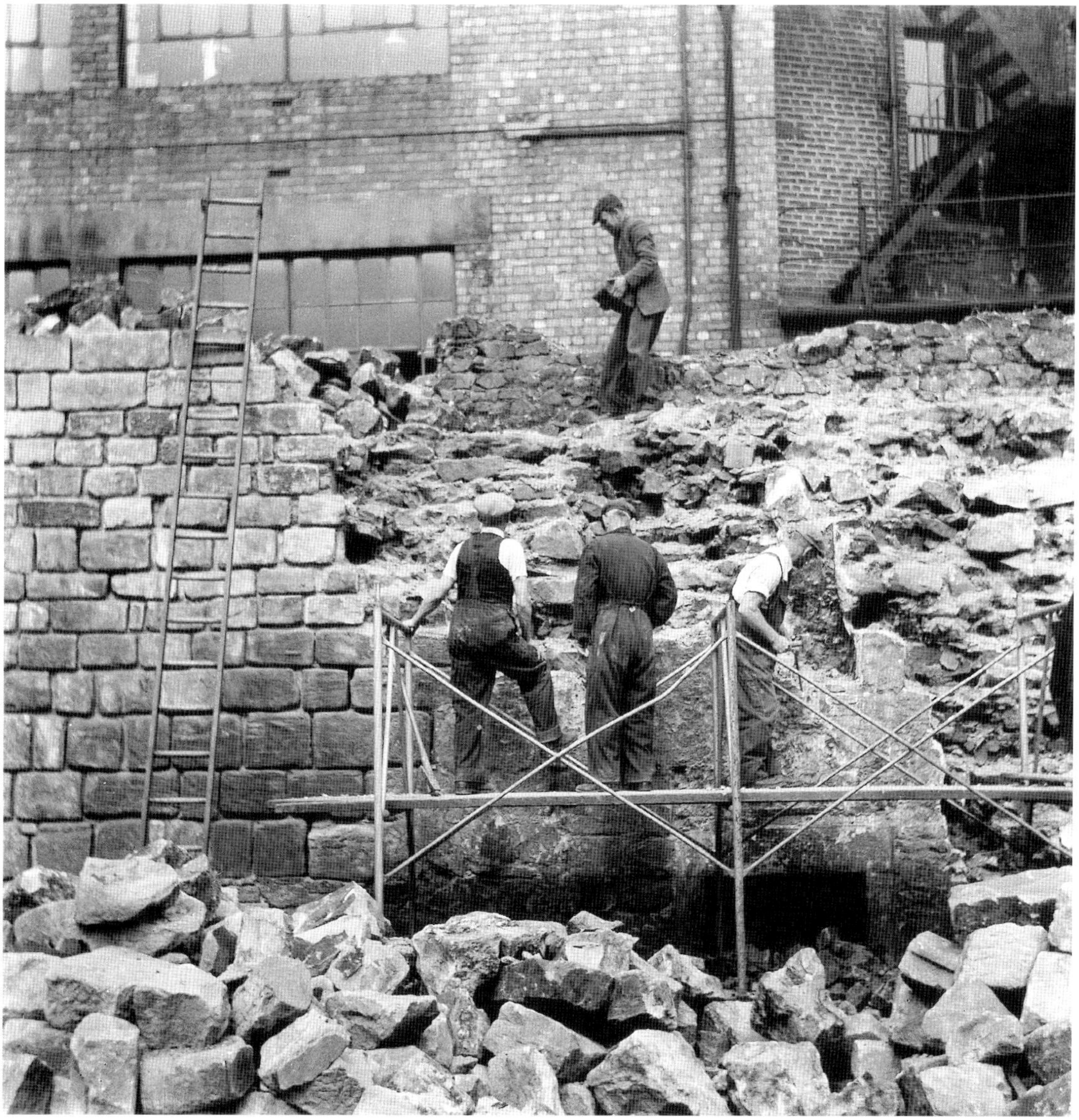

Durham Tower, Bath Lane, 7 July 1959.

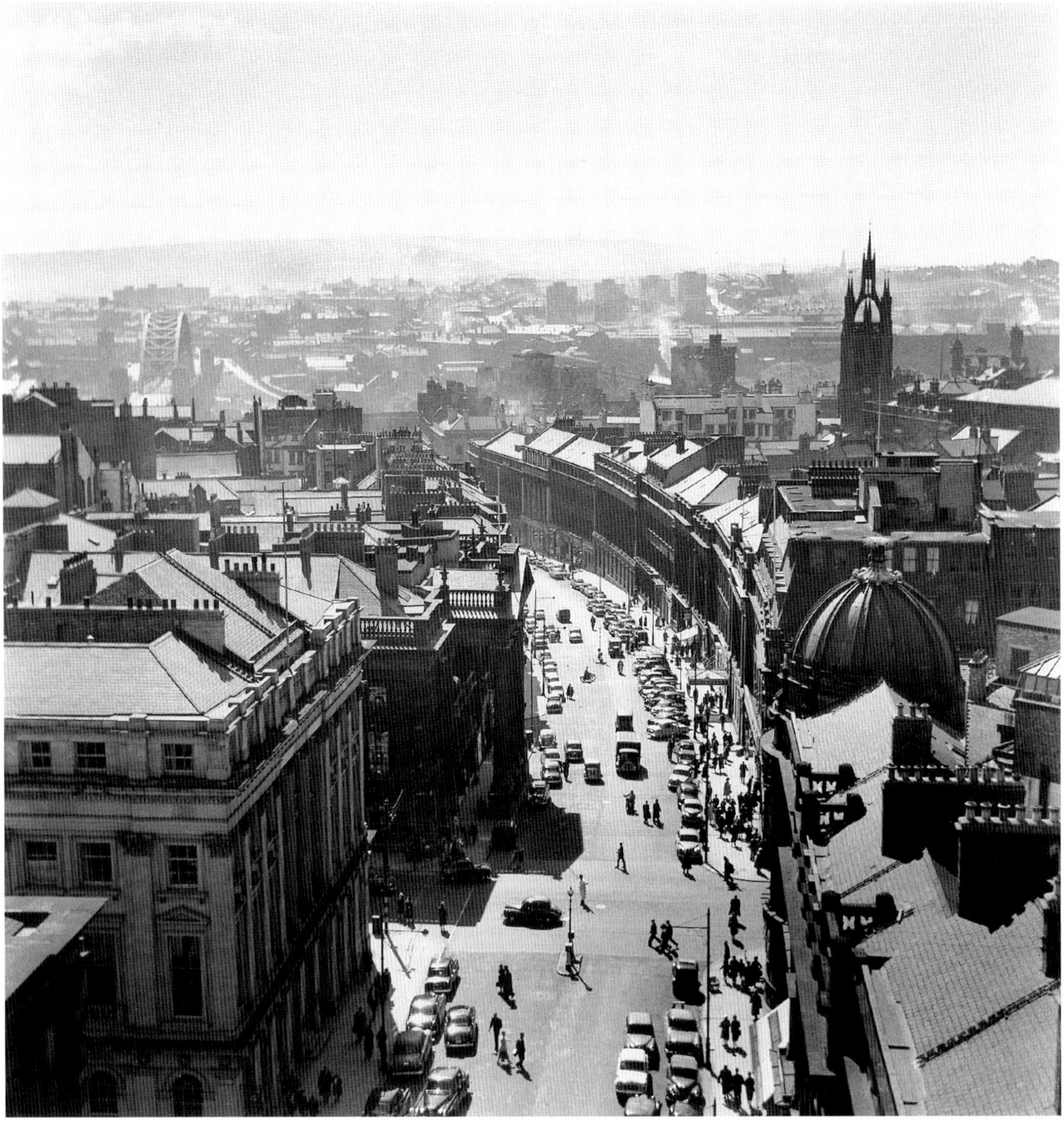

Grey Street from Grey's Monument, 1957.

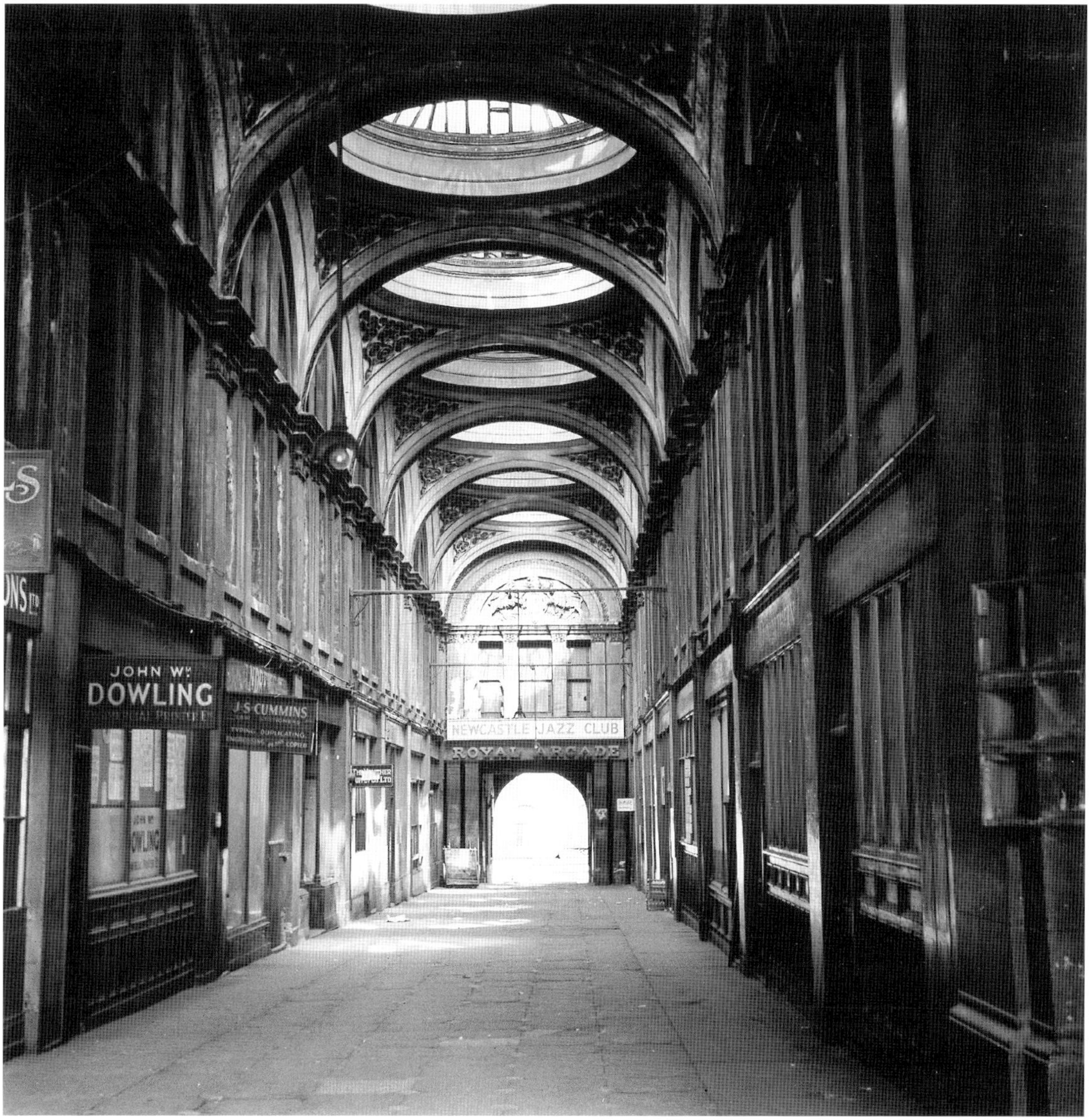

The Royal Arcade, 1960.

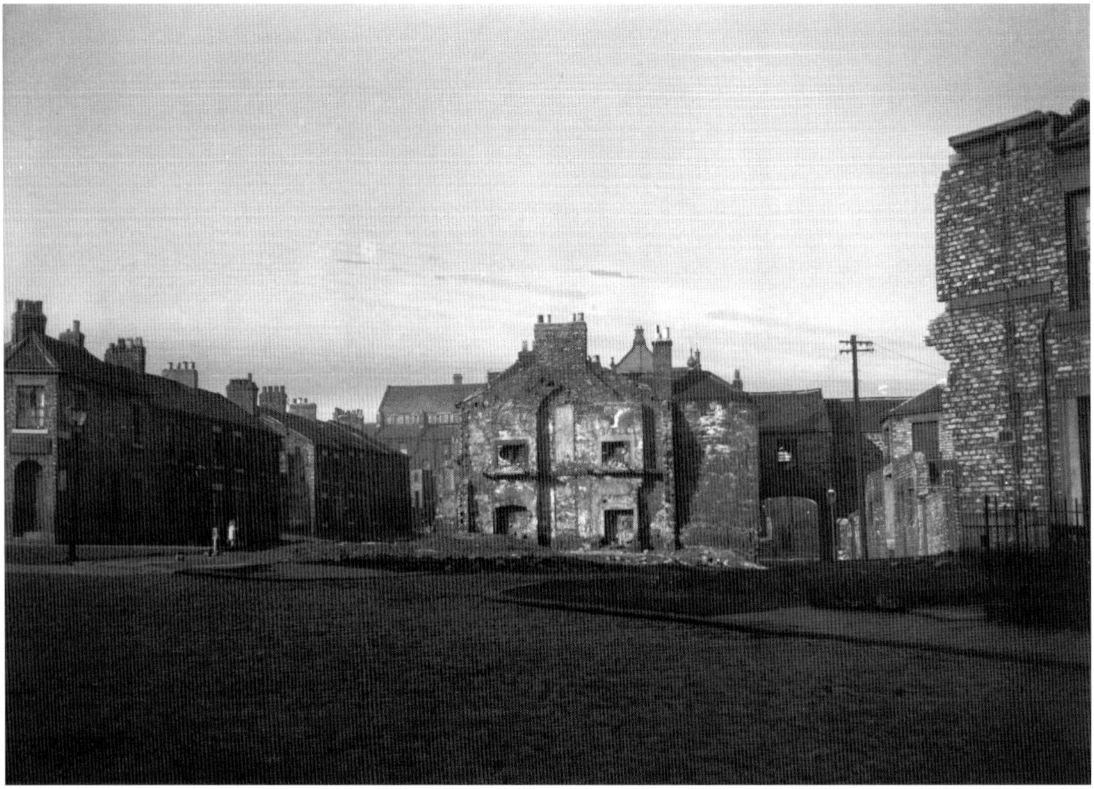

George Street, 1957.

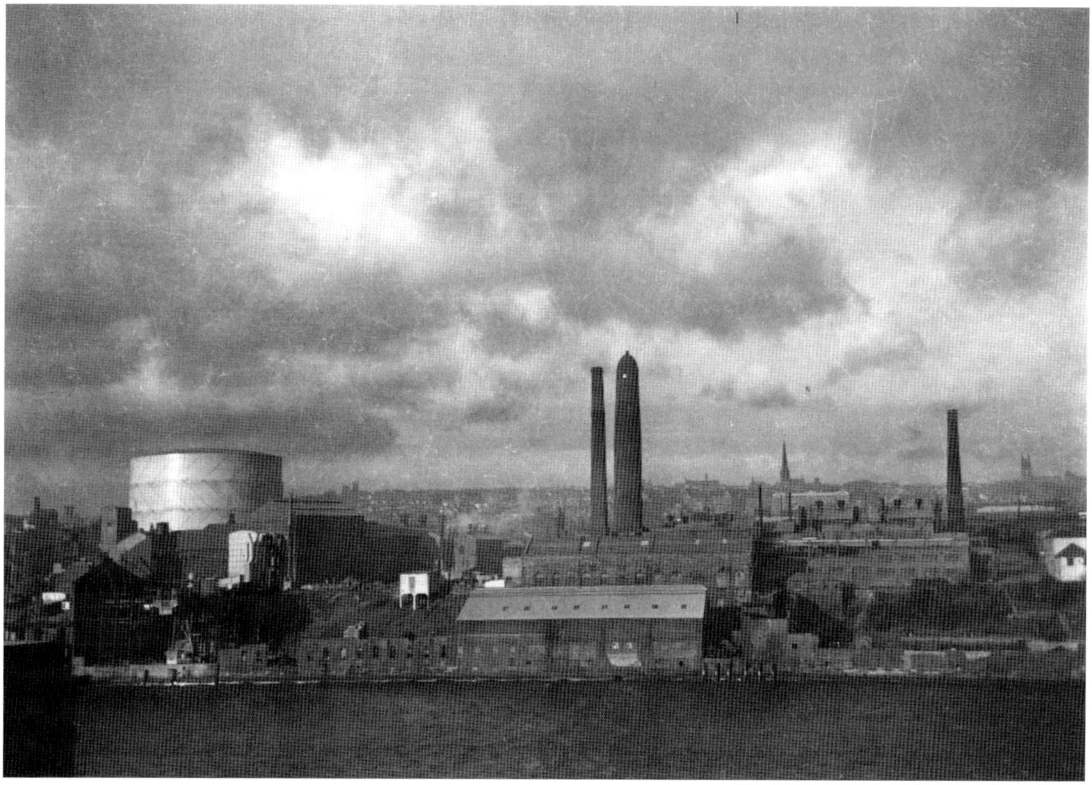

Low Elswick from Gateshead, February 1956.

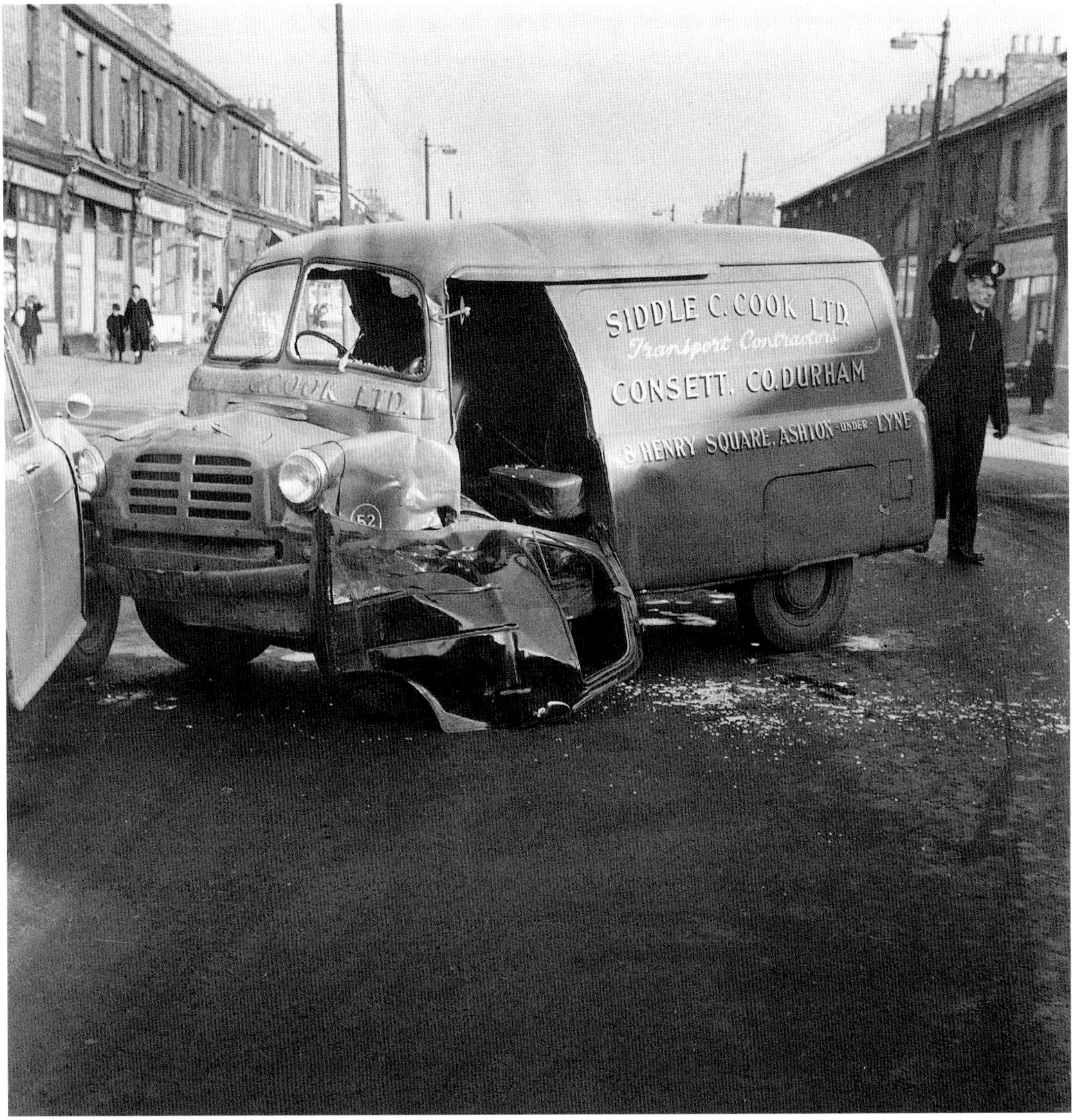

Scotswood Road, 1960.

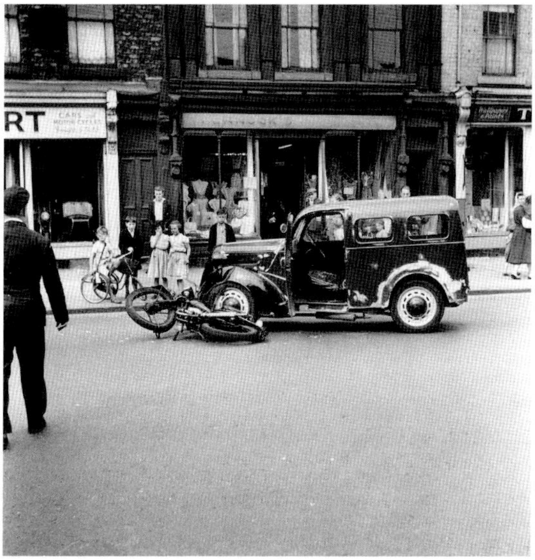

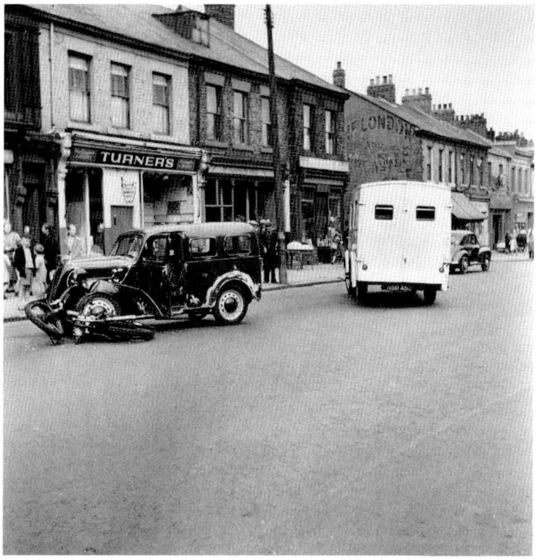

Scene of crash in Scotswood Road between motor cycle and car. 28 August 1958.
Ambulance arriving at scene of crash.

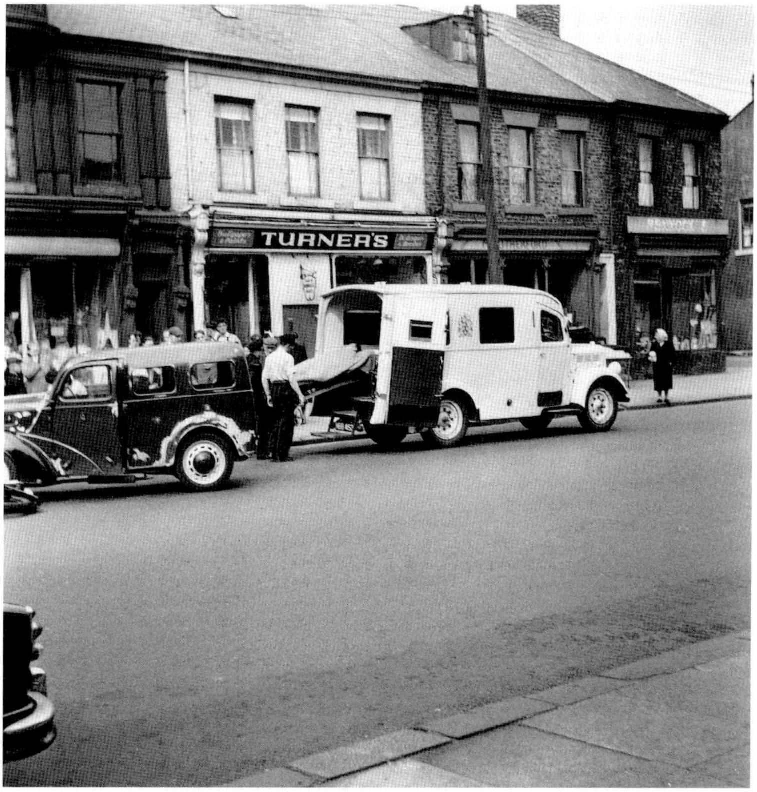

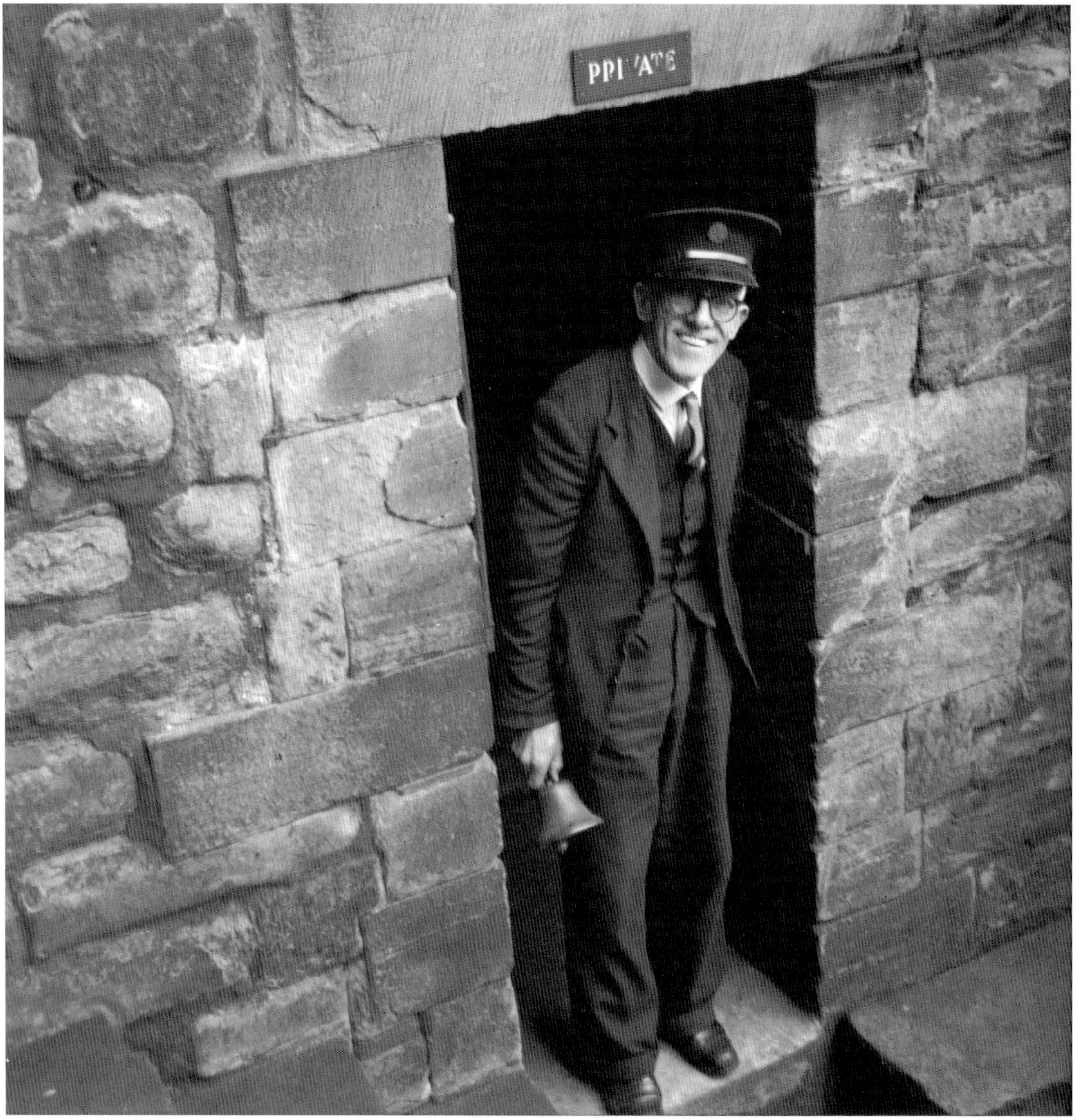

Castle Keep curator.

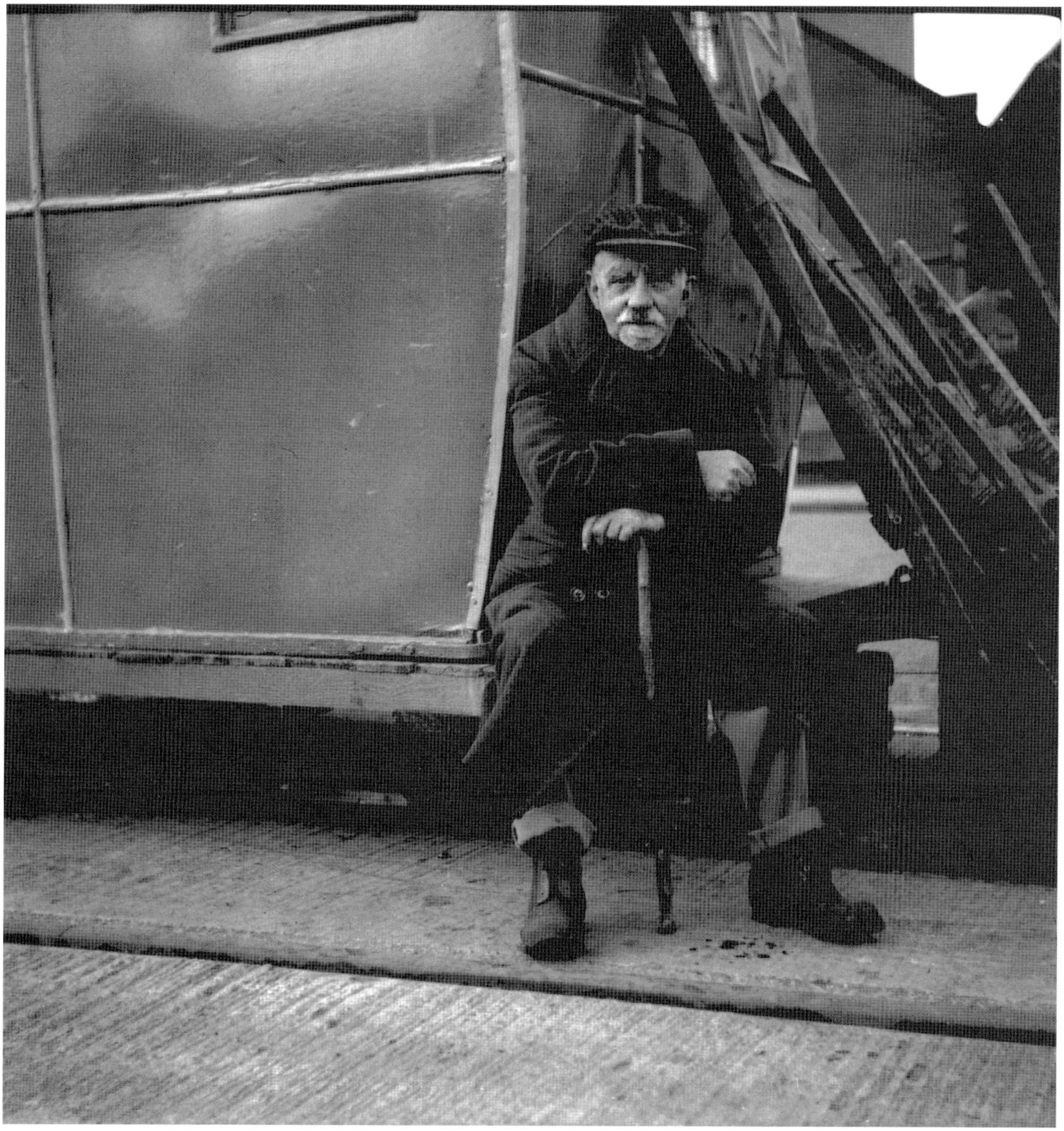

Old man at Quayside, November 1959.

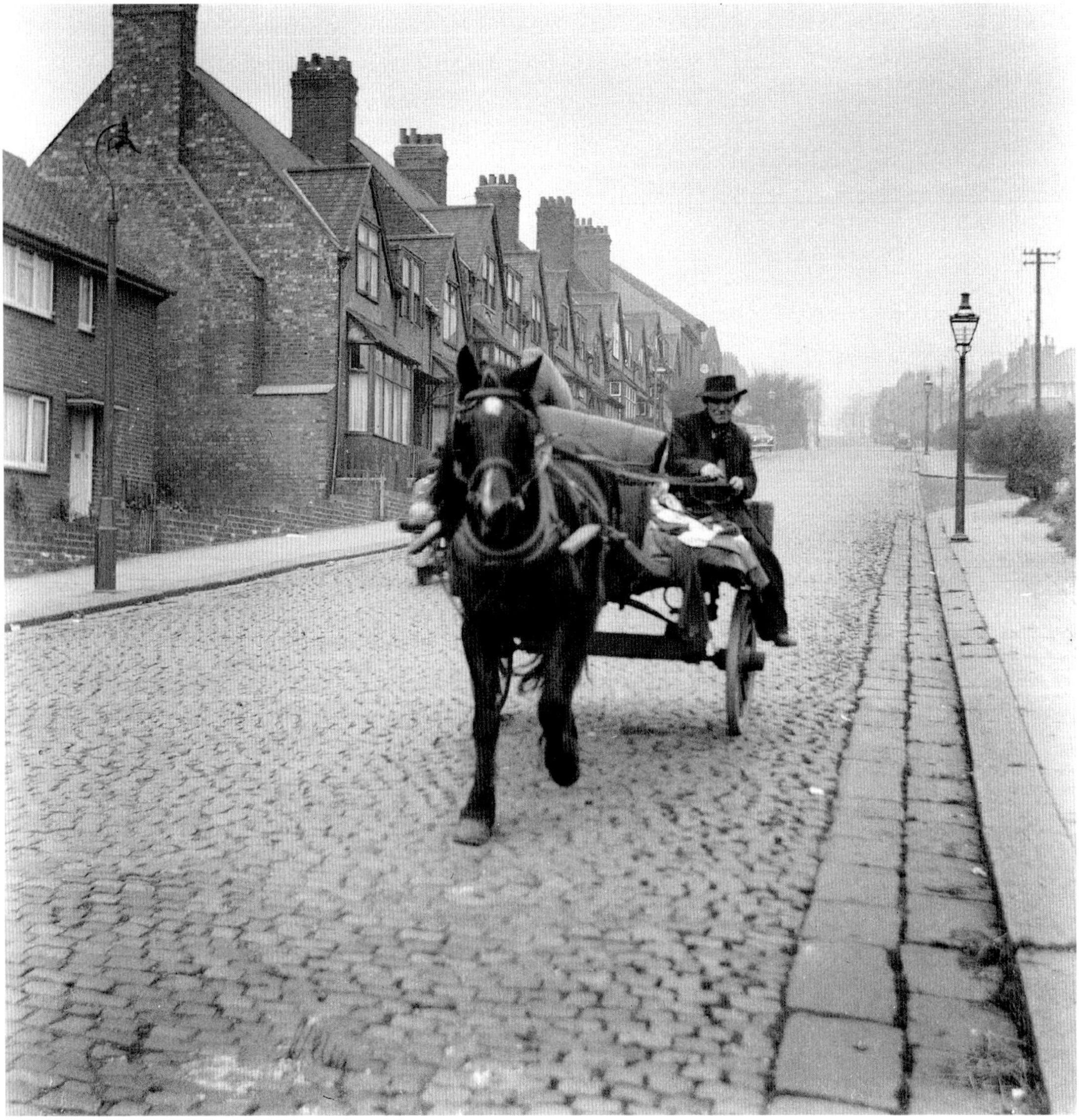

'Isaac Stuart a tatter or rag-man in Delaval Road just below Forest Road, west Benwell, 1959.'

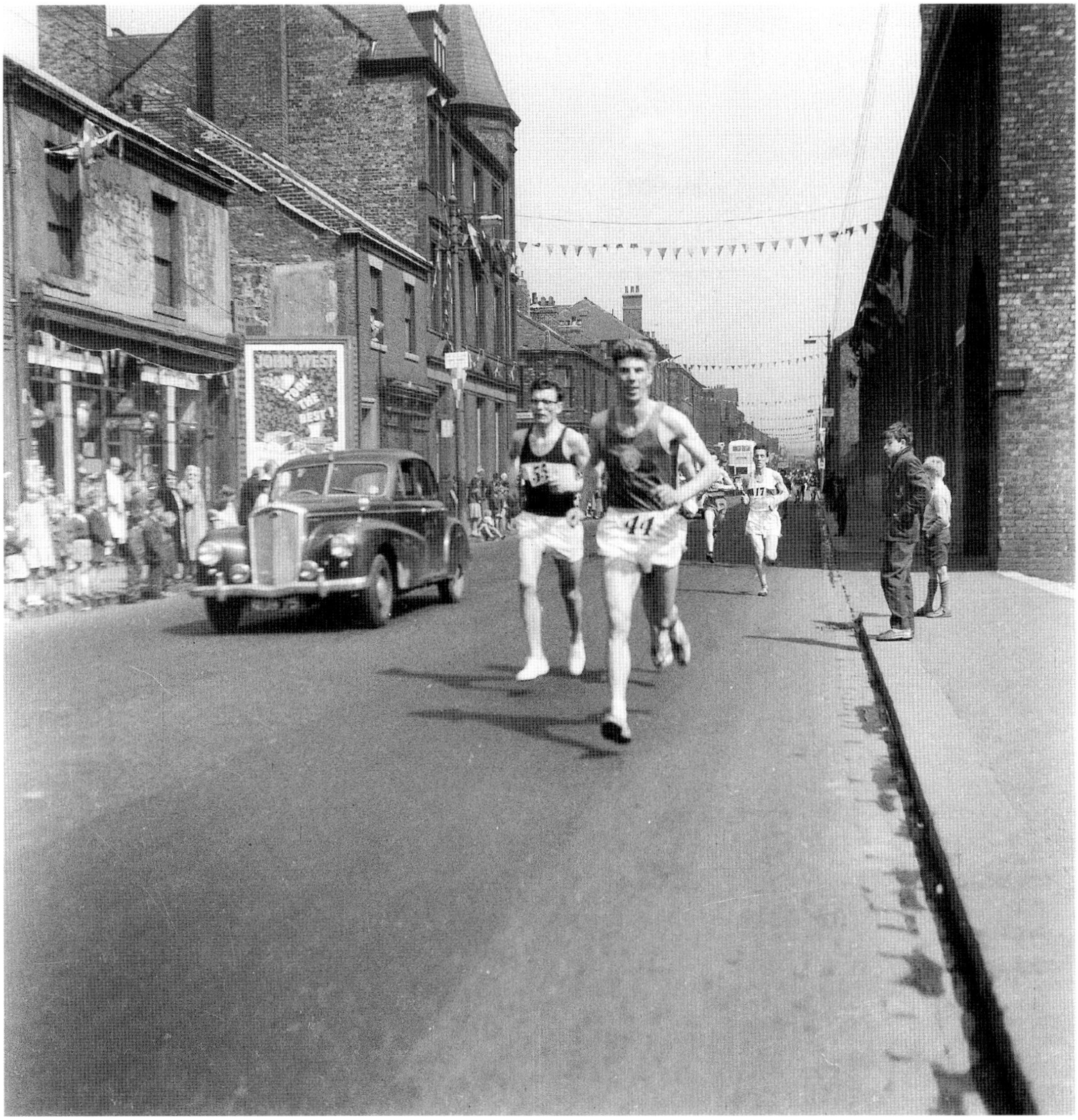

Blaydon Races Centenary celebrations, June 1962.

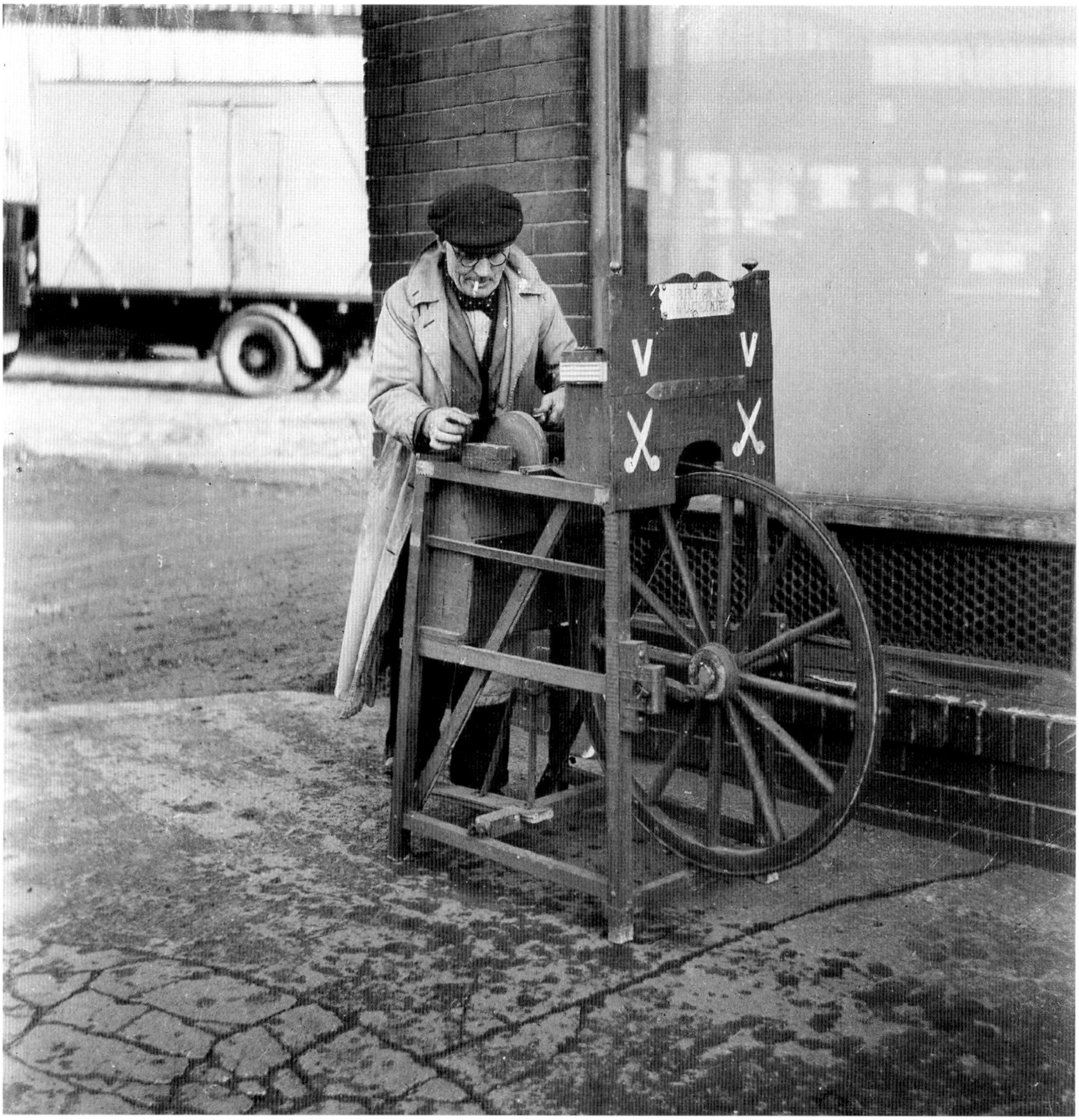

Charles Francis, knife and scissor grinder, 1958.

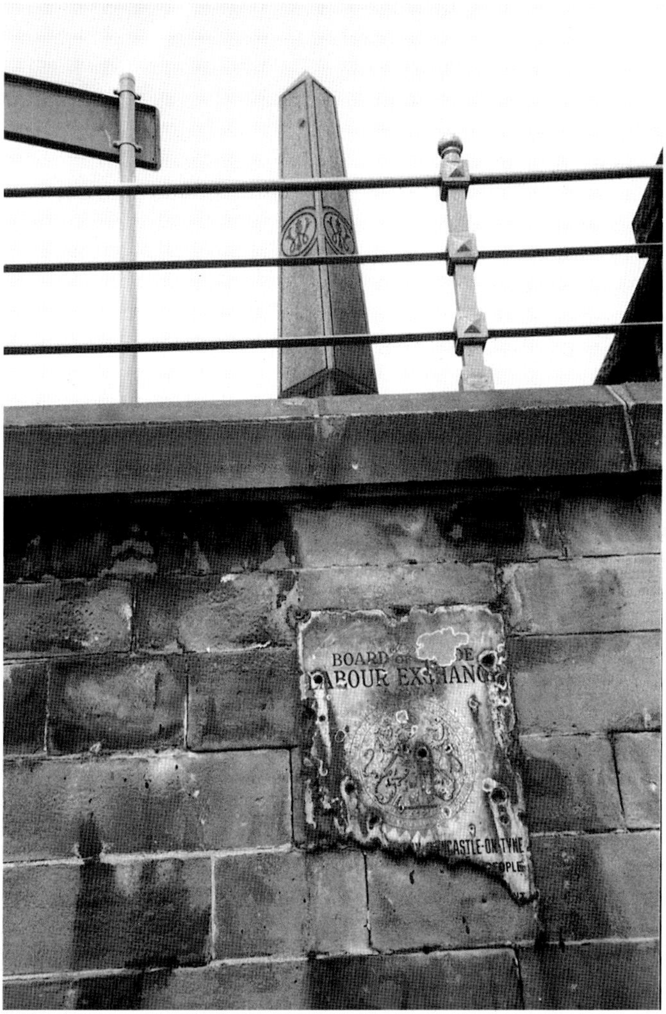

The old Quayside Labour Exchange.

Born in Barry S Wales Went to High Street School until 14 (the leaving off
time in those days) Used to go down woods around Porthkerry Park There were then
three or four fields between top of cliff & woods (Now built on partly I believe) Have pictures
around about 1756 of some of docks & area around about Very large exports of coal until
grouping of railways when it declined through GWR diverting it to Cardiff (Anything
I had always wanted to) Could go all over then it was country & seaside all
thrown in August Holiday spent in Hoinyfold near Leicester (about 18 miles away) It
was real country We used to go on a farm with my uncle Tom & went behind the
mower when the corn was cut trying to get a rabbit but never succeeding We used to
pinch apples out of orchards as kids will & also we eat the cattle cake to see what it
was like there was cotton seed & linseed & it was not that bad really Used to get rides
on hay cart etc The worst job I tried was stonepicking As you plough stones are left
on surface when earth particles descend & these are collected & probably used for drainage etc
Makes your back ache though! Altogether we did fairly well I think even if not well to do
Became a apprentice fitter in cement works repair shop Used to work lathe & help out all
— blacksmith — welder, boilermaker etc It was not a posh place but you learned a lot & jobs
didn't grow on bushes just then Went to sea for a few years later My
first trip was "Around the world in 6 months" (Not 80 days) Took coal to Alexandria when
the Ethiopia / Italian war was under way & proceeded to Ras Hafun in Italian Somaliland for
salt for Japan We passed 4 Italian ships in the Canal who were called some vile names
We coaled at Sourabaya (By Night) the coal being lumped aboard by coolies in
baskets which as junior engineer I had to count In Japan salt was unloaded &
women did most of the work Then we went to Dairen near Port Arthur for Soya
Beans for Galveston USA (These ended up in Sweden) In Japan snow was on the mountains
& in Dairen harbour blocks of Ice 2 feet Square were floating We hit the edge of a
cyclone & instead of the canal (Panama) ended up at Astoria on the Canadian
border out of oil & food also In those days the captains of some ships use to
put down 1000 gns (guineas) & get 800 & the food was the same (They never got good pay)
We were brought down to 6 knots instead of 12 knots & naturally the food ran out
& we emptied the ships lifeboats lockers too Deck Lads went into the bilges to scrape
the remaining oil to a pump to get us to [illegible] I forgot to mention that once in an
oil area (where coal was dearer to use than oil) we changed over the furnaces to be
capable of burning oil. We oiled up at San Diego & went through the Panama
wherever the soya beans were sold off at Galveston & we went on to Sweden
(Carrying letters at Caldwars Sweden had been to Galveston & back) where we unloaded It was
nice up there very wild & not over populated Empty to Sunderland & home later
Went to South America later Buenos Ayres, Rosario, San Nicolas & MOSQUITOS at night
Once on way home saw a host of locusts the sky was black with them & some fell
down the engineroom, long as a finger, like big yellow grasshopper Have not yet
found what the relation is but there were also big yellow beetles (shaped like ladybirds)
in amongst them To keep the biggest ships at Buenos Ayres (All Argentina is of
6 different states federated) the Martin Garcia Bar on River Plate is not dredged
or ships of larger size could go to Rosario But the bar is under B Ayres jurisdiction
Ships have grounded on it ours just slid over (Condensers full of mud)
one grounded stops until flood tide One unlucky change of wind can do it
The Second World War was on the horizon & grain was being queued up for
by ships of various nationalities Afterwards got various maintenance jobs around
London & then nearer home in Merthyr Tydfil at the ICI factory there When the
foreman gave me a hammer & chisel to try me out I snapped the shaft
in a jiffy. Being clever he showed me THE PROPER WAY but to his surprise
got the same result Alas every shaft in the stores big & little & told him had
dry rot & were useless We went to Hirwain for a while Under Ministry of Supply
men could be requisitioned & a small arms factory was being built Line Shafting
is not my job really but we did our best Some did not [illegible] the place

'Jimmy Forsyth of Elswick, Newcastle upon Tyne – My Life' written November 1989

Jimmy's brief autobiography is thought to have been written for his friend, the journalist Veronica Johnson, in preparation for a more detailed biography. It exists in typescript, with Jimmy's handwritten amendments, in Tyne & Wear Archives. A fragile photocopied version of the autograph manuscript is in the author's possession, the original is believed lost. In my transcription I have retained the original spelling and punctuation of the autograph version. Jimmy's vivid account of his life in this document reads as if Jimmy were sitting next to you, telling you his story in his own inimitable manner. As with much personal testimony he leaves out what he considers to be unimportant.

His childhood, which clearly left a deep impression on him, is remembered with great humour. Jimmy would go with his mother, Bertha, to Melton Mowbray every August Bank Holiday. They would then catch the train to Leicester and Market Harborough on route to visit Granny Bates in Horninghold for a summer-break. Jimmy would walk to a large house owned by Alexander Cross 'his name was on the milk carts', and there he would 'scrump' apples. Jimmy's half-brother, John, the child of a long-standing affair between Jimmy's father and a neighbour, was brought up by Bertha; Lilian (Lilly), John's sister and Jimmy's half-sister, remained with her own mother. John left home when he was fifteen and went to the Midlands in search of work; it was said he also went to escape his father's temper and to get away from Bertha. Bertha was said to be a very quiet shy person who became estranged from her husband, returning to her mother for extended periods, though she always returned to Barry, and to her husband, where she died in 1958.

In 'My Life' Jimmy goes on to describe his experiences as an apprentice fitter and as a merchant seaman in the lead up to the second world war, and his arrival with his mates as a 'taffy' on Tyneside. He obviously intended to recount his time living in Elswick in more detail but becomes distracted by his annoyance with the planners who swept away his community. No other autobiographical writings have surfaced since Jimmy's death, which makes this document all the more valuable.

Born in Barry S[outh] Wales Went to High Street School until 14 (the leaving off times in those days) Used to go down to the woods around Porthkerry Park There were then three open fields between top of cliff & woods (Now built on partly I believe) Have pictures around about 1956 of some of docks & area round about Very large exporter of coal until grouping of the railways when it declined through G[reat] W[estern] R[ailway] diverting it to Cardiff (As they had always wanted to) could go all over then, it was country & seaside all thrown in August Holiday spent in Horninghold near Leicester (about 18 miles away). It was real country We used to go on a farm with my Uncle Tom & went behind the mower when the corn was cut trying to get a rabbit but never succeeding We used to pinch apples out of orchards as kids will & also ate the cattle cake to see what it was like There was cottonseed & linseed & it was not that bad really Used to get rides on hay carts etc The worst job [I] tried was stonepicking As you plough stones are left on the surface when earth particles descend & these are collected & probably used for drainage etc Makes your back ache though! Altogether we did fairly well I think even if not well to do [I] Became & [an] apprentice fitter in cement works repair shop Used to work lathe & help out all–blacksmith–welder–boilermaker–etc It was not a posh place but you learned a lot and jobs didnt grow on bushes just then In Horninghold my mother's home, one got shopping in the next village Hallaton (Famed for Easter Bottle Kicking Festival) three and a half miles away Naturaly one walked there & back The nearest Market Town was Market Harborough, where one presumably bought clothes & such items & Hallaton could not supply If [one] wanted a fire for cooking etc (No electric or gas) one collected wood (no coal either) from spinneys etc & chopped it up Water needless to say was pumped up in a yard & oil lamp or candles were the only lights So it was early to bed for all Horninghold was I have since found, a Model Village (Presumably built to some squire's needs) & every house had apple trees etc Hallaton was a real village going back a long way (Saxon in name I think) Easter Bottle Kicking was between Hallaton and Medbourne & football itself derives its origins from such medieval practices Cannot describe it as I have never been in the vicinity at Easter as yet Went to sea a few years later My first trip was 'Around the World in 6 Months' (not 80 days) Took coal to Alexandria when the Ethiopia/Italian war was under way & proceeded to Ras Hafem in Italian Somaliland for salt for Japan We passed [an]& Italian ship in the Canal who were called some vile names We coaled at Sourabaya (At Night) the coal being humped aboard by coolies in baskets, which, a s junior engineer, I had to count In Japan salt was unloaded & women did most of the work Then we went to Darien near Port Arthur for soya beans for Galveston USA (These ended up in Sweden) In Japan snow was on the mountains & in Darien harbour blocks of ice 2 feet square were floating We hit the edge of a cyclone & instead of the canal (Panama) ended up at Astoria on the Canadian Border out of food also In those days the captains of some ships used to put down 1,000 guineas and get 800 & the food was the same (they never got good pay) We were knocked down to 6 knots instead of 12 knots & naturally the food ran out & we emptied the ships lifeboats lockers too Deck lads went into the bilges to scrape the remaining oil to a pump to get us to port I forgot to mention that once in an oil area (where coal was dearer to use than oil) we changed over the furnaces to be capable of burning oil We oiled up at San Diego & went through the Panama [canal] where the soya beans were sold off at Galveston & we went on to Sweden (my letters at Carlshaam [Karlshamn] Sweden had been to Galveston & back) where we unloaded It was very nice up there very wild & not over populated Empty to Sunderland & home later Went to South America later Buenos Ayres [Buenos Aires], Rosario, San Nicolas & MOSQUITOES all night Once on way home we saw a host of locusts the sky was black with them & some fell down into the engine room, long as a finger, like big yellow grasshoppers Have not yet found out what the relation is but there were also big yellow beetles (shaped like ladybirds) in amongst them To keep the biggest ship[s] at Buenos Ayers [Buenos Aires] (All Argentina is six different states federated) the Martin Garcia Bar on River Plate is not dredged or ships of larger size could go to Rosario But the bar is under B Ayres [Buenos Aires] jurisdiction Ships have grounded on it ours just slid over it (Condensers full of mud) & once grounded stopped until flood time One unlucky change of wind can do it The Second World War was on the horizon & grain was being queued up for by ships of various nationalities Afterwards got various jobs around London & then nearer home in Merthyr Tydfil at the ICI factory there When the foreman gave me a hammer & chisel to try me out I snapped the shaft in a jiffy Being clever he showed me THE PROPER WAY but to his surprise got the same result Also every shaft in the stores big & little & told him had dry rot & were useless We went to Hirwain [Hirwaun] for a while under Ministry of Supply men could be requisitioned & a small arms factory was being built Line Shafting is not my job really but we did our best Some did not In the place where the line shafts went it was rather dark (Could only just make out our marks on the wall for brackets) Across the line shaft plan in each room was marked a rough square The agent on being informed by me found that the brickies had forgot ? to leave holes for windows In Edinburgh a canteen was built on the wrong side of N[orth]/S[outh] line & had to be demolished for road into the factory Lots of queer goings on Scrap iron lay alongside of a railway near Bridgend Glamorgan the whole war time & was not collected After a while some fitters were needed at ICI factory, Moss End [Mossend], Glasgow So we volunteered (4 of us) to go there & it was a change to travel though bad, for trains were overcrowded at times (Stood all the way once; We got monthly leave). On coming to Newcastle for the same period lost sight of eye in four days & went convalescent at Wylam & very nice too Worked in the Boiler Plant Maintenance at Prudhoe (Site now trading estate) After War came to lodge in Scotswood Road area in a house of ill repute The food was alright & the rest did not concern me over much Was taking childrens pictures when someone said Scotswood Road was being demolished by & by & I took some snaps gradually getting more involved as I saw this was indeed the case Planners unfortunately never live in there[their] constructions or they would be more careful High Rise Flats for instance are only Makeshift establishments Cannot & never will compare to a house of ones own & communities cannot naturally exist in such conditions 90 flats comprise the Cedars & I know about eight or nine of the residents All on my floor are new & as you go out you meet in the lift not as in a street where you pass people on doorsteps Nobody stands at a flat door and you are too quickly away to see anyone Barracks are for soldiers as makeshift dwellings but not any use for ordinary people IF I HAD MY WAY I WOULD BLOW THEM ALL UP as Liverpool is attempting to do Im glad a[I] took the ROAD now as it shows how people lived, I know they had not bathrooms & the water taps were outside but there was a community that knew & therefore helped each other Since [then] I have also snapped the Scotswood & Redheugh Bridges during construction, seen the old ones go & am now taking snaps along the W[estern]/B[y]/P[ass] at the youthful age of 76 years young' Writ by J. Forsyth 26 Cedars Elswick November 1989

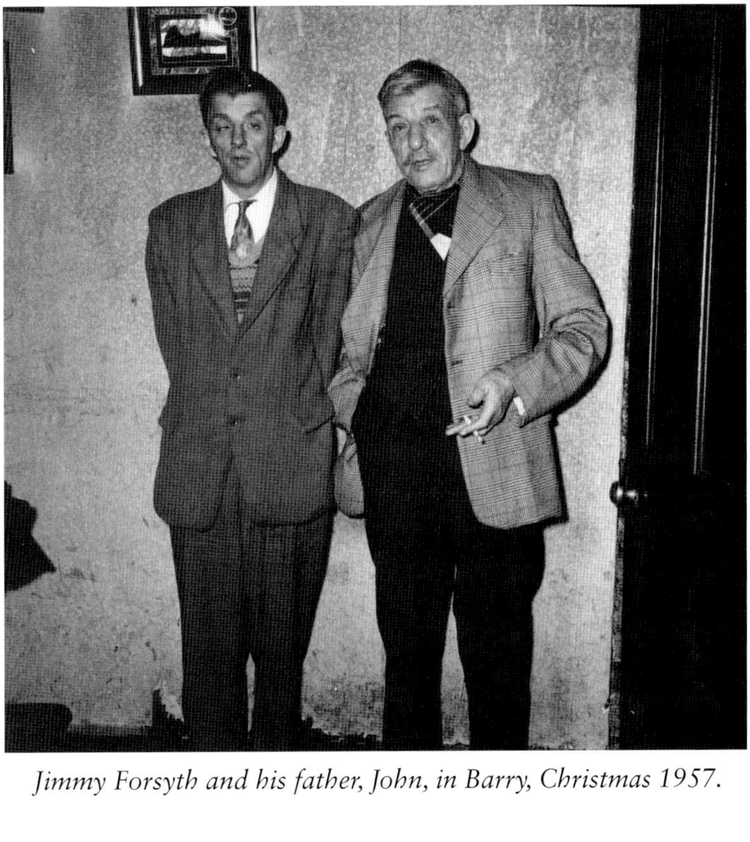

Jimmy Forsyth and his father, John, in Barry, Christmas 1957.

Bibliography

Scotswood Road, Jimmy Forsyth, ed. Derek Smith, Bloodaxe Books 1986.

Looking back at Scotswood Road Pubs, Newcastle upon Tyne City Libraries and Arts 1988.

Old Scotswood Road, A. Desmond Walton with West Newcastle Local Studies, Chalford, 1997.

'Little Brother is Watching You', Gordon Burn, *The Guardian Weekend Magazine*, 30 June 2001.

Out of One Eye The Photography of Jimmy Forsyth, Anthony Flowers and Derek Smith, Tyne Bridge Publishing 2002.

Jimmy Forsyth Photographs from the 1950s and 1960s, Anthony Flowers, Tyne Bridge Publishing 2009.

In addition to the published material on Jimmy I have made extensive use of the albums and documents from Jimmy's personal collection in Tyne & Wear Archives and the following:
Jimmy Forsyth *No Fancy Shades* (edited master 23 September 1986) Tyne Tees Television; *The Tube*, episode transmitted 16 January 1987, Tyne Tees Television for Channel Four; Jimmy Forsyth Metro Radio interview recorded at the Side Gallery 7 October, 1986, (unpublished tape recording); *Lives through a Lens* a BBC *Close Up North* film (broadcast in 2001); *Jimmy Forsyth of Elswick, Newcastle upon Tyne – My Life*, November 1989, (unpublished autograph manuscript); Jimmy Forsyth interviewed by Les Bell at West Newcastle Local Studies 7 February, 1995, (unpublished tape recording); Jimmy Forsyth interviewed by Derek Smith (in preparation for *Out of One Eye)* 2001, (unpublished tape recordings); Mary Evans for background material on Jimmy's family and his early life in Barry (personal correspondence with the author 2008-9); A. Desmond Walton, miscellaneous papers in the collection of Newcastle Libraries; Steve Wood, *Memories of Yesteryears* typescript manuscript, July1999 in the collection of Newcastle Libraries.